LMS
ENGINE SHEDS

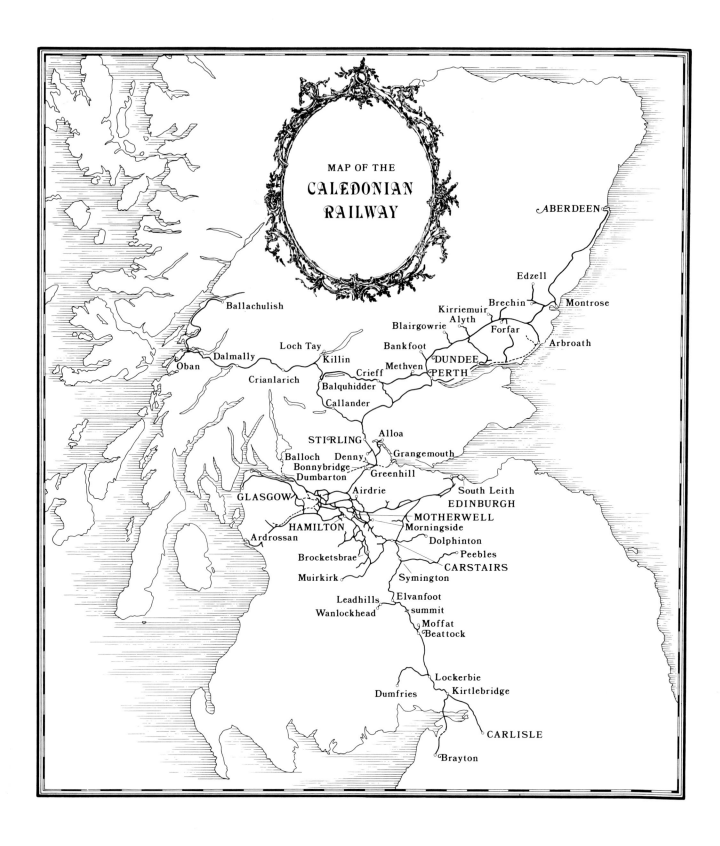

LMS
ENGINE SHEDS

Their History and Development

VOLUME FIVE
THE CALEDONIAN RAILWAY

BY

CHRIS HAWKINS & GEORGE REEVE

WILD SWAN PUBLICATIONS LTD.

ISBN 0 906867 56 8

FOR
STEPHEN SUMMERSON

Designed by Paul Karau
Printed and bound by Butler & Tanner, Frome

Published by
WILD SWAN PUBLICATIONS LTD.
1-3 Hagbourne Road, Didcot, Oxon OX11 8DP

CONTENTS

AUTHORS' NOTE

The next volume, No. 6, will complete the coverage of Scotland, describing the sheds of the former Highland and Glasgow & South Western Companies. It has been the custom to provide an allocation for each shed, fixed at 1945. This has been omitted in the case of the Caledonian; the Scottish companies forming the Northern Division were perceived as 'an entity' and transfers to and from the south were (relatively) few. LMS engines going new to Scotland in the 1920s and 1930s, with exceptions, tended to remain 'Scottish' engines, and in some respects former GSW and HR engines were regarded as of secondary rank, their rapidly diminishing numbers frequently replaced by former Caledonian locos. There is thus considerable logic in taking Scotland 'as one' and the complete 1945 allocation, together with a substantial amount of supplementary data, will be listed in Volume 6.

The Caledonian at Perth, an early *penchant* for the massive.

National Railway Museum

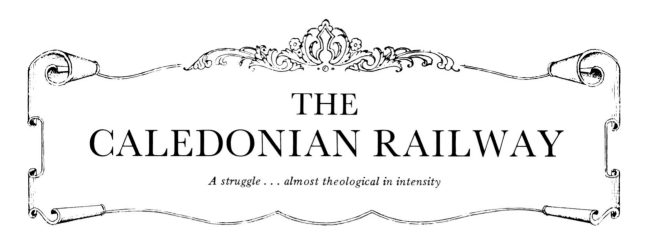

THE
CALEDONIAN RAILWAY

A struggle . . . almost theological in intensity

BORN out of struggle, the infant Caledonian began life in Annandale in the autumn of 1845. In the preceding years 'the severest railway contest in the history of this country' had raged to determine the course of the first line into Scotland. The bitter strife of the Annandale & Nithsdale protagonists has been oft-recounted, providing a fiery background to the triumphant opening, Carlisle to Beattock, in 1847. 'It was widely believed' that traffic would never support more than a single route from England to Glasgow and Edinburgh, and the Caledonian, opening simultaneously to the chief cities of Scotland in February 1848, was accordingly a closely observed venture.

Consolidating its early grasp upon Glasgow, the company expanded steadily 'by a double process of absorption and extension' or so it was described in 1897 by Sir James Thompson, the General Manager, on the occasion of the company's Jubilee. The CR had absorbed at the first pre-existing lines like the Garnkirk and Glasgow Railway, subsequently amalgamating with major lines, like in size and lineage to itself. By 1897 it owned nearly 800 route miles:

> 'Oh, yes. The original mileage of the Company was 122 miles 19 chains, or, if you include the previously existing Glasgow and Garnkirk [*sic*] Railway and the Wishaw and Coltness mineral line, which it absorbed in its progress towards Glasgow, 144 miles. The Company now own 776 miles of line, partly own $152\frac{1}{4}$, and our engines work over a total length of $1,115\frac{1}{2}$ miles of railway.'
> 'In 1865 and 1866 we amalgamated the Scottish Central lines and the group of lines forming the Scottish North-Eastern Railway, and since that time the Caledonian Railway has extended longitudinally from Carlisle to Dundee and Aberdeen, and latitudinally from Edinburgh and Leith to Glasgow and Greenock. It would be tiresome to you and to your readers to detail all the amalgamations which have taken place, but I may say that we have from time to time absorbed thirty-five, lines of railway.'
> (*Railway Magazine*)

The great controversy over the course of the line ('almost theological in intensity') involved colossal legal and parliamentary expense and the whole venture tottered on the edge of financial ruin in late 1849 and 1850. Many works and stations had been left 'incomplete' and what little shed accommodation existed was doubtless both primitive and more or less temporary; there do not appear to have been any grand 'Engine Houses', bold expressions of power and faith seen in some of the pioneering English companies. Very little indeed is known

regarding the early sheds, a situation confused by the disparate, accretionary development of the company. After the company's financial position had been more or less secured, buildings of a more permanent nature began to be established, often in stone, with two or perhaps four roads. They are marked by a strength of style, leavened only a little by arched entranceways. They were invariably straight and there is no hint of a roundhouse in these early years, lest it be the old Dundee and Perth premises at Seabraes (see also p. 58).

An early manifestation of something at least approaching 'standardisation' had appeared by the 1860s with several similar buildings in use – simple constructions with two roads, executed generally in stone. Lockerbie and Peebles were built thus, in local and therefore readily available materials, all of them displaying a common and prominent constructional features – a striking arch, of shallow curve, securing the entrance but incorporated within the main part of the frontage. Buchanan Street (see p. 20) was exceptional – in brick it contrived an altogether lighter, less massive and 'shouldered' appearance. Further buildings in this style might have existed, part of this (loose) grouping but many sheds of this time were long ago swept away.

Stirling, Carstairs and Perth (all 1840s–1850s) and Motherwell were the only substantial buildings (in the sense of size) of any great age remaining by Grouping. Polmadie was an exception but, obligingly, it was disintegrating rapidly and its complete replacement had already been determined. The premier depot of the line, it had perversely been constructed as a colossal timber affair, a hopelessly inappropriate structure increasingly ruinous over the years. Kingmoor, again one of the foremost depots of the line, was also built on this gigantic 'barn' model. In turn it required complete replacement late in the day. Perth remained, much in its mid-nineteenth century pre-Caledonian state, to be entirely rebuilt by the LMS whilst the Caledonian's other great shed, St. Rollox, had been a collection of hovels even to the outbreak of the Great War. It too, as 'Balornock' was then remodelled. Little was left of Carstairs when it was entirely rebuilt by the LMS.

Notwithstanding this apparent tardiness, only lately-remedied, enormous improvements were carried out at intervals over the thirty or so years up to the First World

Grangemouth high transverse roof pitches and associated lifting shop, features as essentially Scottish as Caledonian.

War. Over a dozen major depots were erected in the period, though Polmadie was delayed by war and the Grouping. It cannot be said that strict standardisation was purposed, more that two or three themes, or threads, were present throughout, revived and dusted down of a time; the thirty years after all, spanned the reigns of no less than four superintendents, buildings to the various patterns appearing haphazardly throughout.

Many of the sheds, beginning with Dundee in 1884, were of the 'transverse pitch' type – an arrangement in general favour throughout much of Scotland. Polmadie, though strictly speaking of LMS vintage, can be considered the final expression, a vast building with lofty repair shop characteristic of the larger CR establishments. Sheds to very similar layouts, but with 'north-light pattern' roofs, appeared at intervals, from Greenock in the 1880s to the rebuilt Airdrie at the turn of the century, whilst conventional 'pitched' structures

were employed at certain important sites. These included Hamilton, again in the early 1880s and Kingmoor, a late re-building of about 1915. All three main 'styles' were thus inaugurated within two or three years of each other, in the first part of the 1880s. Thereafter the 'Lanarkshire & Dumbartonshire' project saw two new sheds, remote from mainstream development, at Dumbarton & Yoker. The first, Dumbarton, opened with the line in the 1890s, the traffic worked from the first by the CR – its individual appearance reflects a measure of 'independence', if not on the part of the new company, then at least upon that of the contractor. Yoker opened rather later but to a very similar design.

SHOPS

The main Caledonian sheds were equipped with machines and repair apparatus much as (probably better than) their contemporaries in the south, 'outstations'

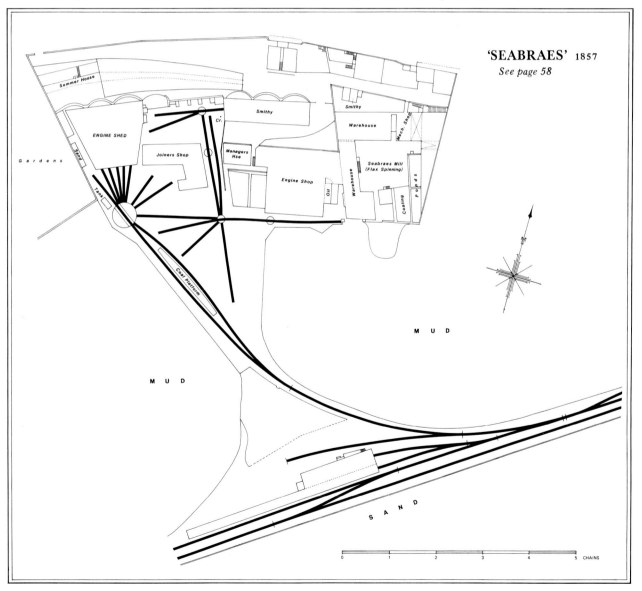

'SEABRAES' 1857
See page 58

Perth in 1913.   *L & GRP, cty. David & Charles*

arranged with due regard to geography, the proximity
of main works and the vagaries of traffic. All the repair
shops were provided with one or more hoists, latterly to
a standard of 30 and even 40 tons, whilst a remote byway
like Lockerbie could boast hand-operated shear-legs.
Absolutely basic provision meant a 7-inch vice and
bench, as say at Leadhills, whilst Lockerbie in 1917, in
addition to the lifting gear, had 'two vices, $5\frac{1}{2}$ inch and
$6\frac{1}{2}$ inch, one grindstone 36 inch with trough (hand
power), one anvil and one Smiths Fire with steel chimney'. Main shops were provided strategically; Carlisle at
the southern extremity enjoyed a full range of equipment
and all manner of machinery including a 4 ft. 6 in. wheel
lathe. Polmadie had a 5 ft. 5 in. example and had habitu-
ally tackled almost anything, short of boiler making and
wheel pressing. Its foremen were carefully chosen, an-
nointed servants wielding great power. Polmadie indeed
reconstructed an 0–6–0ST in 1919; two were taken apart
in the Polmadie 'back shed' and one decent engine made.
Balornock (St. Rollox) relied on the nearby works for
such jobs while Perth, ancient and dilapidated, was
singularly ill-equipped; similarly it relied upon the works,
conveniently close and equipped with, among much else,
two wheel lathes. Aberdeen, a shed of some considerable
importance and, like Kingmoor, at an extremity of the
system, was built rather late – it contained a typical
range of machinery:

    '1 Planing Machine 4' 6″ × 2' 6″ × 2' 6″
     1 Large Turning Lathe, 16″ centre, 12' 3″ bed
     1 Small Turning Lathe, $6\frac{1}{2}''$ centres

    1 Screwing Machine
    1 Radial Drilling Machine
    1 Stationary Engine with Flywheel
    1 Stationary Boiler, with Loco. Type Smokebox
    1 Smithy Fan
    1 Grindstone
    1 Smiths Hearth
    8 Bench Vices
    Anvils, shafting, stands, etc.'

In June 1923 ex-Caledonian Railway sheds with
'repair facilities', as regarded by the LMS, comprised the
following:

Lifting, tyre turning and axlebox boring:
Kingmoor, Motherwell, Polmadie.

Lifting and axlebox boring only:
Hamilton, Dawsholm, St. Rollox, Dundee, Aberdeen,
Edinburgh.

Lifting only:
Beattock, Carstairs, Greenock, Stirling, Oban, Perth,
Forfar.

The main workshops of the Caledonian were at
St. Rollox, with a smaller establishment at Perth. The
LMS General Manager submitted a comprehensive
report to the Locomotive Committee on 27th October
1926 on the future of the various inherited shops with a
view to economy, wherein he proposed 'that locomotive
repair work in Scotland be concentrated as far as possible
on St. Rollox and also that the shops at Perth be closed

and the work transferred to St. Rollox'. This theme was pursued in January 1928 when the Committee was informed of arrangements to concentrate all new construction at Derby and Crewe and to abandon St. Rollox and Horwich as locomotive building centres; the last new construction at St. Rollox was a batch of ten '4F' 0–6–0s, Nos. 4467–4476, turned out later that year. Further consideration was given to the reorganisation of the Northern Division in February 1929, when it was proposed that all heavy repairs in Scotland (this would include ex-CR engines at Kingmoor) would be concentrated at St. Rollox, with Inverness and Kilmarnock reduced to light and service repairs only. This marked the completion of the reordering first considered in 1926. St. Rollox continued in use under BR and only finally ceased steam repairs in the early 1960s, as diesel power was phased in.

TURNTABLES

Between 1904 and 1908 the Caledonian purchased at least six turntables of 70 ft. diameter, both from Cowans Sheldon, its traditional supplier, and from Ransomes and Rapier of Ipswich. 'Standard' turntable diameters had grown rapidly in only a few years, recorded in Western Division Engineers Department minutes at the turn of the century: '5th July 1898. The maximum diameter of Turntables is at present 50 feet. Proposal to increase the maximum in future to 54 feet. Estimates extra cost £130 each Turntable. New Turntables are not to be less than 54 feet'. On 16th October 1900 there came an exactly similar minute, announcing the new maximum as 60 feet.

CR turntables in 1915 were listed as follows

ABERDEEN (FERRYHILL)	70 ft.
ALYTH	42 ft.
ARBROATH	50 ft.
ARDROSSAN	51 ft.
BALLACHULISH (GLENCOE)	60 ft.
BALLOCH	45 ft.
BALQUHIDDER	60 ft.
BEATTOCK	54 ft.
BEITH (see Volume VI)	42 ft.
BLACKWOOD	42 ft.
BLAIRGOWRIE	42 ft.
BOTHWELL	42 ft.
BRAYTON	42 ft.
BRECHIN	51 ft.
BRIDGE STREET (GLASGOW)	55 ft.
BUCHANAN STREET (GLASGOW)	60 ft.
CALLANDER	60 ft.
CARLISLE (ETTERBY)	70 ft.
CARSTAIRS	51 ft.
CONNEL FERRY	50 ft.
CREW JUNCTION (EDINBURGH)	50 ft.
CRIEFF	51 ft.
DALMALLY	48 ft.
DAWSHOLM	50 ft.
DOLPHINTON	42 ft.
DUMBARTON	51 ft.
DUMFRIES	60 ft.
DUNDEE WEST (ENGINE SHED)	70 ft.
DUNDEE EAST	42 ft.
EDINBURGH (PRINCES ST)	51 ft.
EGLINTON STREET	51 ft.
FORFAR	54 ft.
GOUROCK	51 ft.

GRANGEMOUTH ENGINE SHED	70 ft.
GRANGEMOUTH ENGINE SIDINGS, GRANGE DOCK	70 ft.
GREENHILL	60 ft.
GREENOCK ENGINE SHED (LADYBURN)	52 ft.
GUSHETFAULDS	40 ft.
GUTHRIE	43 ft.
HAMILTON CENTRAL	42 ft.
HAMILTON ENGINE SHED	50 ft.
IRVINE	50 ft.
KILBIRNIE	50 ft.
KILMARNOCK (G, B & K)	42 ft.
KIRRIEMUIR	42 ft.
KIRTLEBRIDGE	42 ft.
LANARK	42 ft.
LOCKERBIE	42 ft.
MONTROSE	45 ft.
MORNINGSIDE	42 ft.
MOTHERWELL*	70 ft.
MUIRKIRK	50 ft.
NEWTYLE	40 ft.
OBAN	50 ft.
PEEBLES	60 ft.
PERTH ENGINE SHED	70 ft.
POLMADIE	51 ft.
PORTPATRICK	40 ft.
ROTHESAY DOCK ENGINE SHED (YOKER)	60 ft.
RUTHERGLEN	50 ft.
ST. ROLLOX ENGINE SHED	52 ft.
SEAFIELD	60 ft.
SOUTH SIDE (GLASGOW)	42 ft.
STIRLING	52 ft.
STRATHAVEN	40 ft.
STRANRAER (P & W JOINT LINE)	50 ft.
SYMINGTON	42 ft.
TYNDRUM	42 ft.
WEMYSS BAY	43 ft.

* TURNTABLE TEMPORARILY OUT OF USE OWING TO COAL SINKINGS (Motherwell in fact suffered this problem periodically.)

COALING AND OTHER ASPECTS

Austere, ugly even, timber-clad coal stages, or 'benches' of Scottish usage, (as sand 'kiln' for sand 'furnace') mounted on earth ramps characterised the Caledonian sheds. Inside these darksome places wheeled iron tubs, familiar throughout the country, were hand manoeuvered to a drop-platform overhanging the bunker or tender. The Caledonian was closely allied to the LNWR over very many years and a mechanical coaler much akin to the pioneering edifice at Crewe eventually appeared at Polmadie. This was after grouping but its conception and much of the planning pre-dated 1923. Like the Crewe model, it was not a striking success – at least it wore out quickly and was replaced, again at a period of transition, in the late 1940s. Ash disposal meant simply hand shovelling from pits or track level into open wagons and in this the CR did not differ from other leading companies.

The sheds on the Northern Division were in the main well built and required little in the way of re-roofing in later years. Dawsholm eventually received something approximating to an LMS 'louvre' roof following fire damage but dilapidation on the former CR was attributable more to bombs or subsidence than to imperfect construction. Carstairs and Perth, crumbling and ancient, were untouched in the 'thirty years' (see p. 1) and were entirely reconstructed as standard LMS 'single-pitch' depots, arranged on the 'service-sequence' model. As such they were generically indistinguishable from sheds of widely varied origins, the LNWR, the L&Y or even the Furness. See *LMS Engine Sheds, passim.*

The Caledonian did not employ a shed code and at no time, it seems, was a shed location placed on engines, 'every foreman knew a "stranger" had to be returned as soon as possible (officially at least) to its home shed with its own crew.' All special notices of additional trains carried an indication of the originating depot so all would know whence the loco came. Caledonian engines were generally at the same shed for years, returning 'home' from works visits in the charge of a crew (generally its own) from the home shed. The Caledonian had various 'Engineers Divisions', arranged geographically. These were responsible for building work, plant etc and did not specifically coincide with the locomotive arrangements. For the latter a Running Superintendent was employed, the last, John Barr, taking all the LMS lines in Scotland under his control after 1923.

The Scottish companies conveniently formed the Northern Division of the LMS; little happened at first but eventually, of course, an elaborate coding and reorganisation was arrived at. The LMS 'Concentration and Garage Scheme' was implemented (see other volumes, in particular Vol. I) in 1935 but was not fully thought through with respect to Scotland. Kingmoor was afforded 'concentration' status, as the largest pre-grouping depot in Carlisle and was detached from the Northern Division, coded 12A between the LNW and MR groups. Garage sheds of LNW, MR Furness, CR and GSWR origin gave to the Kingmoor District a unique variety and exceptional interest.

The remaining Scottish sheds were grouped into three districts of widely disparate size, under the Caledonian depots Polmadic, Motherwell and Perth. This left obvious anomalies, important and well-equipped depots at Corkerhill (GSWR) and Inverness (HR) left ostensibly as 'garages'. The situation was resolved under a scheme devised in 1940, recoding most of the sheds and increasing the groups (or rather 'Districts') to six. Polmadie and Perth were reduced in extent, Motherwell exchanging Hamilton and Grangemouth for Dalry Road and Carstairs, whilst St Rollox, Corkerhill and Inverness were constituted as separate Districts. New plates began to appear on engines towards the end of 1940 fitted, with Northern Division convention, high up on the smokebox door (of ex-Scottish company engines). St Rollox had abandoned the front numberplates ordered in the 1920s but, on their re-imposition by BR, the shed plates were moved to the familiar site in the lower part of the smokebox door.

The Scottish Region was in the vanguard when the time came for the BR recoding and many new plates were already affixed by July 1949, the earlier codes made available from such diverse places as Bank Hall L&Y (27A) and Norwich GE (32A).

'Barracks' were provided for lodging enginemen on the Caledonian – by 1915 no less than three were available: 'Dormitories have been provided at Carlisle, Grangemouth and Oban, for the accommodation of Enginemen, brakesmen, and others running to these places. The Lodging allowance will be as stated in the "Conditions of Service".'

The great timber gables of 'Etterby' engine shed, with 0–8–0 No. 600, around 1903. Fires did occur, of course, not the least in wooden buildings but the big Caledonian sheds were far from 'tinderboxes'. Wood was frequently protected from corrosion by layers of soot and failure was frequently due to the chemical degradation of metal attachments, or concrete. If a fire took hold through some ill-chance, then such a building would be in great peril, but its downfall was more likely to come about from below, the slow insidious work of damp and mould at its roots.   *Locomotive Publishing Co.*

The Engine Shed, Aberdeen, scene of endless wrangling. The North British finally settled on terms roughly equivalent to those originally offered, once the brouhaha over lighting up, sand buckets, water and ashes had settled. The North British took possession of its three 'northernmost roads', "Mr. M'Intosh" making the necessary arrangements for the transfer of engines from the old two-road shed close by. This was afterwards given over to wagon repairs.

H. C. Casserley Collection

ABERDEEN FERRYHILL

The Caledonian shared their premises at Aberdeen with the North British, an arrangement condemned to endless altercation and squabbling.

The Aberdeen Railway had been authorised in 1845 as an extension of the Scottish Midland Junction, thus continuing the 'West Coast Route' to Aberdeen; at the same time the promotion of the Great North of Scotland Railway was underway – it had been authorised in its turn in 1846 and the Board of the Aberdeen Railway held many of the shares, for the intention was for both companies to work jointly, sharing an awkwardly sited terminus at Guild Street. The Great North of Scotland failed to attract the necessary finance but the Aberdeen Co. proceeded with its own line to a temporary halt at the River Dee, until the future of its erstwhile partner could be made clear. In 1847 powers were given for both companies to amalgamate, but in July of 1850 the Act was repealed, the new Board of the Aberdeen Co. having despaired of the faltering GNSR. In the repeal Act, the Aberdeen Railway was empowered to make a terminus of its own in Guild Street, east of the site first chosen for the joint station; by April 1850 it had reached Ferryhill where the Board had already agreed to erect a temporary station – since the ground at Guild Street was of limited extent it was decided to place the 'Engine House' at Ferryhill.

This original shed appears to have first served as a store for the contractor, the Aberdeen Railway putting in two lines of rail for locomotives; early records are not clear but suggest that two engines could be accommodated with a further two partly under cover. As a temporary measure and until a larger one could be acquired a 20 ft. turntable intended for Montrose was hastily put in. This was presumably in use by 1851, a period when the Scottish Central Railway, the Scottish Midland Junction and the Aberdeen Railway worked together with a traffic 'pool' – a time when the Ferryhill shed was 'much increased in length'. This is the story according to D. H. Littlejohn's writings but his information would be derived 'from pre-existing legend' and its seems more likely that the shed was lengthened *after* the Caledonian had taken over the Scottish North Eastern; if indeed the shed was in as poor a state as many of the bridges and structures on the line, it is most probable that a complete renewal was undertaken.

The building stood on the west side of the main line near the River Dee (a stretch labelled 'Pot and Ford Fishing' in 1866) a short distance from the Ferryhill Foundry, where the 'Deeside Railway' (the GNSR) was later to join Aberdeen Railway metals. The shed measured some 166 ft. by 38 ft., standing, by the late 1860s, in a reasonably open district close to the substantial detached residence, 'Polmuir House'. 'Devanha Distillery' stood nearby, destined to expand such to rival in size the engine shed itself. The depot at this time had still to make do with a very small turntable; it was eventually replaced by a unit some forty feet in diameter and relegated for coal wagons. By the end of the century the shed had indeed been greatly extended at the rear, increasing in length to something like 230 feet, under the very eaves of the sad 'Polmuir House' and a 50 ft. turntable was in use. The very earliest building

had entirely superseded, new construction perhaps very soon taking place upon the original foundations. Drummond, by the mid 1880s, would almost certainly have looked askance at the restricted proportions of Ferryhill shed, but the exact dates of any changes are unknown – they may very well have taken place in several stages. On 4th of September 1894, certainly, the Board agreed that the 'Engine Shed at Aberdeen' should be 'enlarged', with a fitters shop included.

The North British Railway had acquired the right (included in its original powers for access to Aberdeen) to stable locos at the shed and proved a vexation to the Caledonian from an early date. Money, as ever, came between them: '11th December 1884 ... have had an account against the North British Company for Engine Stabling at Aberdeen from July 1878 to July 1883 ... amounting to £415 ... charging at the rate of £30 *per* Engine *per annum*'. The Caledonian, less than enthusiastically, were now prepared to settle for £20 p.a. Drummond subsequently provided a monthly statement detailing the NBR's activities at Ferryhill and on 13th January 1885, referring to the current half year, reported 'They have had five Engines stabled here during the whole of that period'.

Over the years Caledonian policy remained essentially one of containment; every NB working represented, in effect, financial (and political) failure. The North British would receive no encouragement to their Aberdeen activities and the smallest changes or concessions came about only after endless wrangling. Ferryhill shed was thus the subject of a more or less continual correspondence, the rate increasing sharply on the opening of a new 12-road shed in 1908. The papers are too voluminous to reproduce in full but the following extracts are more or less typical; they indicate the shed's opening to have been 1908, though the new 70 ft turntable was authorised on 20th of March 1906, arrangements terminable on 6 months' notice by either party.

ABERDEEN ENGINE SHED.

CORRESPONDENCE EMBODYING ARRANGEMENT

between

THE CALEDONIAN RAILWAY COMPANY

and

THE NORTH BRITISH RAILWAY COMPANY

As to the Use of a Portion of This Shed by the Engines of The Latter Company.

Edinburgh, 29th July, 1908.

R. MILLAR, Esq.,
Caledonian Railway,
Glasgow.

Dear Sir,
ENGINE SHED, ABERDEEN.

I understand the new engine shed which has been erected by your Company at Ferryhill, Aberdeen, will shortly be brought into use, and should be obliged if you would let me know what portion of the accommodation you propose to allocate to this Company.

Yours faithfully,

W. F. JACKSON.

Glasgow, 9th October, 1908.

W. F. JACKSON, Esq.,
North British Railway,
Edinburgh.

Dear Sir,
ENGINE SHED, ABERDEEN.

Referring to your letter of the 29th July last, I have now looked into this matter, and I find that this shed is now nearly ready for occupation, and I propose allocating to your Company the three northmost shed roads. Besides the shed accommodation, each of these roads is capable of holding an engine clear of the crossing outside the shed, and your Company could also have the use of the siding outside the shed when required to stable any extra engines. There are water columns between the roads, and the yards will be well lighted.

In regard to the charges to be made for your Company's occupation, I am prepared to advise my Directors to agree to those under-noted:—

CHARGE FOR STABLING, £2 per month per engine. Isolated cases, 1s. 6d. per day for use of shed.

LIGHTING UP CHARGE, 1s. per time, which includes coal, wages of staff, and firing of furnace.

TURNING CHARGE, 6d. per engine turned.

SAND CHARGE, 3d. per bucket.

WATER CHARGE, 75 per cent. of capacity of tender would be the quantity of water charged against your Company at the rate which this Company have to pay for it.

ASHES REMOVAL, A proportion of the total cost of the removal of the ashes from the shed, according to the number of engines.

I may say that the average for the year for this runs about £116, and your Company's proportion thereof would be about £45.

I shall be glad to hear from you in regard to this at your early convenience.

I am,
Yours truly,
For the GENERAL MANAGER,
JNO. SCOULLER.

Edinburgh, 12th October, 1908.

THE GENERAL MANAGER,
Caledonian Railway,
Glasgow.

Dear Sir,

ENGINE SHED, ABERDEEN.

I have received your letter of 9th instant, and will write again on the subject.

Yours faithfully,
pro W. F. JACKSON.
J.C.

Glasgow, 22nd October, 1908.

W. F. JACKSON, Esqre.,
North British Railway,
Edinburgh.

Dear Sir,

ENGINE SHED, ABERDEEN.

Referring to your letter of the 12th instant, this matter is becoming rather urgent, and I shall be glad to hear from you definitely at your earliest convenience.

I am,
Yours truly,
G. CALTHROP,
per J.S.

Edinburgh, 14th November, 1908.

G. CALTHROP, Esq.,
Caledonian Railway,
Glasgow,

Dear Sir,

ENGINE SHED, ABERDEEN.

Referring again to your letter of 22nd ultimo, the matter has now been looked into, and as regards the charges proposed to be made against this Company for the use of the new engine shed, etc., I have the following observations to make, viz.:—

STABLING, I shall be glad to know why it is proposed to increase the existing charge of £20 per engine per annum to £24. Are we to have the use of fitting and repairing shop or crane if required, and is the charge of 1s. 6d. for isolated cases to mean the engines of men booked off for not less than 9 hours, or what is to be the minimum?

LIGHTING, Perhaps you will be good enough to let me know how the charge of 1s. is arrived at, stating the amount applicable for coal, wages, and firing of furnaces.

TURNING, No payment has been made hitherto by this Company under this head, as this facility was covered by the payment of £20 per engine per annum for stabling accommodation.

SAND, 3d. per bucket seems to me to be an exorbitant charge to make, and I shall be glad if you will inform me how this figure is arrived at.

WATER, The present method is to charge 2,000 gallons per tank, and I should like to know

why you now propose to alter this arrangement.

ASHES REMOVAL, A direct charge does not appear to have been hitherto made under this head, and perhaps you will see your way to delete this item from the list of charges.

Our Locomotive Superintendent states that he is not satisfied that the accommodation proposed to be allocated to this Company is sufficient for our requirements, but as to this I will write later on.

I am,
Yours faithfully,
W. F. JACKSON.

Glasgow, 25th November, 1908.

W. F. JACKSON, Esq.,
North British Railway,
Edinburgh.

Dear Sir,

ENGINE SHED, ABERDEEN.

Referring to your letter of the 14th inst., I have now had an opportunity of considering the observations made by you in regard to the charges proposed to be levied against your Company for the use of the new Engine Shed, &c., at Aberdeen, and in reply thereto I have to state as follows:—

STABLING, The existing charge of £20 per engine per annum was arranged at a meeting between Mr. Walker, of the North British Company, and the late Sir James Thompson in 1883 without prejudice, and in view of the substantial shed accommodation now provided and the improved facilities for dealing with the movement of engines, and also the fact that the proposed charges are uniform with the practice of other Companies, I think the rent now proposed of £2 per engine per month, with 1s. 6d. per engine for isolated cases – *i.e.*, engines arriving with trains and men booked off for rest – to cover the use of shed and yard, is quite reasonable.

With regard to crane, your Company can have the use of same when it is not being used by our people, the charge for the use of which would be so much per hour, with a minimum charge for each time used.

LIGHTING, One shilling per engine for the supply of burning coal to kindle engines covers the cost of coal, wages, firing up of furnaces, &c., and is the practice on all leading lines.

TURNING, The charge proposed for turning is also a universal one; and while your Company have enjoyed the benefit of getting your engines turned on our table hitherto free of charge, this is no argument in favour of the privilege being continued without payment. The Company have put down a new turntable of the maximum dimensions, and the charge proposed of 6d. per engine to cover the use and tear and wear by your engines is a fair and reasonable one.

SAND, The charge of 3d. per bucket is a very moderate one, and is meant to cover the expense of purchase, haulage to Aberdeen, emptying from wagon to sand kiln, drying, and riddling.

WATER, When your Company's engines commenced running to Aberdeen the carrying capacity of the tenders averaged 2,000 to 2,500 gallons each, and 2,000 gallons was considered equal to 75 per cent. of the then water tank capacity, and the alteration of the charge now proposed should not be looked upon as an increased charge, but more in the nature of rectifying the percentage of water taken by the larger capacity of the tenders now used.

ASHES, In former years the fires of your Company's engines were drawn opposite the ash wagons at the old shed, and one man was sufficient to fill them into ash wagons, but owing to altered construction of your Company's engines the ashes are dropped into pit, and have in consequence to be lifted into barrows and wheeled away. The expense incurred doing this is greater than formerly, and it is only fair that your Company should bear their proportion of the expenditure.

I am,
Yours truly,
G. CALTHROP.

Glasgow, 24th December, 1908.

W. F. JACKSON, Esqre.,
North British Railway,
Edinburgh.

Dear Sir,

ENGINE SHED, ABERDEEN.

Referring to your letter of the 9th instant, our people are again pressing me on the subject, and if you are now in a position to reply to my letter of the 25th ultimo I shall be glad to hear from you.

I am,
Yours truly,
G. CALTHROP.

Edinburgh, 24th February, 1909.

G. CALTHROP, Esq.,
Caledonian Railway,
Glasgow.

Dear Sir,

ENGINE SHED, &c., ABERDEEN.

Referring again to your letter of 24th December last; I have now had an opportunity of looking further into the matter and have to state as follows:—

(1) STABLING, I will not object to the proposed charge of £24 per engine per annum, on the following conditions:—
   (a) That four of the roads inside the new engine shed be allocated to this Company.
   (b) That you concur in the suggestions made in connection with the various matters referred to under heads 2, 3, 4, 5, and 6.

(2) LIGHTING UP, I regret I cannot concur in the proposed charge of one shilling for each engine, but I would be disposed to agree to a charge of 9d. per engine. The last mentioned charge seems to me to be a very full one.

(3) WATER, I am sorry I cannot agree to the new proposal. I think the charge formerly made, viz.:— 2,000 gallons per tank at 6¼d. per thousand gallons, is a full one, and should be continued. If you are unable to concur in this view, I would suggest that it be remitted to the Locomotive Superintendents of the two Companies, with a view to ascertain the quantity of water actually taken for, say, a fortnight, and thereafter report result.

(4) SAND, I cannot concur in the view that the proposed charge for sand is a moderate one, particularly when it is kept in view that the charge for lighting up embraces the coal used to dry the sand, it being dried in the kindling kiln. The proposed charge works out at 13s. 4d. per ton, allowing 42 lbs. to each bucket, which is certainly an excessive rate. I think the former charge was a very full one, and should not be disturbed.

(5) TURNING, I regret I cannot concur in the view that the proposed charge is a universal one. That is not our experience. I am strongly of opinion, as previously stated, that the facility is covered by the payment in respect of stabling accommodation.

(6) ASHES, You would appear to be under a misapprehension. I am informed the ashes that are dropped into the pit when cleaning the fires of the engines are cooled and thrown out of pit by our own staff, and taken to the place where the ashes are deposited in the usual way. I do not think, therefore, the present arrangement should be disturbed.

(7) USE OF CRANE AND FITTING AND REPAIRING SHOP, I should be obliged if you would state precisely the terms on which you would be prepared to grant this Company the use of the crane and fitting and repairing shop.

Yours faithfully,
W. F. JACKSON.

Glasgow, 15th April, 1909.

W. F. JACKSON, Esq.,
North British Railway,
Edinburgh.

Dear Sir,

ENGINE SHED, ABERDEEN.

I have now had an opportunity of submitting to my Directors your letter of 24th February last, and I am instructed to state that they regret your Company has not seen its way to accept the offer made in the late General Manager's letter to you of 9th October last, in regard to the charges to be made against your Company in respect of the accommodation provided for your Company in this engine shed, and for the work to be done for, and the articles to be supplied to, your Company at that shed.

The charges proposed were made specially moderate with the view of coming to an amicable arrangement, and as this object has failed, no other course is open to my Company except to withdraw the offer which has been made – which I now do, leaving the matter to be settled by arbitration in terms of the statute.

In any arbitration proceedings my Company reserve the right to claim such increased charges as they may consider reasonable and necessary in the circumstances.

I am,
Yours truly,
G. CALTHROP.

Edinburgh, 20th April, 1909.

G. CALTHROP, Esq.,
Caledonian Railway,
Glasgow.

Dear Sir,

ENGINE SHED, ABERDEEN.

I have received your letter of 15th instant. You seem to have had the impression that you were making a liberal proposal to me, and I also had the view that in my suggestion I was acting very liberally.

Of course, if there is no way of settling the matter but arbitration, we will have no alternative but to resort to this course. I think, however that if we had an opportunity of talking the matter over we might probably come somewhat nearer each other than we have come, and I propose, therefore, to put the subject on the agenda for the meeting of the two Companies to be held on 3rd proximo. I

hope you will concur in the adoption of this course.

Yours faithfully,
W. F. JACKSON.

The arrangements were afterwards discussed in further detail at meetings, both in Glasgow and London, the final terms being listed by Calthrop of the CR in a letter of 16th July 1909, fully a year after negotiations had first been entered into:

Glasgow, 16th July, 1909.

W. F. JACKSON, Esqre.,
North British Railway,
Edinburgh.

Dear Sir,

ABERDEEN ENGINE SHED.

Referring to the correspondence which has passed between us, and to our meeting on this subject, when you intimated that you were prepared to accept this Company's terms if I reduced the annual payment in respect of the turntable from 20 per cent. of its cost to 15 per cent. I have now considered the matter, and for the sake of a settlement I am prepared, on behalf of my Company, to accept the 15 per cent, per annum on the cost of the turntable instead of the 20 per cent. stipulated for.

The payments to be made by your Company to mine in respect of the use of the Engine Shed at Aberdeen will therefore be as follows:—

CHARGE FOR STABLING, £2 per month per engine. Isolated cases, 1s. 6d. per day for use of shed, as explained in my letter to you of the 25th November last.

LIGHTING, 1s. per time, which includes coal, wages of staff, and firing of furnace.

TURNING CHARGE, 15 per cent. per annum on cost of turntable (£1,200).

SAND CHARGE, 3d. per bucket.

WATER CHARGE, 75 per cent. of capacity of tender, at the rate at which this Company has to pay for the water.

ASHES REMOVAL, A proportion of the total cost of the removal of ashes from the shed according to the number of engines.

USE OF CRANE AND FITTING AND REPAIRING SHOP. – 5s. per hour every time crane is used. Minimum charge 5s. Unless your Company's engines require to be lifted off their wheels at crane there would be no necessity for their being taken into fitting shop, but charge for crane would also cover fitting shop.

This arrangement to last till terminated by six months' notice on either side.

I shall be glad to have your confirmation.

I am,
Yours truly,
G. CALTHROP.

Westminster, S.W., 26th July, 1909.

Dear Sir,

ABERDEEN ENGINE SHED.

With reference to your letter of 16th instant, and to our conversation to-day; I am prepared to concur in the arrangement contained in your letter, subject, of course, to the turning charge of 15 per cent. on the cost of the turntable being divided between the Companies in the proportion of the engines turned by each Company respectively, and to the deletion of the clause relating to the use of crane and fitting and repairing shop. This latter has not hitherto been part of the arrangement, and, while I was anxious to have some idea of the terms on which, if we should wish the facility, it could be obtained, I do not think there is any necessity for making it part of the arrangement, as it is extremely unlikely we will require to avail ourselves of it, and certainly on the terms suggested we would not do so.

I shall be glad to hear from you confirming the arrangement, which I presume will take effect as from 1st proximo, and endure until terminated by either party on six months' notice.

Yours faithfully,
W. F. JACKSON.
G. Calthrop, Esq.,
Caledonian Railway,
Glasgow.

Throughout all this NBR Locos continued to use the old two road shed:

Glasgow, 3rd September, 1909.
W. F. Jackson, Esq.,
North British Railway,
Edinburgh.

Dear Sir,
ABERDEEN ENGINE SHED.

I duly received your letter of the 31st ulto. agreeing to this Company's conditions regarding the use by your Company of this shed, except the conditions relating to the use of the crane and fitting and repairing shop, which you think has no connection with the question, and stating that if I agree to delete that condition the matter may be taken as settled. As this Company has no interest to insist on the retention of the condition I have withdrawn it, and thus settled the matter.

I have instructed Mr. McIntosh, our Locomotive Superintendent, to make the necessary arrangements for your Company's engines vacating the old shed and occupying the lines apportioned to them in the new shed, and no doubt he will communicate with your people as soon as he is in a position to do so.

Of course it must be clearly understood, now that the condition as to the use of the crane and fitting and repairing shop is not included in the arrangement come to, that if your Company should at any time require the use of the crane and fitting and repairing shop, special arrangements as to terms of user will require to be made with this Company prior to such use.

I am,
Yours truly,
G. CALTHROP,
per J. S.

Edinburgh, 6th September, 1909.

G. Calthrop, Esq.,
Caledonian Railway,
Glasgow.

Dear Sir,

ENGINE SHED, ABERDEEN.

I am in receipt of your letter of 3rd instant, and have given our Locomotive Superintendent the necessary advice in the matter. The new arrangement will, of course, take effect as from the date on which we obtain possession of the new accommodation.

I quite understand that in the event of our requiring the use of the crane and fitting and repairing shop, special arrangements as to terms of user will require to be made with your Company prior to such use.

Yours faithfully.
W. F. JACKSON.

At last allowed use of the new shed, NBR engines were not at first permitted to take coal; this concession the CR steadfastly refused to concede and the question did not really arise again until the outbreak of war in 1914:

THE CALEDONIAN RAILWAY COMPANY.

LOCOMOTIVE DEPARTMENT.

Aberdeen Station,
19th October 1914

Wm. Pickersgill Esq.,
Loco. Supt.,

Dear Sir,
Aberdeen & Edinburgh Passenger Trains

Your R4/18987 of 14th inst. & enclosures.

I have looked fully into this matter and it appears to me to be the inserting of the thin end of the wedge as, if the NB Engines are to be coaled here, the goods engines will follow in the same practice and demand coal. It is generally known that once a small concession is granted it becomes a demand very soon.

It is pointed out in letter from NB. Loco. Supt. that more than seven engines would require to be coaled. At present there are five engines of the Atlantic type working into Aberdeen and working out the 6.15 a.m. 10.20 a.m. 1.20 p.m. 5.35 p.m. and 7.35 p.m. Passenger Trains, also there are another three engines which are coaled daily out of NB wagons – one pass' & two goods shunting engines. The number of engines quoted is of course the miminum that would require coal during the Winter Season and it is a question what amount would really be required in the height of the Summer Season when specials are run & trains in duplicate. From information, I have learned that it is also proposed to coal some of the engines of NB goods trains at Aberdeen to save time at Dundee and allow trains to run throughout & so lessen the time taken on journey.

The Coaling Stage here is a small one as it has only one tip and accommodation for 16 ten cwt boxes. During the busy Summer Season, at the like of the Glasgow Fair & Aberdeen Holidays, when we have a great many special trains of our own, necessitating the coaling up of engines for Glasgow and the coaling of Aberdeen engines for Perth runs, through want of time at Perth & also the coaling of Perth engines, it will be a very difficult matter to cope with the coaling of NB engines also, as there will be a great many more of them & as you are aware they all arrive at Sheds about the same time as CR engines, seeing both Company's trains are booked to arrive within a few minutes of each other.

During the month of May this year, owing to the heavy traffic & Aberdeen engines not being coaled at Perth, I found it necessary to increase the Staff of Coalmen from three to four men – 2 by day & 2 by night. Previous to this alteration there were 2 by day and 1 by night, but the nightshift Coalman had to be assisted 6 hours nightly by Cleaners. The total Staff was not increased by this, as I arranged for a Shed Labourer overtaking the work. I may say the four men are fully employed and even with extra man, assistance had to be given during busy season in order to get the engines coaled in shorter time. Should it be agreed to coal NB engines another Coalman would be required

during the Winter months & perhaps two during the Summer.

This last few weeks I have observed that the NB Loco Staff here has been increased by one fitter, one boilermaker and one boilerwasher, all three men having been transferred from Dundee with a view to overtaking work formerly executed at Dundee. Prior to this arrangement only one or two engines of the shunting class were washed out at Aberdeen during the month & as these were engines of a small type only 2,000 galls. of water were charged for each washout, through NB Monthly Account sent you, but since boilerwasher was transferred, engines of the large Atlantic Type have boilers washed out also. This will necessitate an increased consumpt of water and I would suggest that the average amount be increased to 5,000 gallons for this class of engine when washed out.

Yours truly,

In 1915 the North British were still attempting to wrest the use of the coaling bench, the unwelcome 'thin end of the wedge'. To share it, the Caledonian determined, in circumspect fashion, 'would be an awkward arrangement' and offered an extra road on the north side for coal wagons. Seven NB engines were reckoned to require about 14–15 tons daily and this siding remained in place until the end of steam in the 1960s. Through all this it appears that the NB's most effective argument had been safety; their locos 'had to coal so high at Edinburgh for the return trip that we are afraid of it falling off and causing injury'.

The coaling agreement eventually concluded between the Aberdeen protagonists was to last 15 years, though later the NBR was caught out in breach of the articles; the Caledonian replied with a court case abandoned only when its chastened rival agreed to abide strictly by the terms. The NBR in truth could not really overcome its resentment at the defeat suffered in Aberdeen. The company never lost a sense of pique over the 1866 Act, amalgamating the Scottish North Eastern into the Caledonian and checking the aims encapsulated in their own Tay Bridge bill (which would have allowed NB local traffic between Aberdeen and Montrose). The NBR was permitted only to set down at Stonehaven northbound, and southbound uplift passengers for Dundee and south thereof. When the company got to Aberdeen they found that there was no ground available in the city where an engine shed could be erected; a compromise was made by seeking accommodation at Ferryhill *until* suitable land could be obtained. This alternative was never seriously examined and soured relations thereafter. The NBR indeed, it seems, found it very easy (almost it preferred it) to cause offence at Aberdeen, and the Great North of Scotland Minutes recall instances where North British enginemen had at times availed themselves, 'without leave' of that company's Aberdeen turntable. By January 1916 water was the subject of dispute and the Caledonian reviewed some of its figures. The annual charge from the Aberdeen Corporation, for 52,000,000 gallons was

Aberdeen on 3rd September 1948. The shed roof by this time had deteriorated badly, doubtless eliciting demands for restorative action from the LNER, who would not be required to foot the bill. Numbers of LMS locos at Ferryhill continued to decline in puzzling fashion; maybe it was that more locos could be actually based at Perth following its renewal, but in truth the Aberdeen shed was never overcrowded. *The Railway Observer* of July 1937 records LMS express trains to and from Aberdeen 'were worked almost exclusively by Stanier 5XP and 5P 4—6—0s'. The item went on to describe Compound 4—4—0s on secondary duties and 'Royal Scots' occasionally turning up, with the only regular working of a Caledonian 4—4—0 (often 14486) described as the 12.15 p.m. ex-Perth stopping train to Aberdeen, the engine leaving as pilot to a 5P 4—6—0 on an express goods leaving the city 'about 4.40 p.m.'. 14457 and 14502 were noted on this job, the engine working the 1.34 p.m. ex-Perth (Saturdays) usually returning light.

'On 12th June 1937 4—6—0 No. 5357 worked this turn, but returned piloting No. 5176 on the 4.40 p.m. fast goods. No. 14457 working

the 12.15 p.m. ex Perth same day returned light. On 12/6/37 4—6—0 No. 5356 was noted on a troop special into Aberdeen. 4—6—0s Nos. 5356-61 have recently arrived at Perth, but are not yet fitted with staff-changing apparatus for single line working.

'Aberdeen-Stonehaven local services are worked by 0—6—0s which return tender first from Stonehaven. Nos. 4109, 4187, 17400, 17566, 17655, have been noted. An express goods leaving Aberdeen about 8.15 p.m. is regularly worked by 2—6—0s Nos. 2913, 2915 on alternate days. Another goods leaving about 9 p.m. is worked by "Caley" 4—6—0s, Nos. 14632/33 having been noted. The 1.55 p.m. fish train to the South is still worked by "Royal Scot" Class 4—6—0s occasionally piloted by Stanier 5XPs. Those noted have been 6145 piloted by 5581 (25 vans), 6130 piloted by 5579 (26 vans). Goods shunting at the Joint Station (Deeside Goods) is performed by 0—6—0Ts Nos. 16240, 16326/59.'

J. L. Stevenson

No. 4997 at Ferryhill on 16th June 1949. It may be that the paucity of engines at Aberdeen may be explicable in terms somewhat beyond a single concentration of engines at Perth with its superior facilities. It is not known if the CR-NBR ill-feeling carried over into Grouping but it may have suffered neglect through its role as 'no-man's land'. Given the wrangling over the simple coal bench, it is not hard to imagine how the 'thin end of the wedge' difficulties would be compounded by a modern mechanical coaler and the consequent heavy expense. It is significant that the LNER installed its own mechanical apparatus at Kittybrewster, the ex-Great North of Scotland establishment to the north. *H. C. Casserley*

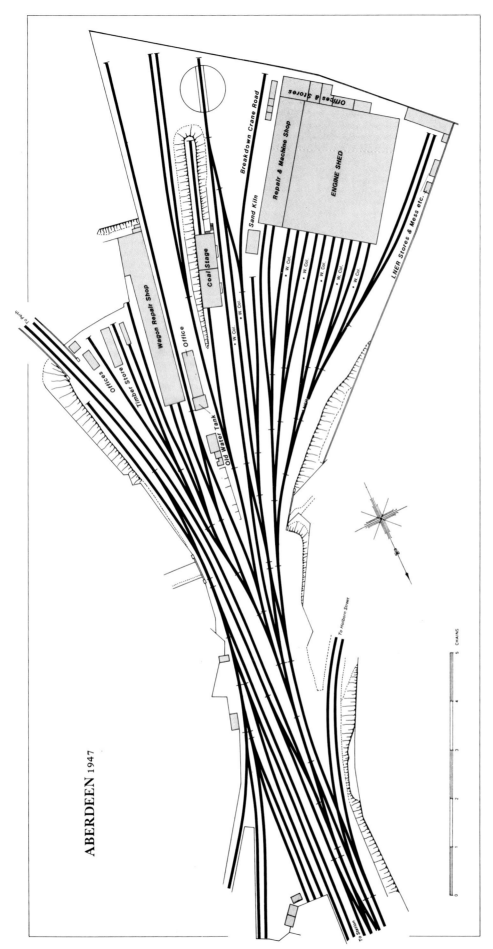

ABERDEEN 1947

£642, that is 2.9631d. per thousand whilst the amount charged to the NBR was 5d – a detail it was felt, better perhaps for the latter not to be aware of...

The new Aberdeen shed of 1908 was most generously provided for with respect to accommodation – only 27 locos were allocated in 1922, fifteen 4–4–0s, ten 0–6–0s and a pair of 0–6–0Ts. Ferryhill had a share in the main line work to the south and received small numbers. Of the principal passenger classes of the 1922 complement, no less than seven were the first Superheater 4–4–0s, arriving new in 1912–1914. The engines could stable on seven roads in the running shed (three of course, were given over to the NBR) whilst a well equipped two-road fitting shop with the usual 30 ton hoist, was provided. By the end of 1947 only fifteen LMS locos were at Aberdeen but in September 1933 the total had stood at nearly thirty – including a pair of new 'Crab' 2–6–0s, Nos. 13212 and 13213 and a number of LMS 0–6–0s and 4–4–0s, '4Fs' Nos. 4108, 4109, 4187 and 4188, with '4Ps' Nos. 918 938, 1183 and 1184. Ex-Caledonian engines comprised 4–4–0s Nos. 14316, 14458, 14459, 14485, 14486, 14489, 14490, 14501 and 14502; 0–6–0s Nos. 17368, (which as 698 had gone new to Aberdeen in 1893) 17393, 17400, 17566, 17655; 0–6–0Ts Nos. 16326, 16327, 16345 and 16359; with solitary 0–4–4T No. 15234. The LNER at Ferryhill at this time were considerably worse off; they had no less than 30 locos in their restricted quarters, mainly 0–6–0s and 0–6–0Ts. Presumably by this time Ferryhill LNER was administered from Kittybrewster. March 1953:

'4P' 4–4–0
41134, 41176, 41184

'5MT' 4–6–0
45245, 45367

'3F' 0–6–0T
56240, 56251, 56278, 56326, 56348

'A2' 4–6–2
60525 *A.H. Peppercorn*, 60531 *Bahram*, 60532 *Blue Peter*

'V2' 2–6–2
60819, 60824, 60827, 60851, 60888, 60898, 60919, 60955, 60970, 60973

'J35' 0–6–0
64482, 64485

'J36' 0–6–0
65247, 65297

'J39' 0–6–0
64795, 64975

'C15' 4–4–2T
67478

'C16' 4–4–2T
67496, 67501

'N15' 0–6–2T
69125, 69128, 69129, 69201

WD 2–8–0
90020, 90041, 90097, 90455

Total 40

The LMS began working their Aberdeen trains with Class 5s (later joined by BR versions) but these were never allocated to Ferryhill. LMS Pacifics were also used for a time, off Crewe-Perth lodging turns, out from Perth with the 7.15 a.m. ex-Glasgow and returning on the 3.30 p.m. 'Postal'. 'Royal

Bound otherwise for obscurity, Ferryhill was made remarkable in the last years by a number of **A4 Pacifics** sent to St. Rollox and Ferryhill for the '3-hour' trains. Above: *Bittern*. Below: *Empire of India*. *N. E. Preedy*

Scot' 4–6–0s could also appear on these turns. The LMS presence was already faltering by Nationalisation after which ex-LNE types rapidly gained the ascendency. A dozen or so 'V2' 2–6–2s were present by 1950, taking over the 'Postal' and other major turns to Dundee (LNE) and Perth (LMS). Fifteen ex-

LNE and ex-NB engines, with six WD 2–8–0s were there but only five 0–6–0Ts remained to represent the Caledonian; in addition three '4P' 4–4–0s were available, Nos. 41134, 41176 and 41184. LNER Pacifics, including eight 'A4s' by 1965, were afterwards a feature at the shed.

Ferryhill was coded 29F under Perth in 1935, becoming 29B in the 1940 re-arrangements. It was revised to 61B by BR in 1949, a code it still retained on closure to steam in March 1967. It continues to serve as a diesel depot, with the roofing over some (including the ex-NB) roads removed.

The LMS interest in the shed at Arbroath amounted to a single road, generous provision for a Forfar 0—4—4T. On 16th June 1936 the engine was No. 15195, together with LNER J83 0—6—0T No. 9805.

W. A. Camwell

ARBROATH

From 1838 Arbroath was the terminus of two distinct lines, the 'Arbroath and Forfar Railway' leading away north to Guthrie and Forfar, and the 'Dundee and Arbroath Railway' hugging the coast southward to Dundee. They later met (February 1848) 'end on' at Arbroath Junction station where both maintained a goods shed. The Arbroath and Forfar additionally operated a short branch to 'the Shore' serving the 'Old Tide Harbour'. The Dundee and Arbroath Railway works and shed were first located at Broughty Ferry, much of it later removed to Arbroath, where an 'Engine House' had been erected, a single road shed some 110 ft. in length immediately to the south of the station. It was also provided with a 15 ft. turntable connected in turn directly with the Dundee and Arbroath goods shed – this connection led under the Keptie Street bridge, which divided station from shed.

In 1870 the North British, under their Tay Bridge Act, obtained mining powers over the Dundee and Arbroath section; in 1879 powers were further arranged to make the line, together with the Arbroath and Forfar as far as St. Vigean's junction, a Joint Line.

Engines off the Arbroath and Forfar line were accommodated in a two-road shed to the north of the station, on the east side of the line, where a street, 'Guthrie Port' crossed the tracks on a bridge. This shed measured about 30 ft. by 85 ft. and a 15 ft. turntable

was provided on one road, together with a pit and coal stage.

The situation (admittedly far from clear) is complicated still further during the period 1838–1848, when (it is thought) the Aberdeen Co. took the lease of the Arbroath and Forfar. In 1838 it was noted in the local press: 'The company's workshops and carriage shed are adjacent to their Arbroath station ... the leasing of the railway by the Aberdeen Company and the intended making of a direct junction with the Dundee Railway ... will make it necessary for the present workshops to be removed and we learn that new and larger workshops will be erected in the vicinity of Spink Street where it will be crossed by the new railway.' From 1866, in any event, the shed underwent some (further?) change – the 'SNER Works' were to be 'downgraded' to a running shed with all heavy repairs concentrated at Perth. There followed later a complete reordering of the ground belonging to the Arbroath and Forfar Railway when a 'joint' station between the two Arbroath companies was determined upon – the NBR indeed is said to have erected a small shed in 1880, their Montrose service suspended on the fall of the Tay Bridge. Temporary accommodation was even provided by the Caledonian.

At some date (improvements were much talked about in 1890) the older sheds, whatever their precise arrangement and evolution, were dispensed with, all engines working into Arbroath being cared for at a new three-road shed erected to the north, by St. Vigean's

Junction, where the NBR line to Montrose took its leave of joint metals. This building, the easternmost road 'reserved' for the Caledonian, was in use by 1901 and in all likelihood opened in 1897. The turntable, a Cowans Sheldon balanced unit, 'originally 49 ft. 10 inches' in length ('50 ft.' in 1915 and later enlarged to 52 ft.) being installed in that year. As late as 1953 the 'table was listed under 'St. Vigean's.'

Arbroath was afterwards operated by the Caledonian as a sub shed of Forfar, 29D in the LMS reorganisation of 1935. Former NBR engines (mostly 'C16' 4–4–2Ts for the Dundee and Arbroath line) were very much in the majority but a Caledonian 0–4–4T doggedly remained for the Forfar workings. 4–4–0Ts were also used on a time and No. 15021 was at work in July 1930. In 1951 the *Railway Observer* described 0–4–4T No. 55162 as having been 'sub shedded at Arbroath for many years.'

The Forfar tank seems not to have been finally dispensed with until about 1950/51. Ex-NBR engines then worked to Forfar, as a through train from Dundee, towards the end often a 4–4–0 turn. The shed was in truth under-utilised, becoming a favourite locomotive store in BR days and contained, for instance, on 28th October 1955 ex-CR '2P' 0–4–4Ts Nos 55173, 55226, and ex-NBR 4–4–2T No. 67486.

In BR days Arbroath was classed as a sub-shed of Dundee Tay Bridge, closing at the last in 1959.

The shed on 1st September 1948. 0–4–4Ts were long familiar at Arbroath, though a *Railway Magazine* item of February 1923 refers to ancient Caledonian engines 'still at work', 0–4–2s shunting Abroath yard. No. 1670 was described as recently taking over from similar engine No. 1255. *J. L. Stevenson*

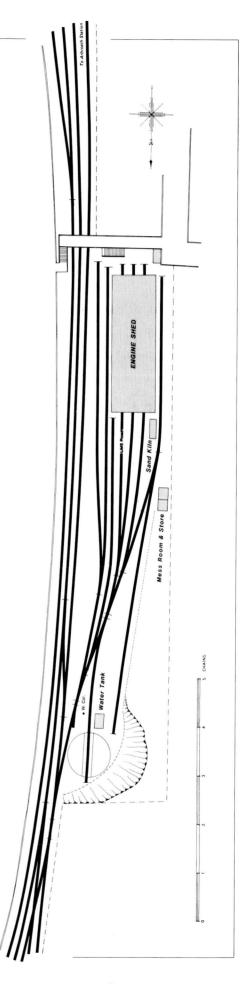

ARBROATH 1935

To Arbroath Station

ENGINE SHED

LMS Road

Sand Kiln

Mess Room & Store

Water Tank

W Col

CHAINS
0   1   2   3   4   5

23307. *Ballachulish looking down Loch Leven.*

Brian Hilton Collection

The Ballachulish branch was an astonishing foray into the Highlands, an exploit into a little-known country of dark hills and gloomy lochs, and endless rain.

No. 17411 at the shed on 28th September 1935. Only one road seems to have been used, a frequent practice at these remote sheds, where traffic never developed to the full. The quarry workings were more or less moribund by 1914 and the Ballachulish slate, ancient even by local standards, seems to have petered out as a branch traffic during the First World War.　　*W. A. Camwell*

BALLACHULISH

The attractive two-road shed at Ballachulish was built with the branch from Connel Ferry; this remarkable line, inching northwards to the Great Glen, was completed in 1903, the locomotive facilities finished shortly after services began. Colonel Yorke of the Board of Trade approved the line in August, attaching the following comment: 'Turntables are under construction at Connel Ferry Station and at Ballachulish but are not yet completed. Until these turntables are ready for use tank engines only, fitted for running in both directions, should be used on the line.' The Ballachulish 'table, a 60 ft balanced unit, had been delivered from Cowans Sheldon and both were in use by mid-October – the weekly special notice of Friday, 16th October, 1903 declares that tender engines could appear 'when required'. The original passenger engines were the small Drummond 0–4–4Ts (latterly numbered in the 15103–15114 series), with 0–4–2s of the 1878/1881 series on goods work. Brittain 4–4–0s (two were specially provided with six-wheeled tenders, giving a greater coal and water capacity, during the First World War) then took over the workings for a while; McIntosh 0–4–4Ts had first appeared around 1910 and were to characterise the passenger service more or less until the end. 0–6–0s, 'Jumbos' etc. seem first to have been employed during the Great War.

0–4–4T No. 55243 on the 10.30 a.m. to Connel Ferry on 30th July 1958. The 0–4–4Ts characterised the branch service for years, though 4–6–0s did appear at times (see text). Around 1907 the Prince of Wales travelled the line, an event remembered locally for the royal appetite for women more than the 'Oban Bogie' 4–6–0 which brought him to his Bibby Lodge holiday.

B. Hilton

The Ballachulish turntable could also deal with CR 4–6–0s and by the 1930s at least a summertime morning passenger train Oban–Ballachulish and return was occasionally worked by a member of the old '191' class and No. 14623 was so employed on 15th August 1938. Ballachulish was from the first a 'sub-shed' of Oban and locos for the lengthy branch through Appin alongside Loch Linnhe were drawn from its complement.

Ballachulish had a coal stage but the awkwardness and inconvenience involved in heaving coal from its low platform into bunkers led to a convoluted sequence of changeover manoeuvers, varying over the years and difficult to document with absolute precision. Engines for much of the time appeared to be exchanged on a daily basis, the Ballachulish loco requiring coal replaced at Connel Ferry by a fully-loaded Oban example. At other periods the Oban – Ballachulish trains crossed elsewhere, at Glencruitten and Benderloch and crews simply swapped footplates. From the first the

The shed on 19th August 1950. It is not entirely clear when it went out of use as far as engine stabling is concerned. E. M. Patterson in a description of the branch (*Trains Illustrated*, July 1955) notes that '. . . all motive power is drawn from the Oban shed, 6¼ miles from Connel, and returns to Oban at the end of the day.'. 0–6–0s must presumably have still required to turn, but many photographs in latter years do show the building more or less closed up.

L & GRP, cty. David & Charles

Ballachulish on 21st September 1951. Freight working for years was dependent upon the Kinlochleven aluminium smelter, though foodstuffs and other supplies had briefly been of note for a prisoner of war camp on Loch Leven side (the prisoners built the road between Ballachulish and Kinlochleven, running close to the shed). Coaling was not popular at Ballachulish; the Oban stage was used wherever possible and various 0–6–0s had a temporarily made-up tender.   *A. G. Ellis*

0–4–4T, however employed, required periodical attention at Oban Shed, washing out etc. The 0–6–0 when in use often enjoyed a (temporary) raised extension box for the necessary extra coal.

As the long reign of the McIntosh 0–4–4Ts came to an end and their numbers dwindled, those engaged in the west warranted increasing attention; on 10th May 1956 No. 55215 was working the line and in 1957 a *Railway Magazine* correspondent reported ... 'passenger trains are hauled by ex-Caledonian 0–4–4 tanks, and the locomotive shedded at Ballachulish runs to Oban once a day for coaling.' Freight traffic was usually handled by Drummond 0–6–0s, though a Pickersgill example, 'able to take heavier loads', had evidently appeared in the summer of 1956, and had been retained during the winter ... 'when a Sunday ballast train has to be worked over the northern end of the line, the Saturday evening train from Oban is hauled by one of the 0–6–0s, which

then works on Sunday.' Towards the end of summer 1958 the branch was 'still worked exclusively by locomotives of the former Caledonian Railway'; 0–4–4Ts Nos. 55208, 55215 and 55263 were occupied on Ballachulish trains, goods work in the charge of 0–6–0 No. 57571. On 29th April 1961 Nos. 55207 and 55260 were in use on the branch, the CR tanks displaced only at the very end by BR standard 2MT moguls. By mid-1962 a BRCW Type 2 diesel was in change of branch services and with this the shed must necessarily have gone out of use.

BALLACHULISH 1930

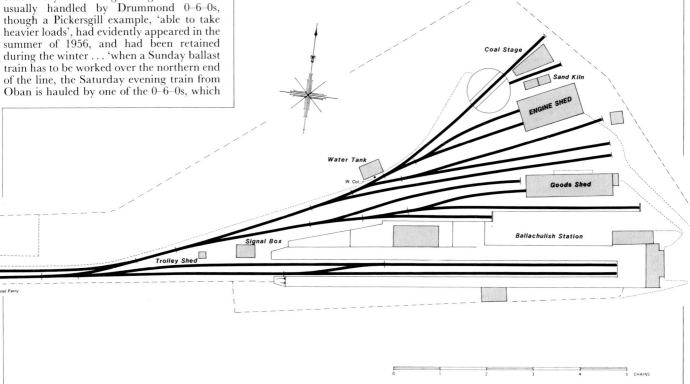

Buchanan Street shed, below 'Dobbies Loan', on 16th September 1935. It is not clear when the shed closed; the building seems to have gone by the end of the Second World War but the turntable remained in use, quite probably until the station closed.   *W. A. Camwell*

BALORNOCK – ST. ROLLOX

Balornock appeared less than a decade before the Caledonian's demise and represented the penultimate stage in a prolonged re-organisation and updating of the company's Glasgow working. Extraordinarily cramped and inadequate premises had sufficed in the city for many years, only partly relieved with the opening of the giant Polmadie shed. Workings from Oban, Perth and the north were dealt with at Buchanan Street station or (in the case of freight) the yards at Robroyston, (Sighthill was exchange), St. Rollox and, of course, the extensive Buchanan Street goods depot, and it was with this traffic that 'Balornock' concerned itself. By the eve of the Great War this had expanded such that the existing stabling provision was ludicrously inadequate and a replacement depot, on a scale to rival the great Polmadie building (a heroic but crumbling essay in timber), was at last authorised. Despite the First World War, construction pressed ahead, the new depot being more or less ready for use in 1916, when its 70 ft. Ransomes and Rapier turntable was installed. This was to bring about the abandonment of two small sheds nearby, 'Buchanan Street' and 'St. Rollox' (the Works).

The former was the earliest, dating from at least 1851 and in all likelihood erected in 1849, shortly after or contemporaneously with Buchanan Street terminus itself. It was a two-road brick shed, 84 ft. by 33 ft., with a pair of roads, 'Coke Stage', 'Water Crane' and minute 20 ft. turntable. The depot was tucked away in a restricted site, constrained on the north side by the Broomhill Foundry and at the rear by a bridge variously labelled on plans 'Dobbies Loan', 'Dobbiesloan Street' and, at times 'Dobbies Lane'. The first-mentioned is the present name. Extension eastward was rendered impossible by

steeply rising ground, on the slope of which lay a section of the now defunct Monkland Canal. After about 1862 the yard was rearranged somewhat and minor additions made to the shed itself. A turntable of conventional dimensions was installed, a 48 ft. example, requiring, in this restricted site, excavation of a low embankment and the repositioning of the coal stage (a triangular, open wooden structure). At some time subsequent to the opening of Balornock, Buchanan Street shed must have gone more or less out of use though the building remained in place well into the 1930s; indeed, the Buchanan Street pilots, both passenger and goods, could regularly be found, at slack times, within its dark and ancient confines. At its peak, the Buchanan Street goods station required no less than three pilots, one of which worked 24 hours each weekday. To allow it a few moments for coal replenishment and other incidental attention, a spare engine came from Balornock for an hour or so when necessary. The exact arrangement varied with the current notions of the contemporary regime at the depot; one passenger pilot, an 0–4–4T, sufficed in latter years but the practice certainly had an ancient lineage. When Buchanan Street station was constructed a connection was ordered into the old Garnkirk and Glasgow works/shed, to reduce time spent travelling to and from the new station. The 48 ft. Buchanan Street turntable was replaced by a Cowans Sheldon 60 ft. unit in 1905 but the final fate of 'the engine shed at Dobbies Lane' remains unclear. The building itself had been reduced to rubble by 1952 but the 'table was in use certainly as late as 1959 and possibly until final closure of the station itself, in November 1966.

The Caledonian also established a shed near to their St. Rollox Works. These in turn

had grown up near to the site of the original Garnkirk and Glasgow terminus – the CR establishment indeed arose from the early shops of the Garnkirk and Glasgow Co. On opening of the line, a building at the northeast corner of the Glebe Street (Townhead) level crossing was taken over for a 'workshops' but by 1835 a replacement had been erected. This shop-cum-shed, a primitive but effective 'Locomotive Carriage and Wagon Works', stood at the Inchbelly level crossing. At this point Castle Street now passes under the line leading to the original terminus, which was located at Glebe Street, about a quarter of a mile further on. When the Caledonian took over the Garnkirk line in order to obtain access to Glasgow, the early works were enlarged, in time for the through Carlisle workings which began in February 1848. These services used Glebe Street (also referred to as Townhead) until Buchanan Street became available the following year. It had always been the intention, even before the new line came into use, to erect a shed and works at St. Rollox but, with the Caledonian all but broke, postponement was necessary. The scheme was laid aside and it was 1855 before the first part of the new project, 'the double bay' could be completed. As a temporary measure engines were brought over from the primitive Garnkirk and Glasgow accommodation and housed in what then existed of the new works. The contractor was at this time offered the job of constructing a new engine shed 'adjacent to the works' but he declined and the work was given to another builder, who also agreed to alter the Garnkirk and Glasgow 'works' into a boiler shop. Construction went ahead, interrupted by the calamitous events of February 1856; on the night of the 6th/7th 'a hurricane', sweeping across Glasgow, completely demolished a side wall of the new shed. Reconstruction was put in hand straight away, the shed at last opening (it is presumed) when the St. Rollox Works came properly into use in June 1856. There were major extensions, both in 1864 and 1870 – another shed 'on ground eastwards of the workshops' was contemplated but does not seem to have been finally approved until 1880. On 27th April a 'new engine shed' was ordered to be erected, partly at least 'to relieve the works', and this building, 210 ft. by 59 ft. with water tank, in the eastern part of the works yard, was in use by December. It was a through building, four roads entering at the western end whilst two were continued through onto a turntable some 42 ft. in diameter. The general arrangement of the depot was highly unsatisfactory, an elongate disposition alongside the St. Rollox 'High Bank', carrying the running lines into the various coal chutes and so on by the canal at Port Dundas. The turntable partly impinged onto this embankment, requiring a brick retaining wall and the 'Coaling Station' was perched in a remarkable position yet further to the east. A simple loop was put in, by the running lines above, for coal wagons, the 'High Bank' serving in effect as a coaling ramp for a single road in the depot and yard beneath. This dismal structure sufficed until the new shed

was made ready in 1916, operating under an increasing burden of overcrowding, poor provision and ill-suited arrangement. In 1907 a new water supply was authorised at a cost of £150 and in 1909 a further £160 was expended at 'the Running Shed, St. Rollox' on urgently-needed outside pits. The building had long proved an inconvenience to the works and was demolished on the completion of Balornock; the roads and pits, however, with the large water tank, remained in place for many years.

The new building, 'Balornock', on a scale to match the other great sheds of the Caledonian, was officially brought into use on 13th November 1916; the contract had been placed with P & W Anderson for £27,997 7s. 6d on 29th December 1914 and engines were moved from 'St. Rollox' to 'Balornock' as the new shed neared completion. The turntable was ordered from Ransomes and Rapier at £685 and in March 1917 £680 was authorised for a new coal siding at 'Balornock New Engine Shed'. Thus christened, the new shed slowly reverted to its parent appelation, though in reality it was quite remote from the works, built to the north-east where various lines and loops trailed through empty fields near the village of Provanmill. 'Broomfield Road' also passed through this area and it formed the rear

boundary of the shed. Generally speaking, 'Balornock' can be regarded as a CR/LMS term – 'St. Rollox', BR.

Responsible for some eighty locomotives almost from opening (it is hard to visualise how their requirements were accommodated before), Balornock was concerned with a range of duties, mainly to 'the north'. There was of course, infinite variation; the shed worked the 'south fast goods' on alternate nights, for instance, leaving Buchanan Street every weekday at 7 p.m. It even conveyed, among other commodities, a tank of Loch Katrine water. Kingmoor had the great part of the work Carlisle–Glasgow but Balornock was responsible for much of the relief. Local passenger work to Cumbernauld, Motherwell via Coatbridge, Glenboig etc. belonged to Balornock but work to and north of Stirling was shared, for the most part, with Perth. Similarly much of the Oban traffic was worked by Balornock engines, with crews often provided from Stirling and Oban. While principally the depot for Buchanan Street, Balornock did have work out of Central, providing the engine, for example, for the 4.00 a.m. to Stirling and Aberdeen and a corresponding arrival from Aberdeen around midnight.

The depot was equipped for a wide range of repairs to its substantial locomotive fleet

Site of the old 'works' engine shed, in September 1935. The two roads before the water tank terminated inside the shed, the other two continuing on to a turntable and the precariously-sited coaling stage, more or less where the 'City of Glasgow Union Railway' crossed under the CR running lines. The site remains easily discernible (until recently at least) and still served as a dumping ground for old stock, lately abandoned DMUs and passenger vans.

W. A. Camwell

Balornock (*above*) in 1935, and (*below*) in August 1936. It had come into use during the First World War, put up in the dismal country beyond Broomfield Road. Everything was ordered in solid Caledonian fashion, with two-road repair shop and open roads at the rear.

L & GRP, cty. David & Charles and W. Potter

4—4—0 No. 14488 on 21st June 1938. The shed had been equipped with a 70 ft 'table from the first, the Caledonian 'standard' for any location likely to see the new 4—6—0s, and it remained in place through to the end of steam working.   *H. C. Casserley*

but, although the value of its equipment fell only a little short of that at Polmadie, certain major items were absent. The various elderly wheel lathes at St. Rollox Works were only lately superseded by a single, up-to-date model, enabling outside contract work to be dispensed with, and wheels removed in the Balornock 'shop' were customarily and necessarily sent to the works for attention – the transfer from 'shop to shop' could be accomplished if necessary within an hour. This kind of support could no doubt be of great advantage on occasion but undoubtedly the system had its drawbacks – there were always certain matters the running side preferred not to come too closely under the eye of central authority.

Like many other ex-Caledonian sheds, Balornock found itself for a while relatively free from direct LMS influence, at least in the matter of locomotives; it was CR engines, if anything, that tended to 'travel' in the first years. The only manifestation of the 'greater corporate whole' was a handful of Horwich moguls, familiar engines in Scotland and reputedly highly popular, in tune with a local taste for the massive. Forays by Derby 4—4—0s and 0—6—0s were to minimal effect on the CR but Stanier's designs, becoming available in real quantities from the late 1930s were to make a lasting impact in Scotland, allocated *en masse* at various strategically situated depots. The allocation at the beginning of 1934 is therefore of considerable interest in that no less than eighteen CR-designed 4—6—0s of six different classes were still present. Three of these classes had become extinct by 1937 and, apart from the '60' class engines, twenty of which had been built in 1925, the remaining 4—6—0s were

4—6—0 No. 14622 on 9th September 1933.   *T. Middlemass*

The Balornock coal stage, with Broomfield Road bridge beyond, in September 1936. In contrast to the shed buildings, Scottish coal 'benches' were often of relatively flimsy construction, planking on a wooden frame. Coaling was never mechanised at St. Rollox and the coal shelter, with minor repairs, remained in use until the end.   *W. Potter*

Clan Munro at the coal bench. St. Rollox saw the various 4—6—0 classes but they were used in minor capacity until the Stanier engines arrived in numbers. LNER B1 4—6—0s unexpectedly worked out of the shed during a stage in the reconstruction of Queen Street station, which necessitated the diversion for some months in 1966 of the Glasgow-Fife services.   *H. F. Wheeler*

4–6–0 by the Balornock coal ramp.

H. N. James

withdrawn by 1946. St. Rollox found itself host to the last '191' class 4–6–0, No. 14621 when that engine was withdrawn in November 1945.

The war proved something of a watershed as far as locomotives were concerned and it is of interest to compare allocations:

31st January 1934

CR 4P '55' Class 4–6–0
14605

CR 4P '908' Class 4–6–0
14609, 14610

CR 3P '191' Class 4–6–0
14619, 14620, 14625, 14626

CR 5P '956' Class 4–6–0
14803

CR 3F '179' Class 4–6–0
17906, 17907, 17908, 17909

CR 4P '60' Class 4–6–0
14650

LMS/CR 4P '60' Class 4–6–0
14632, 14633, 14635, 14639, 14649

LMS 'Crab' 2–6–0
13179, 13180, 13181, 13182

CR 2P 'Dunalastair III' 4–4–0
14340

CR 3P '139' Class 4–4–0
14456, 14457, 14460

CR 3P Pickersgill 4–4–0
14473, 14474, 14481, 14482, 14487, 14488, 14497, 14498

CR 2F 'Jumbo' 0–6–0
17248, 17251, 17254, 17259, 17269, 17283, 17294, 17311, 17330, 17333, 17334, 17379, 17380, 17411, 17412, 17422, 17460

CR 3F '812' Class 0–6–0
17554, 17557, 17558, 17579, 17580, 17617, 17620, 17621, 17624, 17626

CR 3F Pickersgill 0–6–0
17656, 17657

CR 2F '498' Class 0–6–0T
16151, 16156

CR 3F '782' Class 0–6–0T
16232, 16233, 16234, 16235, 16251, 16252, 16289, 16365, 16370

CR 2P '439' Class 0–4–4T
15178

CR 'Pug' 0–4–0ST
16005

[16005 was a Neilson-built engine very similar when rebuilt to the '611' class tanks – it had come from Greenhill (see page 153) in 1925 and remained within the works until scrapped in 1940. It was never at Balornock shed after arrival at the works, though found itself, for political or accountancy reasons, on the official complement.]

31st December 1947

LMS 5 4–6–0
4880, 4881, 4922, 4923, 4956, 4957, 4995, 4996, 5115, 5116, 5117, 5153, 5154, 5155, 5156, 5157, 5158, 5159, 5176, 5177, 5178, 5179, 5355, 5356, 5358, 5359, 5362, 5423

LMS 4P 4–4–0
918, 1126, 1128

CR 3P Pickersgill 4–4–0
14474, 14475, 14483, 14487, 14494

MR 4F 0–6–0
3848, 3849

LMS/MR 4F 0–6–0
4194, 4253, 4254, 4255, 4256, 4257

CR 2F 'Jumbo' 0–6–0
17240, 17251, 17253, 17254, 17269, 17305, 17311, 17318, 17333, 17350, 17352, 17374, 17380, 17394, 17434, 17453, 17454, 17455, 17457

CR 3F '812' Class 0–6–0
17554, 17557, 17558, 17617, 17631

CR 3F Pickersgill 0–6–0
17686

CR 2F '498' Class 0–6–0T
16151

CR 3F '782' Class 0–6–0T
16233, 16234, 16252, 16289, 16330, 16370

CR 2P '439' Class 0–4–4T
15121, 15124, 15159, 15178, 15204

Total 85

'St. Rollox' at the end of 1947 had no less than 28 class 5 4–6–0s, the new engines having swept away all the old CR 4–6–0s and many of the 4–4–0s. The 'Black five' complement included the four locally named examples, much sought after by enthusiasts keen to view the distinctive nameplates. They remained together at St. Rollox until March 1957 when 45154 *Lanarkshire Yeomanry* and 45156 *Ayrshire Yeomanry* went to England. The other two remained in Glasgow until the withdrawal of 45157 *The Glasgow Highlander* in December 1962 and the removal of 45158 *Glasgow Yeomanry* in January 1964. It was withdrawn from Ardrossan a few months later.

The LMS 4–6–0s were augmented in early 1957 by ten of the Caprotti-fitted BR versions, 73145–73154, St. Rollox sharing the engines with Patricroft on the LMR. They represented the final development of the classic class 5 4–6–0 and remained at St. Rollox more or less until closure. Although officially not part of the allocation, the works shunter, immaculately maintained, was notable over many years. In post-war years it was 'pug' No. 16025, retaining a Dawsholm (27K) shed plate in 1945 and repainted in early 1950 in the distinctive BR black lined livery. It was withdrawn in 1960.

St. Rollox was at a disadvantage in BR days in that mixed traffic, class 5 4–6–0s remained the largest passenger engines available to it. In the early 1960s, with dieselisation not proceeding in quite ideal fashion, the

The shed on 21st September 1948. On the railway, by this time, it was always referred to as 'St. Rollox', though 'outsiders tended to call it Balornock, no doubt to distinguish it from the Works'.

J. L. Stevenson

4—4—0 No. 54474 on 19th June 1949.

H. C. Casserley

No. 45116 on 27th October 1951, in condition fine enough to be 'ex-works'. Engine-working off St. Rollox was usually enhanced by up to half a dozen such engines, of assorted types, running in 'and consequently in rather delicate condition'.

A. G. Ellis

0—6—0 No. 17558 (*above*) on 4th February 1950 and (*below*) semi-derelict 4—4—0 No. 54474 in July 1958.   *A. G. Ellis and Tony Wright*

Like many of the major Scottish depots, St. Rollox came to rely heavily on the Class 5 4—6—0; numbers of BR engines also came new to Scotland and probably here, more so than in the south, the mixed traffic 4—6—0 was put to thoroughly flexible use. *K. Fairey*

Caprotti-fitted class 5MT on the St. Rollox turntable, 26th June 1957. These engines were received very well at the depot and were put to use on the Buchanan Street-Aberdeen services. Success owed much to their *en bloc* allocation, so that drivers and fitters, through regular work on them, became quickly accustomed to the different techniques involved. The new camboxes fitted to the later Caprotti engines (44686, 44687, 71000 and 73125-54) without doubt represented a great improvement over earlier types and, but for the demise of steam, the gear must have seen a much wider application. The advantages lay not so much in performance, thermodynamically, *per se*, as in the ease of maintenance and the free running characteristics imparted to the engines. *Brian Morrison*

stage was thus set for the extraordinary transfer of displaced ex–LNER 'A4' 4–6–2s to the shed. Following trials in early 1962, four of the Pacifics were made available for the Aberdeen 3-hour service, two to Ferryhill and two, 60027 *Merlin* and 60031 *Golden Plover*, to St. Rollox. 'V2' 2–6–2s could also be seen at St. Rollox in the early 1950s and eventually all sorts of ex-LNER power could be found at the shed alongside the 'A4s', various Pacifics as well as 'B1' 4–6–0s. The latter in particular appeared in some numbers during the reconstruction of Queen Street station.

St. Rollox remained almost entirely unaltered throughout its existence; the wooden coaling shelter was in fair condition considering its age and the harsh usage received, and no aids to ash disposal or coaling seem to have been provided. Even the great transverse pitches of the shed itself remained relatively unscathed. The diesel presence increased slowly through the 'sixties, the locos administered to in the former repair shop. In 1965 the steam allocation was reported to be as low as ten engines, not all of them active, whilst more than twenty

diesels were based there, many of them shunters.

Coded 29G under Perth from 1935, the shed was recoded 31A in the 1940 reorganisation with Stirling, Oban, Grangemouth and Dawsholm as 'garages'. In the 1949 BR scheme it became 65B in the Eastfield District. St. Rollox, 'Balornock', closed from 7th November 1966 and the whole site was afterwards cleared. Latterly surrounded by multi-storey blocks of flats, it has never been reoccupied.

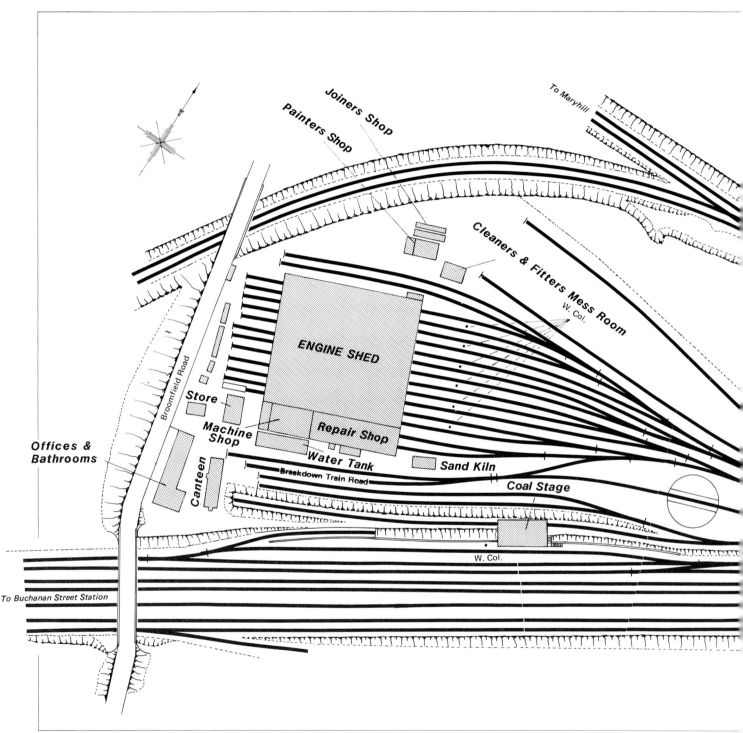

St. Rollox on 14th August 1960. It occupied a spacious site, unrestricted by the running lines to either side; the site was perfectly suited to a comprehensive rearrangement in pursuit of quicker servicing turnrounds, but such a renewal does not appear to have been considered.

K. Fairey

BALORNOCK ST. ROLLOX 1940

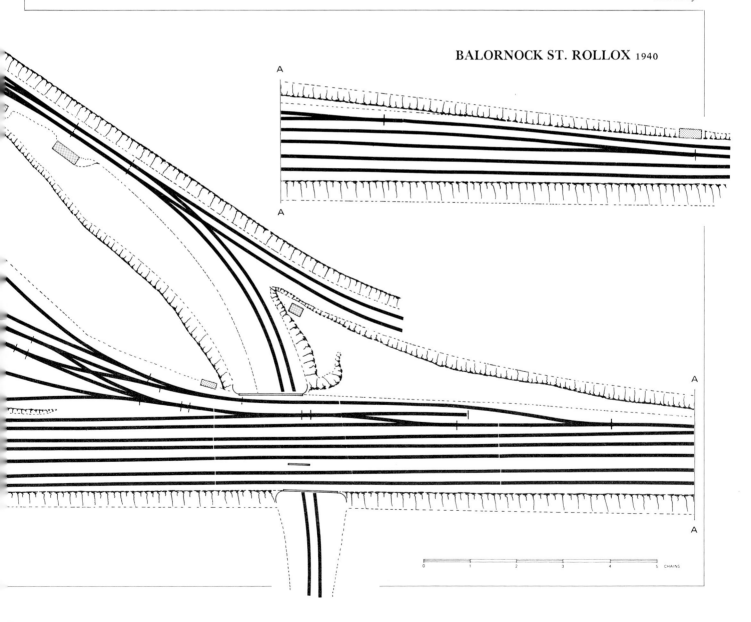

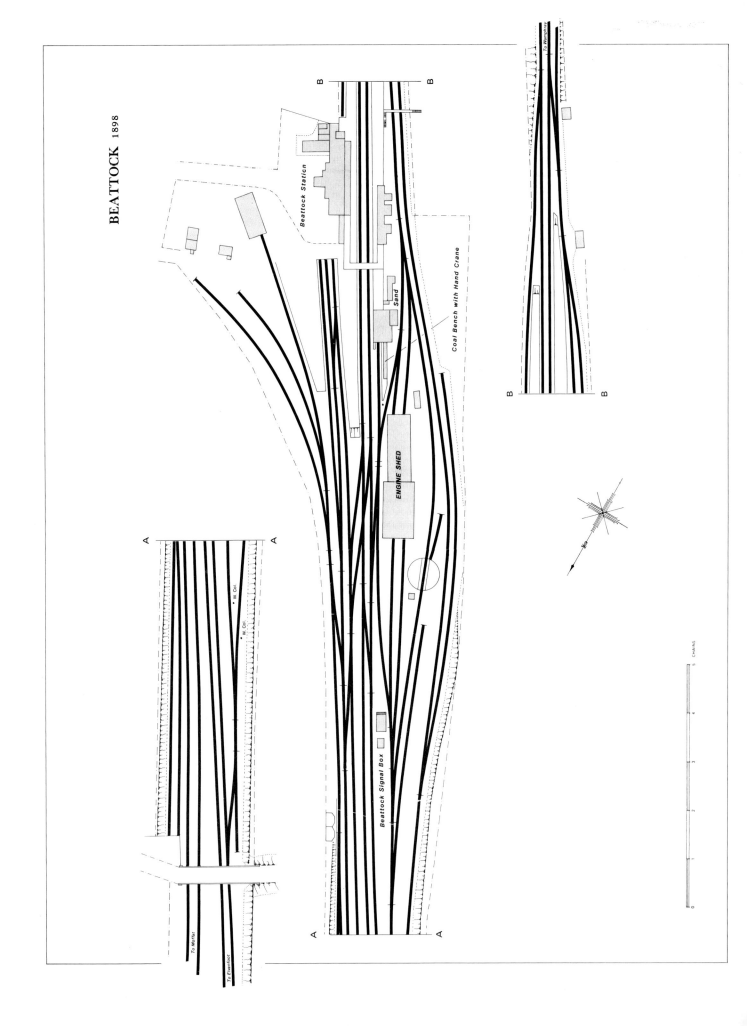

BEATTOCK 1898

Beattock Station

Sand

Coal Bench with Hand Crane

ENGINE SHED

Beattock Signal Box

To Wamphray

To Moffat

To Elvanfoot

W. Col.

W. Col.

CHAINS

Amongst the most intriguing of the Beattock bankers were the hulking 'Wemyss Bay' 4–6–2Ts; they had been ousted from Polmadie by new 2–6–4Ts and spent a few years 'on the bank' before final withdrawal, replaced again by 2–6–4Ts. July 1947.
B. Hilton

BEATTOCK

Accommodation was arranged at Beattock very early, from September 1847. It grew subsequently in accretionary fashion, leaving the shed by the 1890s an oddly hybrid building with turntable and coal stage laid out in antique and eccentric manner. The shed itself was built in stone; the turntable, originally some 42 ft. in diameter, lay in the north of the yard but in 1899 was resited a distance away at the southern extremity of the down platform. A balanced 54 ft. unit, it came from Cowans Sheldon nearby at Carlisle. Apart really from the Moffat and other branch workings (fascinating enough in their turn), Beattock was strictly a banking engine shed; the daunting heights facing northbound trains proved a lasting barrier, requiring throughout steam days a complex organisation – special signal sections, banking crews and accommodation for their families. 'Banking' took place from the first, the Board of Trade allowing it when all vehicles had buffers, piloting when bufferless(!) For many years brake wagons were required to be attached in either direction if there was less than a specified number of hand-brake fitted vehicles in the train. In 1857 mention was made of 'increasing accommodation' at the shed and in 1869, the company determined on a further (again its exact nature is unspecified) 'increase in accommodation'.

Always a potential blockage to the West Coast workings, Beattock, as traffic grew, required ever more elaborate regulation, the resulting complexity drawing inspectors and more company 'officers' rather than 'servants'. The former were generally accommodated in the village with many signalmen, permanent way staff and others housed in a remote community of scattered cottages by the line up to the Summit, at Auchencastle, Greskine and Harthope. These isolated

tenants needed to visit Beattock (and Moffat) at intervals for essential shopping and a staff train known as the 'Siege' was duly operated – a Beattock engine and a single carriage to a platform at the summit. The working (unadvertised of course) utilised one of the bankers (under the Scottish title of 'pilot') and generally tied in with the change of shifts at the summit signal box, when new men (any not actually living at the summit) might go 'up', with any finishing their shifts coming back. Shift changes daily demanded all manner of operational agility (bankers were ideal 'lifts'), given the remote and element-susceptible nature of 'the bank', and the area was left more or less to run itself in accordance with day to day traffic needs. The local Traffic Inspector and the Locomotive Foreman ordered affairs as seemed best.

The arrangements latterly familiar at Beattock – a down (west) side loop south of the station for holding the bankers, connected directly (and separately) to the engine shed, together with the necessary facilities at the summit for their return down the bank – appear to date from the last part of the nineteenth century. The minutes contain a number of references to water columns, tanks, loops etc. some of which relate specifically to the bank arrangements (both foot and summit) rather than the shed. In 1883 and 1886 respectively, for example, approval was given for 'enlargement of water tank at Beattock' (£50) and 'new water column at Beattock' (£45). In 1896 various alterations occurred, with no less than £2,100 authorised on 20th October for 'water tank, column and pipes, loop line and sidings, footbridge.' On 11th January 1899 a new water column 'of largest type' was ordered 'at Beattock Summit' and on 13th February 1904 a petition was accepted and £50 approved for the settlement thereof, from the engine drivers at Beattock, for an engine pit 'on the Dead End Siding.' Some years after this, the shed

suffered weather damage to an unspecified extent: '1912. Approved, £300 for new engine pits at the south end of Beattock shed ... recommendation from the Locomotive Superintendent ... in the rebuilding of the engine shed at Beattock, which was damaged by storm last winter.' Again in 1916: '£200 approved for engine pits at Beattock shed and Ross Yard.' Finally on 30th November 1920 £175 was approved for 'new water closets Beattock Engine Shed.' The pre-war price was estimated at £50, prompting a 'special charge against the Government' for the difference.

It is already quite clear that Beattock held a place in the motive power hierarchy well above that normally merited by its size and complement. It was in the charge of a locomotive foreman, was provided with shear-legs (in later years employed mainly on stock repairs) and its engines, a hardworked and well maintained collection of tanks, were vital to the proper operation of the company's principal main line. It was not always so; the original pilots were 2–4–0s for passengers work and 0–4–2s for goods but around the 1870s older engines of both types were being sent to work out their last days. This set the pattern for several decades, Beattock operating miscellaneous engines largely ousted from duties elsewhere and in truth past their best. This practice continued until the time of McIntosh, until about 1902 when standard 0–4–4Ts were sent to work the bank (though an occasional 4–4–0, nearly ready for shopping could appear). 0–4–4Ts Nos. 431, 432, 433 and 434 (15237–15240) were turned out in 1922, to augment the existing tanks; thicker cast iron buffer beams, it was decided, made them specially suitable for banking. A succession of CR 0–4–4Ts were thus in use over many years, some remaining, remarkably, well into the BR period. The complement on 30th September 1933, for instance, stood at eleven, made up as follows: '2P'

0–4–4T: 15161, 15163, 15164, 15181, 15217, 15226, 15237, 15238, 15239, 15240; '3F' 0–6–0 No. 17679. There was an 0–6–0 allocated at various times over the years; it was useful, for instance, on workings arising out of the Moffat sheep sales and when unavailable, or if further assistance was required, a Lockerbie or Carstairs 0–6–0 might be sent down, depending on the destination of the animals and the loading. The shed was responsible for all work on the Moffat line, passenger and goods, and 0–4–4Ts might work turn and turn about Moffat branch and banking. If the livestock train was light and bound for points south of Beattock, it was not unusual for it to be in the charge of one of the tanks, taking it (as a conditional working) as far perhaps as Lockerbie. The Moffat branch indeed was of great interest over the years, the 0–4–4T workings punctuated by some peculiar visitors. Ex-LNWR steam railmotor No. 10697 (LNW No. 5504) was at Beattock for the Moffat line from 1930 to 1933 but spent more time with the fitters than on the branch. Sentinel steam cars were subsequently in the area, on the Wanlockhead branch, and presumably the unfortunate Beattock fitters were once again acquainted with the shortcomings of steam rail motor working. Later, as LMS days drew to a close, a second ex-LNW motor was at the shed, the last survivor No. 29988 (No. 10698 prior to 1933) withdrawn in November 1948.

A curious period then followed, with further Crewe products at Beattock. 2–4–2T No. 6639 was transferred from Dumfries at the beginning of 1949 for the branch service but by May it lay out of use at the shed. By this time a second 2–4–2T, No. 46656, had found its way there; it had come to Scotland in 1946, appearing at Hamilton in April, and on 7th May 1949 had charge of an LMS non-corridor and an ex-LNW dining coach on the Moffat service. 46656 remained active at Beattock for some time and was not finally withdrawn until 1952. The 0–4–4Ts again became pre-eminent on the branch and worked the passenger service until its withdrawal on 4th December 1954. In its last years the service 'was designated push pull' but the CR tanks were not auto-fitted. The coach would be propelled from Moffat but the driver and fireman remained on the footplate and a guard was always required. No. 55232 worked the last train and Moffat was left with a daily goods departing Beattock about 9.30 a.m. In earlier years the small Drummond 0–4–4Ts had been used on the branch, with no less than three at the shed, for Moffat and Wanlockhead with a third spare.

Three of the great 'Wemyss Bay' tanks, the Pickersgill 4–6–2Ts of 1917, arrived at Beattock more or less new but did not stay long, the superheater elements suffering from the rapid temperature changes between hard banking stints and periods spent idle. Seven, however, returned in the autumn of 1946, displaced at Polmadie by new 2–6–4Ts. They took over much of the banking work, followed soon by the three remaining survivors. 2–6–4Ts, both Fairburn and standard varieties, had replaced them as the principal banking types by 1953 (when the last

A variety of engines, with varying success, found their way to Beattock for the banking. Despite their size, for much of the time 0–4–4Ts carried out the work; they proved adaptable machines and the Caledonian employed them more than any other Scottish company, using them on commuter trains, branch lines, pilot jobs, shunting as well as banking. John W. Grant in *The Railway Magazine* of January 1959 commented to great effect on the tanks and their construction: 'McIntosh was less an innovator than a man who saw the merits of something already good and then improved on it, generally by increasing dimensions. His engines were strong and straightforward.'   *J. F. McEwan*

4–6–2T, No. 55359, was withdrawn), though other types continued to see intermittent use; in the summer of 1951, indeed, two standard '4F' 0–6–0s were reported on loan from Kingmoor for banking. An interesting trial was carried out with a pair of Fowler 2–6–2Ts, Nos. 40021 and 40030, which arrived in August 1953; not entirely unexpectedly, they were found less than perfect and returned to Kentish Town and Cricklewood in mid-1954. As late as 1959 two 0–4–4Ts, Nos. 55234 and 55260, remained, principally employed on the Lockerbie pilot turn, with an ex-CR 0–6–0 No. 57568, on local goods work. A Beattock 0–4–4T, quite properly, was destined to be one of the last few still at work in Scotland. By 1966 standard 2–6–0s Nos. 76079, 76103 and 76113 had taken over and these remained until the end of steam in May 1967. Latterly two class 20 diesels used the shed until banking finally ended in the late 1970s.

This was an unfortunate end to a long and fine railway tradition, and Beattock, though not a 'railway town' in the strict sense, lost much with the decline of steam banking. In order to overcome potentially expensive bottlenecks, Beattock had indeed come to be laid out in elaborate fashion, the intention being to clear the summit as quickly as may be, avoiding delay wherever possible. The banking engines worked the day through and lay in the separate loop on the down (west) side, south of the station. The leading engine would go off first and, as each returned down the bank, they trailed onto the others in the line. Certain trains were booked to stop at Beattock for assistance (not shown in the public timetable) whilst other trains within the load limit might run straight through. If a driver decided upon banking assistance, through weather, or engine condition, he would whistle a warning to that effect whilst passing Murthat box, about three miles to the south. This was common, at least until

1932, when the box closed, and a signal was at times given as early as Ecclefechan; the 1937 LMS working appendix stipulates a signal whilst passing Kirtlebridge, repeated at Beattock South box. When trains were running late or traffic was heavy, drivers were encouraged in any event to seek assistance, for it shortened the time between the three stages of the bank. The banker was slip coupled at the rear of the train and, when satisfied of its correct attachment, the guard indicated that all was in order to the banker driver and to the train driver. With that the banker gave a cock crow; if the road was clear the train engine replied in similar fashion, the banker repeated the whistle and simultaneously began to shove. When the train topped the summit, the banker gave a long whistle to inform the train crew of its disengagement and then drew ahead of the down refuge siding for the signalman to either set it back or pass it across to the up relief loop. If no traffic was due on the up line, the engine might well proceed down to Beattock immediately or be attached to a goods train waiting to descend. On some occasions, if a train engine (generally goods) was in poor shape, two bankers might be attached at Beattock, and normally the whole cavalcade went into the down loop at the top to uncouple. The whole system was set out to clear northbound trains with all possible speed. It tried to avoid at all costs stopping a following train on the gradient – in wet weather, with wind blowing sand clear of the rails, an operation fraught with all manner of difficulty.

12F since the 1935 scheme, the shed became 68D in 1949. The Kingmoor District (Scottish Region) was broken up in 1958, Kingmoor itself reverting to 12A. The Scottish sheds retained their old codes until the anomaly was resolved in 1962; Beattock then became 66F under Polmadie, until closure five years later.

Beattock on 14th September 1953. A darksome shed in a wild setting, Beattock men spent their time battling the elements as much as running a railway. They inhabited a remote, almost moorland area, offering little respite from cold, rain, snow and wind. By March 1953 the 2—6—4Ts numbered four, taking most of the banking duties, Nos. 42192 (*above*) along with 42213, 42214 and 42215. Tender engines were also frequently to be found at Beattock; when there was not one on the allocation, goods work in the area always brought them to the shed, whilst main line failures were frequently dragged in for 'a look'. By 1966 banking work was much in decline and the bustle and activity at both 'top' and 'bottom' reduced to a hardly noticeable level. The shed itself had always possessed an air of quiet, more so than many sheds, where that feeling of desertion, locos apparently abandoned and ownerless, remained an abiding impression. *B. Hilton*

No. 55355 on 14th September 1953, last of the 4—6—2Ts withdrawn that year. *B. Hilton*

Brechin on 8th June 1936, a solid and impressive building, of a prodigious size, given the complement. The Caledonian was a relatively wealthy company and could afford its several 'over-estimates' in this vein; this generous accommodation for a handful of tanks is in some small degree a reflection of the great commercial success of the old companies, approaching a zenith around the turn of the century.   *W. A. Camwell*

BRECHIN

The shed at Brechin dates from opening of the station in February 1848, a single road 'Engine House' accommodating one locomotive. The Scottish North Eastern Railway 'Brechin Branch' by 1862 ended in a covered passenger terminus with a substantial goods shed alongside; the small engine shed stood some distance to the east, facing the station, and at first a small turntable was provided, replaced by the CR around 1868. The line became single alongside the shed, before a bridge; on the opposite side of this line stood a substantial water tank. Brechin remained a terminus, with a triangle at its entrance formed by the original line from Bridge of Dun and new lines to Edzell and to Forfar. Increased traffic required more generous engine accommodation and a two-road shed in brick opened on the south side of the line in 1894/95, when the line via Justinhaugh was being built. The new shed was provided with a 50 ft. turntable from Cowans Sheldon, enlarged in later years by the simple expedient of extending the rails out across the walkway.

The shed was never more than an outstation of Forfar which supplied for many years a pair of 0–4–4Ts for the local passenger service. The turntable was available for 0–6–0s, again generally Forfar engines, serving the quite substantial goods sidings and shed. In LMS days there could be up to four tanks working from Brechin with Nos. 15184, 15198, 15200 and 15214 familiar

over some years. A new engine pit was put in around February 1927 but the shed remained a little-used backwater – in the 1930s Forfar at times took to storing engines there, and it did not long survive Nationalisation.

In 1952 the *Railway Observer* reported that 'drastic changes are afoot at Brechin' and

went on to detail the transfer of workings to Montrose ex-LNER shed. The lines to Forfar via Justinhaugh, and Montrose via Bridge of Dun, indeed closed in August, leaving Brechin 'freight only'. There was no longer a need for the shed and it duly closed on 2nd August 1952.

0–4–4T No. 15184 on 8th September 1948.   *J. L. Stevenson*

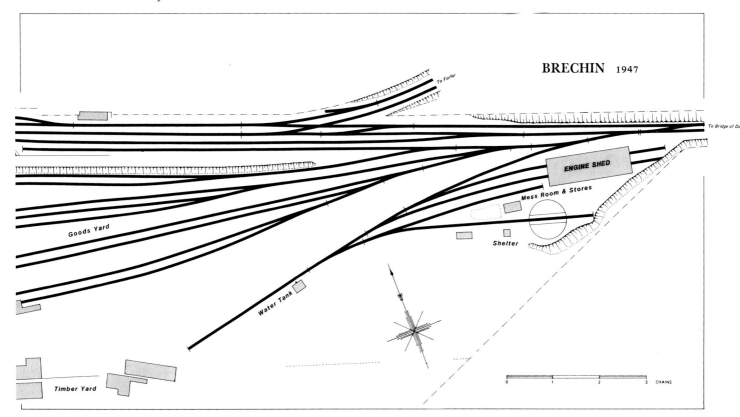

BRECHIN 1947

To Forfar

To Bridge of Dun

ENGINE SHED

Mess Room & Stores

Shelter

Goods Yard

Water Tank

Timber Yard

0 1 2 3 CHAINS

0–6–0 No. 17672 out of use on 8th June 1936. This was presumably a Depression measure, the shed at Brechin proving a convenient and little used store.

W. A. Camwell

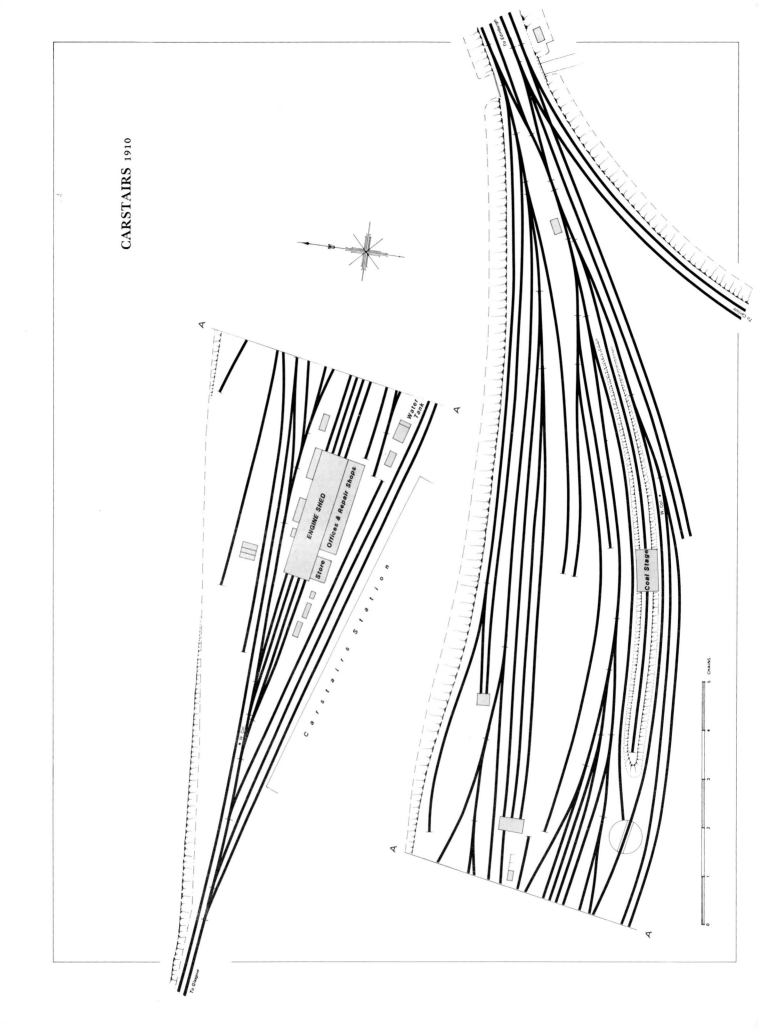

CARSTAIRS 1910

Water Tank

ENGINE SHED

Offices & Repair Shops

Store

Carstairs Station

W. Col.

Coal Stage

W. Col.

To Glasgow

To Edinburgh

To Carlisle

To Edinburgh

A A

A A

A A

5 CHAINS
0 1 2 3 4 5

Carstairs shed, one of the few entirely rebuilt in LMS days. The depot lay astride a junction, owing its importance almost entirely to the complexity of working deriving therefrom. *T. J. Edgington*

CARSTAIRS

Carstairs very soon became a junction of great importance to the Caledonian Railway and a shed was accordingly built at a very early date, documented in admirable fashion in the Stephenson Locomotive Society *Journal* of 1968. It recounts that 'a plan of 1849 is understood to show a shed but the most interesting feature was a four road structure contemporary in date with the station of the early 1850s and clearly the same architect; it had the buttressed walls and laminated timber barrel roof, but with longitudinal vents.' The water tank was the only major item to survive the LMS rebuilding of the shed in 1934–1935, the *Journal* went on to note. The original shed had in fact been a hastily put up timber building which the contractor, Brassey, had used as a store. By 1852 it was reported in poor state of repair, unsafe furthermore, and the scheme the following year for the remaking of Carstairs Junction station included a new engine shed. This was the 'four road structure' of the 1968 *Journal* item.

Carstairs at first had been no more than an isolated country junction, its importance unforeseen. Originally it had been envisaged that trains would run through from England to Edinburgh; such traffic never developed as anticipated and carriages originating at Edinburgh were joined at Carstairs to those from Glasgow and (later) Perth. By the early 1850s it was also becoming clear that pilot engines were necessary for the drag south to Beattock, whilst Carstairs was an eminently suitable base for standby or spare engines.

Soon thereafter it became common practice to replace some engines off Glasgow or Stirling trains at Carstairs.

The shed, still with its four short roads, was responsible for over thirty locomotives by 1922. It had been at least 1860 before the original open wooden coal stage was replaced by a proper coal ramp with shelter and the early turntable was not enlarged until 1896. A Cowans Sheldon 50 ft. turntable was installed in that year (excluding masonry it cost £300), considered adequate for the shed's requirements into BR days. The depot lay, of course, beside a triangle, and turntable needs would never press too greatly.

A new well costing £50 was ordered 'to be proceeded with' in 1880 and in 1913 £200 was approved for a new engine pit 'on the coal road at Carstairs'. On 30th May 1922 a new water column was ordered for the north end of the loco yard, at a cost of £150 and in February the following year improvements to the coal bench were arranged, 'heightened somewhat so as to facilitate the coaling of large modern engines, Estimate £120.'

The depot really was in deplorable condition as the 1930s began, with forty-five locomotives to deal with by September 1933:

LMS 4P 4–4–0
917

CR 2P 'Dunalastair IV' 4–4–0
14350, 14354, 14355, 14357, 14358, 14361, 14363

CR 3P 'Dunalastair IV' Rebuilt '139' Class 4–4–0
14439, 14444, 14446, 14455

CR 3P Pickersgill 4–4–0
14471, 14483, 14484, 14499, 14500

CR 2F 0–6–0
17260, 17298, 17300, 17303, 17323, 17385, 17386, 17399, 17438, 17451

CR 3F 0–6–0
17565, 17569, 17578, 17583, 17586, 17603, 17613, 17619

CR 3F Pickersgill 0–6–0
17670, 17680, 17681, 17682

CR 3F 0–6–0T
16248, 16249, 16308

CR 2P 0–4–4T
15203, 15204, 15227

The LMS local authorities eventually determined upon complete renewal of the ruinous building. Considering it at some length, a comprehensive remodelling began in the latter part of 1934 and continued through to 1935:

J. G. Tod, Esq., C. E.,
EDINBURGH.
    23rd November, 1934.

LONDON MIDLAND AND
SCOTTISH RAILWAY COMPANY.

Extract from the Minutes of meeting of the Scottish Local Committee (Traffic Sub-Committee) of the 16th Ocotober, 1934 approved by the Board of the 25th Ocotober, 1934.

2128. CARSTAIRS. PROPOSED REPLACEMENT OF ENGINE SHED, ETC.

REPORTED that the Locomotive Engine Shed at Carstairs which was constructed about 80 years ago, is in a dilapidated condition.

It was, therefore, recommended:–

  (1) That the Engine Shed should be

The triangle at Carstairs left an impression of sweeping lines and curves, the depot 'almost lost somewhere in the midst of it all'. It meant that odd sidings were available all over the place and engines could be found dotted about, stored or stabled. On 31st August 1952 4–4–0 No. 54461 was in steam with 54449 and 40903 stored out of use.   *H. I. Cameron*

replaced as shown on Plan No. 9438 (Glasgow);
(2) That a No. 2 type 75-ton capacity Mechanical Coaling Plant and a Mechanical Ash Lifting Plant, complete with engine pit and ash road, should be installed.

The estimated outlay to carry out the proposals is £24,048. The scheme involves additions to the Company's existing Capital Assets and the Chief Accountant's approximate allocation is:–

Capital Account............. Dr. £11,366
Revenue Accounts......... Dr. £12,682
                                            Dr. £24,048

It was explained that the increased annual charges will amount ultimately to £1,061.

It was also explained that figures have been included in the estimated cost in respect of the provision of a wheeldrop and traversers but that, when the final estimate and allocation is subsequently reported, such costs will be deleted as the question of the provision of these appliances will form the subject of a separate report.

APPROVED.

A number of details required to be cleared up throughout the early part of 1935; on 19th February, for instance, under the general heading 'Replacement of Engine Shed', £94 had to be found for the 'Heating work required in offices and store.' The value of this investment was enhanced by an increased number of 'standard' locomotives – as Nationalisation dawned Carstairs was operating class 5 4–6–0s (Nos. 4953 and 4955), at least fourteen LMS 4–4–0s (including '2Ps', briefly and without distinction) and '8F' 2–8–0s, Nos. 8301, 8302 and 8331. By an important junction, the shed was concerned with local passenger work to Glasgow, Edinburgh, Lanark and Peebles and by 1954 was operating four compound 4–4–0s, nine 2–6–4Ts and six class 5 4–6–0s. Ex-Caledonian engines, principally 4–4–0s and 0–6–0s, remained very much in evidence throughout the 1950s; correspondence in the *Railway Magazine* of January 1958 regarding

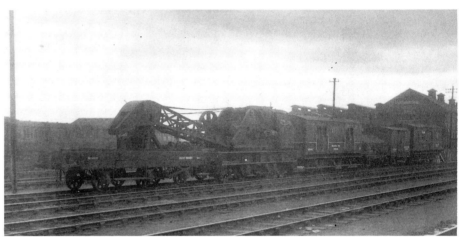

Crane and vans at Carstairs on 21st February 1949.   *W. H. Whitworth*

Ex-GSWR 2–6–0 No. 17826 carrying a Carstairs 27D shedplate, on 19th June 1936.
W. A. Camwell

0—6—0s at Carstairs, Nos. 57604 and 57618 on 17th February 1951. Carstairs men had a wide range of work; clearly shunting was important and, quite apart from far-ranging jobs with their own locomotives, there was a lot of remanning work, regularly as far as Perth or Carlisle, frequently on LMS Pacifics. *H. I. Cameron*

Carstairs on 27th May 1959, brought in whilst the coaling plant was 'out of order'. *H. I. Cameron*

14th August 1960. The condition of the old shed at Carstairs can as yet only be guessed at – the LMS Scottish Local Committee called it 'dilapidated', a sure indication of a more or less ruinous state and in its rebuilt form there was little to distinguish the building from sheds elsewhere on the LMS. Certainly it had been of all-timber construction until about 1913-1914, when some parts were taken down, leaving 'a very rough and ready structure'. There was supposed to have been a fire at the shed and an early reconstruction was discussed, part of an attempt to improve the loop to the Edinburgh line. The Polmadie men avowed that only the grease and soot held it up at all. It remained in use for stock purposes long after steam disappeared and was only finally removed in the early 1980s.

K. Fairey

workings in the previous year noted that an ex-CR 4–4–0 from Carstairs 'usually No. 54477, but recently No. 54461, has worked regularly on the 7.53 a.m. train from Lanark to Glasgow Central. This has broken the monopoly of standard types on the Lanarkshire business trains. The 7.58 a.m. train from Carstairs also has occasionally been worked by a Caledonian 4–4–0 and thus two of these locomotives may be seen on adjacent platforms at Glasgow Central. During November a class "B1" 4–6–0 was noted on both these turns.' The division and assembly of Glasgow and Edinburgh portions of Anglo-Scottish expresses at Carstairs over very many years lent an added importance to the duties of the station pilot. It was therefore appropriate that the shed retained the last CR 0–4–4T to remain active, No. 55189 working until December 1962. It was withdrawn, along with the remaining members of the class, at the end of the year and set aside for preservation. Restored in 1964 with CR chimney in place of the stovepipe and with the original number 419, it is now in the care of the Scottish Railway Preservation Society.

Carstairs, 27D under Polmadie in 1935, and from 1940 28C under Motherwell, spent most of its BR existence as 64D, a 'garage' of the ex-NBR Edinburgh shed, St Margaret's. It returned to the Polmadie District from April 1960 and was recoded 66E – described as 'a stronghold of steam' with 24 locos present on New Year's Eve 1964, the allocation afterwards slowly dwindled. By

The shed actually lay close by the station, and movement, at times seemingly continuous, took place all around. 16th June 1951.

H. I. Cameron

December 1966, shortly before the end of steam in Scotland, it was without locomotives, and in March 1967 was found 'empty but for two locomotives in the yard'. Much of the depot was dismantled following closure to steam but the corrugated sheet building itself was retained, until very recently.

Carstairs on 30th July 1962.

W. T. Stubbs

CRIEFF

This remote country junction saw a most remarkable sequence of change. The little depot was never in possession of more than a handful of locos but had a history (for its size) amongst the most complex to be encountered. The main episodes seem clear enough, within broad limits, but much of the detail continues to prove elusive. The original station was the terminus of the Crieff Junction Railway (running from the main line at Gleneagles (then named Crieff Junction) and opened in 1856. It fronted 'Browns Bow' – 'King Street', and a small brick engine shed was provided, opposite (to the south-east of) the little terminus and close by a (then) sawmill. It was reputedly ordered to the design of the Crieff Junction engineer Bouch, of unfortunate Tay Bridge association.

The 'Almond Valley' line followed in 1866 bringing the town in direct communication with Perth; amalgamation between the Scottish North Eastern Railway and the Caledonian was by this time firmly in prospect and the CR Board ordered that the 'Almond Valley engine shed be located adjacent to that already at Crieff station'. This would have placed the new shed at the 'saw mill' site but a long gap in the records precludes any exact determination of subsequent events. By the 1890s the first shed had long been abandoned, its site and the old terminus taken up with goods sidings etc (a

Three sheds stood together at Crieff, in a unique disposition, their age-relationships as yet imperfectly determined. Before this there had been a further shed (and *possibly* two) at the original station; the repositioning of the turntable and subsequent removal of one of the buildings adds to the confusion. 2–4–0 No. 587 on 30th August 1894.   *Collection John Hooper*

new through station was opened, some yards to the east). A wholly new site had been chosen, further to the south-east on the opposite side of the line and beyond the bridge carrying 'Duchlage Road'. No less than three single road sheds were to stand on this site, their exact age-relationships as yet undetermined. The oldest *seems* to have been the centre building, brick with a turntable (marked 45 ft.) immediately outside. Ord-

nance Survey plans show this shed standing alone in 1899 whilst CR plans dated about the same time show all three, with the turntable increased to 54 ft. and repositioned outside the easternmost shed. There is indeed a flurry of activity around this time, impossible to elucidate satisfactorily but revealing, it is believed, the period in which the two wooden flanking sheds originate. Doubtless there was some connection with the new line

The turntable from the 'middle' shed was removed when a larger replacement was installed outside the easternmost building, around 1910. Doubtless this allowed the old 'table to continue in use while the work went on, and it could quietly be removed on completion. The left-hand shed, the westernmost building, was the flimsiest of the three and was removed, or fell down, it is said, during the Second World War.   *W. H. Whitworth*

Crieff on 19th March 1949. There are some fine contemporary notes on the shed(s) in an article by R. D. Stephen ('I Remember Crieff', *Trains Illustrated* April 1956); passenger services were withdrawn Perth-Crieff and Comrie-Balquhidder as early as 1951, leaving only the Gleneagles service. In the year or so before this the writer records two sheds (as above) at Crieff, 'neither large enough to accommodate a modern engine and tender'. Around 1950 two Pickersgill 4—4—0s were allocated, seldom using the turntable, 'so there was much tender first running'; they were inadequate for the traffic and Mr. Stephen goes on to note the wealth of engine variety, including many of Perth's considerable Class 5 fleet, often working tender first. There is a charming description of the efforts required to stable locos at Crieff; in the wooden shed the tender would protrude at the rear, 'tilted up a steep hill with the buffers buried in a grass bank'. At the other the smokebox

and forward part of the engine would project out of the shed entrance. The yard and buildings remained available for use through much of the 'fifties, despite the drastically reduced services but they were little needed. Engines were coaled up at Perth though in former years they had been dealt with at Crieff, by hand from wagons. For over thirty years (F. Turner, *Trains Illustrated* June 1956) there were 0—4—4Ts at Crieff, only replaced by 4—4—0s at the beginning of the Second World War. Nos. 15160, 15168 and 15216 were outstationed in 1932, the last three being 15159, 15160 and 15168. The last regularly allocated locomotive seems to have been one of the Perth '4Fs'; 4—6—0s rattled off the remaining passenger work to Gleneagles, leaving the '4F' to potter about on whatever freight could be gleaned from the lines out of Crieff.   *J. L. Stevenson*

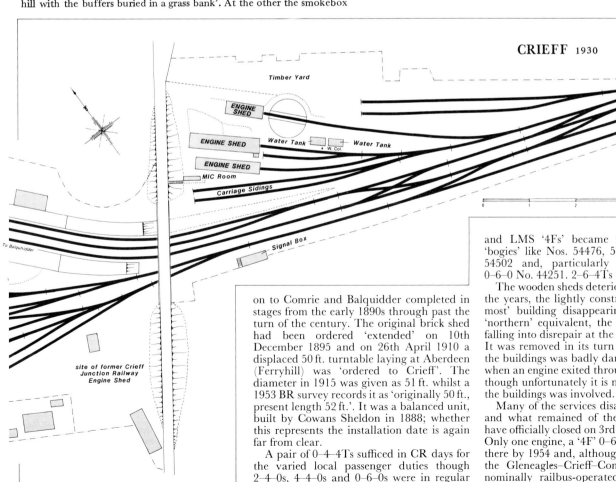

on to Comrie and Balquidder completed in stages from the early 1890s through past the turn of the century. The original brick shed had been ordered 'extended' on 10th December 1895 and on 26th April 1910 a displaced 50 ft. turntable laying at Aberdeen (Ferryhill) was 'ordered to Crieff'. The diameter in 1915 was given as 51 ft. whilst a 1953 BR survey records it as 'originally 50 ft., present length 52 ft.'. It was a balanced unit, built by Cowans Sheldon in 1888; whether this represents the installation date is again far from clear.

A pair of 0—4—4Ts sufficed in CR days for the varied local passenger duties though 2—4—0s, 4—4—0s and 0—6—0s were in regular use throughout the shed's history. CR 4—4—0s

and LMS '4Fs' became familiar latterly, 'bogies' like Nos. 54476, 54500, 54501 and 54502 and, particularly common, Perth 0—6—0 No. 44251. 2—6—4Ts also appeared.

The wooden sheds deteriorated badly over the years, the lightly constructed 'southernmost' building disappearing first, with its 'northern' equivalent, the 'turntable shed', falling into disrepair at the end of the 1950s. It was removed in its turn by 1961. One of the buildings was badly damaged some time when an engine exited through the rear wall, though unfortunately it is not clear which of the buildings was involved.

Many of the services disappeared in 1951 and what remained of the depot seems to have officially closed on 3rd September 1958. Only one engine, a '4F' 0—6—0, was stationed there by 1954 and, although in its last years the Gleneagles–Crieff–Comrie service was nominally railbus-operated, steam in fact often deputised.

DALRY ROAD

The North British held Edinburgh its citadel, scything through the city in bold fashion. The Caledonian crept in humbly to Princes Street and the collection of buildings to be found at their engine shed, Dalry Road, reflected, it might seem, the two companies' fortunes in Edinburgh, greatly different from Glasgow. 4–4–0s Nos. 14445 and 916 on 20th June 1937. The latter, in David L. Smith's SLS account, came new to Hurlford, with Nos. 919 and 920 going to Dalry Road. The new shed at Dalry Road improved working conditions, for its predecessor had degenerated to something approaching a hovel, but the site was not conducive to a well-ordered depot on the scale envisaged in the Slateford Junction proposals.

H. C. Casserley

The main building at Dalry Road, the principal Edinburgh shed of the Caledonian, dates from 1911. It was at least the fourth building on the site, in the fork by Dalry Road station, divided from a cemetery at the rear by the appropriately named alleyway 'Coffin Lane'.

The three buildings extant prior to this reconstruction comprised a two road 'wagon shop', some 100 ft. by 40 ft., a slightly bigger engine repair shop, and a four road shed measuring 153 ft. by 52 ft. A coal stage and ramp occupied the northern part of the site, adjacent to Dalry Road station and a 42 ft. turntable was provided, between the engine and wagon shops. The opening dates of these buildings are not known precisely but the earliest seems to date from about 1861, when various changes took place at the main Edinburgh station, 'Lothian Road'. A small shed had stood on the north side of this terminus since opening in 1848, presumably removed as part of the alterations contained in the 1860 Act. The CR line was taken through Princes Street in 1870 and there is a suggestion of further additions at Dalry Road in 1874/75. Again their exact nature is far from clear; furthermore an 1895 contract hints at final development of the site, but again details are scrappy.

Before the century was out, the cramped triangular site at Dalry Road was proving a hindrance to engine working and bold new plans were drawn up for a replacement shed, some distance away 'at Slateford Junction'.

This new building was on a grand scale relative to the crumbling accommodation at Dalry Road – a ten-road through shed measuring 300 ft. by 165 ft. with an eleventh road terminating inside at a small workshop. It would have been a curious building, in brick with northlight pattern roof, a conventional pitched section covering the shops. 'Slateford Junction' in the event proved rather too ambitious and pondering the problem for a further period of years (in June 1899 a site was considered 'at Gorgie' but the NBR objected to the necessary bridge over their line) the CR eventually determined simply upon a reconstruction of the old shed. Apart from its poor condition, the old building was, of course, far too small and the new shed represented almost a doubling of the covered accommodation. It was erected in large part on the site of the earlier shed, utilising the four approach roads and the examination pits. Detailed estimates were prepared, made ready in early 1911 and presented in the following fashion:

'Dalry Road Engine Shed – Southern and Eastern District, Caledonian Railway.

Earth Work	£55.9s.8d.
Masonry	£1695.0s.0d.
Steel Work	£418.11s.2d.
Carpentry and Joinery	£1810.9s.5d.
Slating	£185.13s.1d.
Plumbing	£594.10s.8d.
Sewers and Drains	£102.5s.0d.
Time Account Work	£115.0s.0d.
General Sundries	£30.0s.0d.

Add surveyor fees 1¼%
The operation shall be commenced at once, and be carried on with such speed as will ensure the whole work being entirely completed on or before the 30th of September 1911.'

A tender was accepted on 14th May 1911, of one James Kinnear, at £5,190.19s.5d. He was unable to give an absolute promise of the completion date and the company accordingly reduced his monthly payments 'by 10% during the progress of the work'.

Despite Mr. Kinnear's shortcomings with regard to guarantees, he was able to complete the work more or less on time and in early 1912 McIntosh could recommend a new water column 'in front of the reconstructed loco shed at Dalry Road'. The cost was estimated at £65 and in 1915 a further £450 was authorised for a new sand kiln ('furnace', less accurately, in England) . . . 'as the old one is falling down'. Various other improvements followed over the years, including new lighting approved in August 1924, £24.10s.0d., and a 'new siding', cost £237, in 1928. A turntable had been available at Princes Street station for many years and on the installation of a vacuum-fitted 60 ft. unit in 1937, the short and ageing Dalry Road example appears to have been finally dispensed with. The new Cowans Sheldon 'table was not ready until late in the year, Messrs Thomas Gebbie Ltd. winning the foundation contract with a tender of £922.5s.5d. on 19th October. For many years the tables at both the shed and Princes Street had been under-

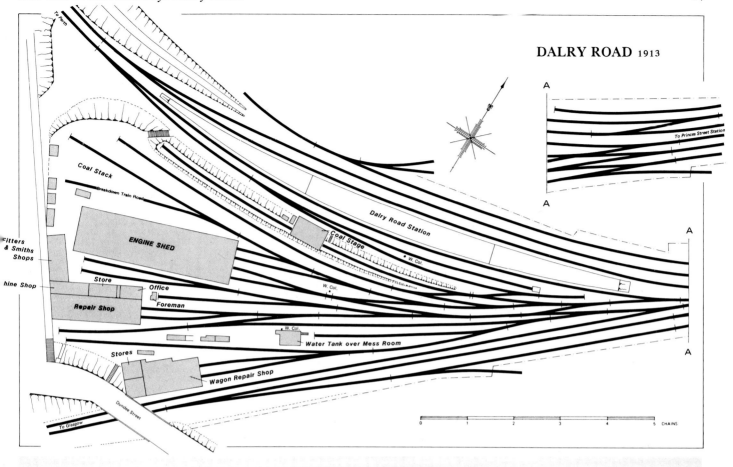

DALRY ROAD 1913

Coal Stack
Breakdown Train Road
Fitters & Smiths Shops
hine Shop
ENGINE SHED
Store
Office
Foreman
Repair Shop
Stores
Coal Stage
Dalry Road Station
W. Col.
W. Col.
W. Col.
Water Tank over Mess Room
Wagon Repair Shop
Dundee Street
To Glasgow
To Perth
To Princes Street Station
0 1 2 3 4 5 CHAINS

4—6—0 No. 14638.

No. 920 on 29th August 1935.   *J. Hooper Collection*

Scottish survival at Dalry Road.   *J. Hooper Collection*

sized and it had become (and remained)
common practice to turn engines on the triangle Dalry Junction – Coltbridge Junction –
Slateford Junction. The restricted site,
coupled with a poor layout, made any turntable operations awkward in the extreme;
when the shed was crowded it was easier to
use the triangle.

The old wagon shop had disappeared by
about 1930 but the wooden repair shop, with
the depot offices and other rooms at its rear,
remained until the end. It contained a 30-
ton hoist and survived the years only through
regular attention to its long-suffering
timbers. The wooden coaling stage soldiered
on in similar fashion and just about the final
improvement at Dalry Road seems to have
been new mess and lavatory accommodation,
approved in 1947 at a cost of over £2,000,
after representations from 'The Regional
Welfare Officer for Scotland and the Ministry
of Labour and National Service'.

With the Caledonian taking second place
to the North British in Edinburgh, Dalry
Road could not hope to rank with the great
Glasgow sheds, Balornock or Polmadie, but
nevertheless at one time more than sixty locos
operated from its claustrophobic confines.
Dalry Road ('Edinburgh' was a management
title never employed at local level) engines
worked to Glasgow Central, Carstairs, Stirling and Perth on a regular basis. Coal traffic
from West Calder, Breich and the Fauld-
house areas meant a number of very strenu-
ous turns, given over gratefully to the class 5
4–6–0s when they first arrived. In addition
Dalry Road men were possessed of a remarkably varied route knowledge and would work
specials almost anywhere, particularly on
Sundays. They ranged as far afield as Carlisle
and Ayr; indeed at one time through carriages were available to the latter place.
There were also many duties in and around
Edinburgh itself, local passenger trains, all
kinds of goods, shunting, dock work and so
on. The complement stood at sixty-six in
1933, the LMS represented only by some ten
locos, 'Crabs' Nos. 13214 and 13215; '4F'
0–6–0s Nos. 4103, 4104, 4319 and 4320;
4–4–0s Nos. 919 and 920; and Dock Tanks
Nos. 11272 and 11273. The remainder,
lending the shed a distinctly Caledonian
air, was made up as follows:

CR 2P 'Dunalastair III' 4–4–0
14337, 14338, 14347, 14348

CR 2P 'Dunalastair IV' 4–4–0
14349

CR 3P 'Dunalastair III' Rebuilt 4–4–0
14434, 14437

CR 3P 'Dunalastair IV' Rebuilt 4–4–0
14438

CR 3P '139' Class 4–4–0
14445, 14450, 14451

CR 3P Pickersgill 4–4–0
14465, 14472, 14491

CR 2F 'Jumbo' 0–6–0
17247, 17358, 17375, 17429, 17430, 17431,
17432

CR 3F '812' Class 0–6–0
17559, 17560, 17576, 17600, 17607, 17608,
17609, 17622, 17623, 17625, 17645

CR 3F Pickersgill 0–6–0
17662, 17677, 17686

0–4–4Ts Nos. 15210 and 15229 at the crumbling coal stage in July 1947.   *H. C. Casserley*

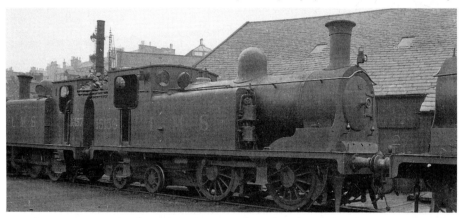

The lines in and around Edinburgh boasted a considerable variety and both CR and NBR maintained an assortment of tanks, of variously peculiar aspect, for 'specialist' work. The sharply
curved Balerno branch had its own 0–4–4Ts, numbered 104-111 and 167-170, small and elegant
engines. Behind the (inevitably) christened 'Balerno' tank is 16157, a short wheelbase 0–6–0T
'Beetlecrusher', again suited to the Balerno goods. Many of these small tanks attracted epithets,
few of them, one suspects, in use by railwaymen. The 'Balerno' 0–4–4Ts were also supposed to
have been called 'Threepenny Bits'.   *H. N. James*

0–4–4T No. 15140.   *H. N. James*

Most of the outside roads at Dalry Road seem to have been used for preparation work — at busy periods indeed it was hard to find any corner of the perversely arranged yard without an engine tucked in somehow. The turntable had long been sited in the 'wrong' part of the yard to render the term 'service sequence' an instance of nothing less than hyperbole. Given the limitations of the site and the availability of both the Slateford Junction triangle and a new turntable at Princes Street, it was easier simply to dispense with the undersized 'table at Dalry Road and put the extra sidings to some good use. *Photomatic*

CR 2F 0–6–0T
16157

CR 3F 0–6–0T
16253 16282, 16283, 16288, 16312, 16313, 16329, 16372

CR 1P 'Balerno' 0–4–4T
15150, 15151, 15152, 15155, 15156, 15157, 15158

CR 2P 0–4–4T
15119, 15169, 15205

The most interesting feature of the complement at this time was the continued presence of no less than seven of the twelve 4′6″ 0–4–4Ts of 1899, built for the sharply curved Balerno branch in Edinburgh and the Cathcart Circle in Glasgow, both of which had closely-spaced stations. The type became extinct in 1938 and the Balerno branch passenger service ceased in 1943. Two Fowler dock tanks, Nos. 11272 and 11273 (later 7162 and 7163) with a single 'Beetlecrusher', No. 16157, provided the necessary short wheelbase goods tanks for the branch. After the war years six Fairburn 2–6–4Ts arriving in 1947, Nos. 2268, 2269, 2270, 2271, 2272 and 2273, found a warm welcome. Employed on suburban work (supplanting CR 0–4–4Ts) with trips to Carstairs, they were immaculately maintained and polished with blue backgrounds to the front numberplates and silver stars on the smokebox door centres. So adorned, the engines were a most appealing sight; well cared-for they established an enviable reputation for reliability.

By Nationalisation the complement had fallen to under fifty, the 4–4–0s and 0–6–0s having suffered the worst, with LMS 2–6–4Ts, class '5s', '8Fs' etc presenting a mark-edly different sight. Dalry Road inevitably saw increasing numbers of LNER types and as early as 1951 locos were reported frequently on loan from Haymarket and St. Margaret's. Various ex-LNER 0–6–0s and 0–6–2Ts were soon a prominent part of the allocation and towards the end of the shed's existence 'Black 5s' and 'B1' 4–6–0s were at work in more or less equal numbers. The last Caledonian engine in use was reported in early 1963, 0–6–0 No. 57634. Coded 27C in 1935, Dalry Road became 28D in 1940 and 64C from the immediate post-Nationalisation years.

The depot closed finally at the end of October 1965, and by the following July both depot and station were demolished.

The Dalry Road complement was stiffened by class 5 4–6–0s and these engines, together with 'Crab' moguls, were responsible for the principal turns in BR days. *Pendon Museum*

Dalry Road in June 1954. The shed had reached an advanced stage of decay though the doors (long vanished) had still been in place in early LMS days. 'Claughton' 4–6–0s turned up on Scotland v. Wales rugby specials and the joiner was called out on a Saturday to 'saw bits off the doors, to get them in the shed'. The shed closed in 1965 and was afterwards demolished.   *Photomatic*

Dalry Road was an illustration of the drawbacks of steam operation. It had survived at least half a century beyond its effective operational life and, although the clutter and dilapidation remains an abiding fascination, such conditions were not conducive to either proper working or the economic servicing of engines. The turnround of a fleet approaching fifty engines, given such tools, constituted a daily miracle of endeavour. 14th April 1963.

D. Banks

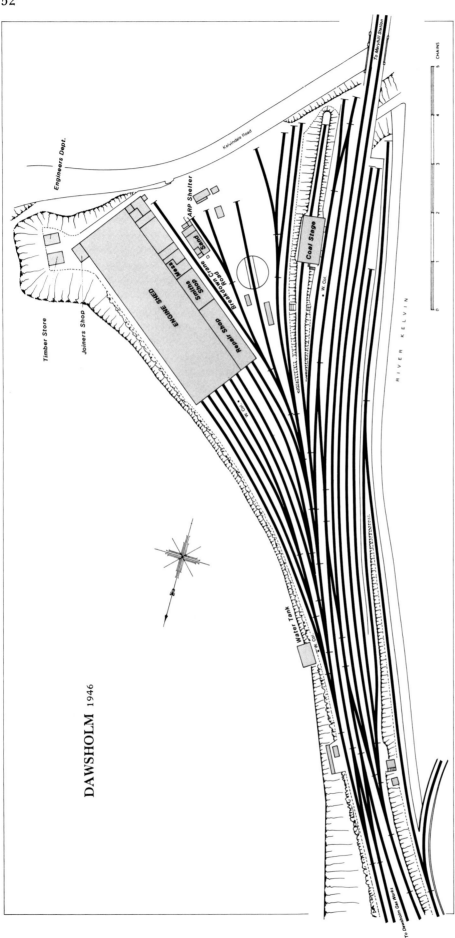

DAWSHOLM 1946

DAWSHOLM

Several years in the planning, Dawsholm opened in 1896, a well equipped shed housing engines employed on the new Low Level lines. The shed was to be built by one George McCall, contracted on 24th March 1896 but found wanting in some now long-forgotten respect – the job was accordingly reassigned to Robert McAlpine at £7,931.12s.8½d., with gas plant houses at a further £817.12s.2½d. The shed's position in the north-west of Glasgow proved convenient for a number of freight workings and responsibility was soon assumed for the new depots at Dumbarton and Yoker. Dawsholm was equipped with the usual wooden coal stage and a 50 ft. turntable, though in 'Glasgow Central Railway' plans as far back as 1888 the latter item is shown at 54 ft., positioned variously about the yard. The two road fitting shop boasted a 40-ton hoist and McAlpine's 'gas houses' remained an abiding feature – tar gas production was centred on Dawsholm for the Low Level carriages and tank wagons were filled for other districts.

There were some forty locos at Dawsholm in 1922, with a further half-dozen or so sub-shedded at Yoker and a handful at Dumbarton and Airdrie, the great majority 0–6–0s, 0–4–4Ts or 0–6–0Ts. The latter were employed mainly on goods and mineral trips, whilst the passenger tanks worked both on the Low Level lines and further afield. The distinctive Lambie 4–4–0Ts built in 1893 with condensing apparatus for working over the Low Level lines, opened from 1894–6, came to the shed on its opening and were a prominent feature for many years. The 0–6–0s handled a variety of goods out of the area, Scotstoun West Yard to Robroyston and elsewhere. In September 1933 the allocation totalled forty-five engines, CR types but for three standard LMS 0–6–0Ts; the Caledonian engines still included three of the surviving Lambie 4–4–0Ts, the class finally becoming extinct in 1938.

The complete allocation in 1933 comprised:

CR 2F 'Jumbo' 0–6–0
17234, 17258, 17306, 17314, 17322, 17346, 17371, 17372, 17377, 17426, 17428, 17456, 17469, 17472, 17473

CR 2F 0–6–0T
16158, 16161, 16168, 16169

CR 3F 0–6–0T
16231, 16297, 16310, 16330, 16350

CR 1P 4–4–0T
15020, 15022, 15023

CR 2P 0–4–4T
15117, 15120, 15121, 15123, 15124, 15135, 15136, 15137, 15206, 15235, 15236

CR 0F 0–4–0ST
16011, 16026, 16028

LMS 3F 0–6–0T
16417, 16418, 16616

The Stanier era brought a number of '3P', 2–6–2Ts to the shed which remained one of the few establishments in Scotland to retain

Dawsholm on 15th September 1946. It was an odd location, almost picturesque, though little of this shows in photographs. The shed stood on a former passenger line, to a short-lived 'Dawsholm' terminus, closed after a brief existence as part of the new Low Level lines. Freight continued to the mid-1950s, mainly to serve Dawsholm Gasworks. On one side the shed was constrained by a rock cutting; on the other lay the valley of the River Kelvin.   *B. Hilton Collection*

15120 at Dawsholm. Many of the passenger engines had long been equipped with condensing gear for the Low Level line but the practice, awkward and more often than not ignored in any case, went out of use, apparently in early LMS days.   *H. N. James*

Dawsholm on 26th September 1947 with from left to right: 17652, 17605, 17341, 17592 and 17472. It was a long time before LMS types found their way to Dawsholm and only the '3P' tanks in the mid-1930s changed the almost wholly 'Caledonian' nature of the shed. The allocation in April 1929: 0–4–0ST No. 16009; 4–4–0Ts Nos. 15020/3/9; 0–4–4Ts Nos. 15119/22/3/30/7, 15206/35/6/68/9; 0–6–0Ts Nos. 11276, 16158, 16162, 16231/95/7/8, 16310/50, 16407/9/17/18, 16615/6; 4–6–2T No. 15360; 0–6–0 Nos. 17234/58, 17306/14/22/43/6/71/2/7, 17426/8/56/69-71/3; Sentinel No. 2253; Railmotor No. 4153.

                                                                                                    G. S. Lloyd

0–4–4T No. 15122 in 1930.   *J. F. McEwan*

Dawsholm in 1961. Ex-NBR engines, principally Reid 0–6–2Ts, had come from Stobcross on closure of that shed around 1951. The 'N15s' shunted Stobcross goods and other places but also had trips quite far afield, to Yoker, Maryhill, etc.

K. Fairey

this class in any numbers. In 1945 Nos. 153, 158, 159, 176, 177, 185, 186, 187, 188, 189 and 200 were employed, accompanied by three of the CR 4–6–2 'Wemyss Bay' tanks, Nos. 15359, 15360 and 15361. They left in 1946 ending a long association – No. 954 had arrived new in 1917, to work the fast Balloch and Dumbarton-Glasgow express, morning and evening with some local trips in between. A few '8F' 2–8–0s were present in 1945 and by 1947 the overall complement totalled nearly sixty engines, falling by 1950 to about forty, a reduction partly explained by Yoker's elevation to 'garage' status, with its own 'separate' allocation. Its engines, of course, continued to be repaired at Dawsholm. In addition to Yoker, Dawsholm was variously responsible for the sheds at Dumbarton and Airdrie and in about 1951 took on the engines, men and duties of the old NBR shed at Kelvinhaugh/Stobcross, a joint yard long shunted by Dawsholm's own engines. It afterwards provided a convenient running-in turn. In 1954 the allocation comprised eleven of the familiar 2–6–2Ts, one 'Pug', two dock tanks, two '3F' tanks and seventeen 0–6–0s of CR origin, together with nine ex-NBR engines, mostly 'N15' 0–6–2Ts. There were also three Great Northern 'N2s' and six WD 2–8–0s. BR moguls later accounted for many of the old 0–6–0s.

When the preserved 'Caley Single' No. 123 was restored to steam in 1958, it was based at Dawsholm and in the following year was joined by GNS 4–4–0 No. 49 *Gordon Highlander*, ER 4–6–0 No. 103 and NBR 4–4–0 No. 256 *Glen Douglas*, completing a quartet which attracted an inordinate number of visitors to this otherwise obscure shed. The HR 'Ben' class 4–4–0 No. 54398 *Ben Alder* which had also been set aside for preservation arrived in 1961 for storage pending a restoration which was regrettably never carried out; finally LNER 4–4–0 No. 62712 *Moray-*

Dawsholm on 28th August 1961, with 0–6–0s Nos. 57259 and 57607, and 2–6–2T No. 40187. WD 2–8–0s came to Dawsholm for the heaviest freights and six were there by 1953. They were used in pairs on iron ore specials from Rothesay Dock to the works at Ravenscraig, Motherwell. Dawsholm was the principal depot for the goods and shunting engines on the Lanarkshire & Dumbartonshire line (G. H. Robin, *Railway Magazine* January 1959).   *K. Fairey*

shire came to the shed and on closure in 1964 all six were transferred to Parkhead, ex-NBR.

The onset of dieselisation caused many engines to be stored pending withdrawal and on 3rd March 1961, for instance, the melancholy assemblage was made up of CR 0–6–0T No. 56171 and 0–6–0s Nos. 57245, 57314, 57470, 57472 and 64471.

Little had been done over the years at Dawsholm, though a new toilet costing £50 was installed in 1910 with new lighting ordered the following year. McIntosh had complained of the latter's inadequacy and £23 was authorised for replacement of the 'flat gas' burners by 'incandescent fittings'. The shed roof had not been built particularly to CR tradition; it was in poor condition by

the end of the war, a decline hastened by fire in 1948. General replacement work began in 1949, making 'slow progress' and late in that year it was noted: 'the back wall has been strengthened and the east wall demolished'. The new roof was not finally complete until 1950 – Dawsholm could then boast the louvre style (see, in particular, Vols. 1 & 2) a distinctly imported look typical of the big English straight sheds.

27K under Polmadie in 1935, Dawsholm, after a spell as 31E in the wartime re-organisation, received the Scottish Region code 65D. It closed, despite 'assurances to the contrary' on 3rd October 1964, the men transferring to a diesel signing-on point established at Yoker.

DUMBARTON

Akin to Yoker and arising out of the same Lanarkshire and Dunbartonshire building episode, Dunbarton shed opened for goods and mineral work on 1st May 1896 and for passenger traffic on 1st October. It was a simple affair, a two-road brick shed in the fork by Dumbarton East Station, with access from the goods depot spur alongside. A Cowans Sheldon 50 ft. turntable and small coaling shed were provided at opposite ends of the yard, with a water column and tank between. Part of what amounted to a new locomotive organisation on north Clydeside, Dumbarton from the first came under Dawsholm shed, four or five 0–4–4Ts forming the basis of its complement. These worked between Balloch and Glasgow and could easily be exchanged when attention was required at the Dawsholm fitting shop. The shed was an obscure byway and remained more or less unaltered through till closure. Like Dawsholm it was inadequately provided for with respect to lighting and almost the only improvement recorded over the years was the new lights installed in 1912.

On 30th September 1933 the allocation is recorded as eight locos, half of them 0–4–4Ts, Nos. 15115, 15116, 15127 and 15218, a pair of 0–6–0s, Nos. 17470 and 17471 and two further tanks, 0–6–0T No. 16250 and 0–4–2ST No. 15001. The latter engine had never-

Goods Depot

theless been transferred away, to Inverness, the previous year but is of interest as the surviving 'Killin Tank' (see p. 92). It had been found useful over some years for one of the Turkey Red factories (no less), in the Vale of Leven. A Westinghouse fitted short wheelbase was necessary, hauling out fitted vans of cloth bound for various parts of the country; the trade declined after about 1919 and finally ceased in the early 1930s. The Dumbarton 0–6–0T did local shunting work at various yards along the line, depositing complete trains usually in the Scotstoun West yard.

LMS 2–6–2Ts arrived at Dawsholm, eventually replacing many of the 0–4–4Ts; in 1949, of five engines normally working from Dumbarton, three, Nos. 187, 188 and 189, were of this type. The 2–6–2Ts had come new to Scotland around 1935, with Nos 99, 100 and 131–138. They were employed on the Low Level lines and would variously have made use of the shed – a fresh batch numbered from 150 upwards arrived in late 1939

Dumbarton, 'a small brick built engine shed', close by Dumbarton Goods Junction and Dumbarton East station, on the Caledonian's 'Lanarkshire & Dunbartonshire Railway'. An outstation and later 'sub shed' of Dawsholm, its locomotives took their share of secondary duties on the Caledonian lines on north Clydeside. 0–6–0 No. 57426, 16th June 1949.

W. A. Camwell

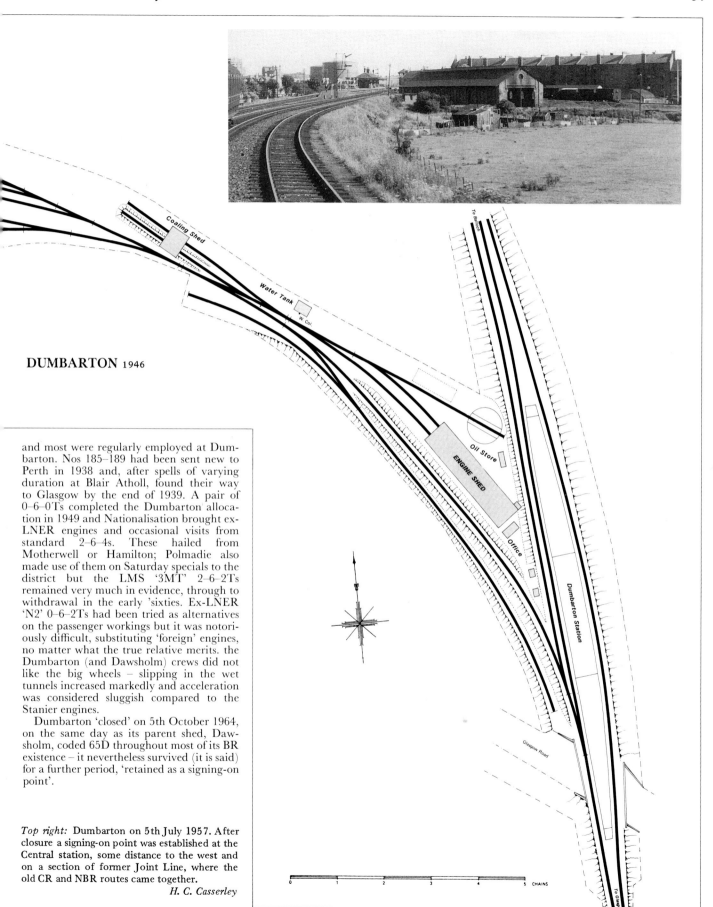

DUMBARTON 1946

and most were regularly employed at Dumbarton. Nos 185–189 had been sent new to Perth in 1938 and, after spells of varying duration at Blair Atholl, found their way to Glasgow by the end of 1939. A pair of 0–6–0Ts completed the Dumbarton allocation in 1949 and Nationalisation brought ex-LNER engines and occasional visits from standard 2–6–4s. These hailed from Motherwell or Hamilton; Polmadie also made use of them on Saturday specials to the district but the LMS '3MT' 2–6–2Ts remained very much in evidence, through to withdrawal in the early 'sixties. Ex-LNER 'N2' 0–6–2Ts had been tried as alternatives on the passenger workings but it was notoriously difficult, substituting 'foreign' engines, no matter what the true relative merits. the Dumbarton (and Dawsholm) crews did not like the big wheels – slipping in the wet tunnels increased markedly and acceleration was considered sluggish compared to the Stanier engines.

Dumbarton 'closed' on 5th October 1964, on the same day as its parent shed, Dawsholm, coded 65D throughout most of its BR existence – it nevertheless survived (it is said) for a further period, 'retained as a signing-on point'.

Top right: Dumbarton on 5th July 1957. After closure a signing-on point was established at the Central station, some distance to the west and on a section of former Joint Line, where the old CR and NBR routes came together.

H. C. Casserley

DUNDEE

The Caledonian shed at Dundee had an unusual history – complex and tangled beginnings resolved in bold fashion, only for the building to suffer premature abandonment.

The Dundee and Newtyle Railway, a leased line diverted by the Dundee Perth and Aberdeen Junction Railway westwards in a loop via Lochee West and Liff in 1861, had an 'Engine House', to the north of Dundee, by the lower entrance to the Law tunnel in the district of 'Coldside'. This line, as the Dundee and Newtyle Harbour branch, continued through the city, southwards along 'Lindsay Street' and 'School Wynd' to connect with the Dundee and Perth Railway terminus, roughly on the site of what was to become Dundee West station – it closed in 1861. The shed, 'Ward Road', measured 56 ft. by 37 ft. and was equipped with a 15 ft. turntable and lengthy coal stage at its southern end. Labelled 'coal depot', the latter comprised an open wooden platform with retaining wall. The shed itself was eccentrically disposed, having two roads, one only entering at each end. It served as both engine shed and repair shop and it, too, closed in 1861.

In 1840 the Dundee and Arbroath Railway was connected to the Dundee Harbour Trustees Line which ran along the northern boundary of the docks to the Dundee and Perth Railway in 1847. This line between the two ran east–west along 'Dock Street' (forming the perimeter of Victoria Dock, in the 1850s the largest in Dundee). The Dundee and Arbroath had their original terminus at 'Road Yards' from June 1839, then at 'Trades Lane' from 1st April the following year. The company opened 'Dundee East' from 14th December 1857, though Trades Lane had been thus labelled, by Bradshaw, until 1855 – elsewhere Trades Lane had been referred to as 'Dock Street'. The original engine shed had been built at Trades Lane, on the south side of the line, moving in February 1858 to the new Dundee East. This shed had three roads, measured 83 ft. by 38 ft. and was provided with smithy, store, office and bothy. Access was direct from a 36 ft. turntable, an 80 ft. wooden 'coal shed' standing on its approach road. The D & A shops, shed etc. had originally been located at Broughty Ferry, the establishment later removed to Arbroath (see also p. 14). The Dundee and Arbroath was subsequently jointly worked by the CR and NBR (from 1880) and by 1900 facilities at the station, 'Dundee East' comprised simply a turntable, on the north side of the line east of the station, at a point labelled 'Camperdown Junction'.

The real forerunner of the Caledonian 'Dundee West' shed in the 1850s lay to the west of the Dundee and Perth Railway terminus but nevertheless east of the modern CR shed. It lay in fact, almost exactly halfway between the latter day Dundee West station and engine shed. The development of

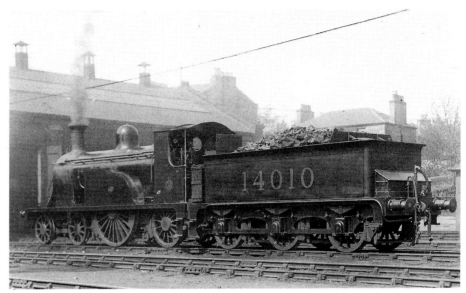

No. 14010, allowed out from Perth on 29th May 1930 (see page 109).   *H. C. Casserley*

the railway at Dundee, the opening of the Tay Bridge, the arrival of the North British, etc. led to a vast reclamation programme, the whole of the area destined to become Tay Bridge station, shed and yard, and Dundee West engine shed, consisting in 1858 of respectively sand and mud flats. In the early years this whole area, later to take on such permanence, was a tidally-swept margin of the Firth of Tay, crossed only by the tracks of the D & P, running in from Perth. From its opening, this line's main shed and workshops were located at 'Seabraes', opened in March 1847 on a remarkable site above the ephemeral mud, on ground of a rather more permanent nature. This required a causeway approach above ordinary spring tide level,

and came off the main embankment leading to the station some 500 yards to the east. It was further developed, 'near shore' into a wide area of reclaimed ground. On this 'approach causeway' a coal platform some 100 ft. in length was provided, tracks running either side directly onto a 36 ft. turntable. The very foundations of this table lay on reclaimed ground and five roads led off northwards into 'an Engine Shed' arranged as a sort of truncated half-rhombus (if such a thing can exist), its rear wall measuring some 110 ft., the front only 62 ft. The sides varied from about 88 ft. to about 93 ft. A joiner's shop stood alongside the shed and a series of small turntables connected the main table with a smithy and a large 'Engine Shop'. A

Doubt remains about Dundee and its operation (similar might be said of Aberdeen), an apparent underutilization explicable only in terms of a wholly pivotal role for Perth. One side effect was a dazzling collection of ancient engines, of wholly primitive aspect. 0–4–2 tender engines nevertheless had a long and excellent tradition in Scotland and only English unfamiliarity casts them in an outlandish light. Many of the army of 2–4–2Ts, for instance, so familiar in England, would appear crazily-lurching machines on Scottish lines.   *G. Coltas*

Dundee yard on 30th April 1936. Engines (apparently stored) are Nos. 17589, 17563, 17397, 17590, 17605, 17658 and 14382, the line trailing into the distance almost on to the site of the old 'Seabraes' shed.

W. A. Hannan, cty. W. A. Camwell

'Manager's House' stood at the centre of this complex which adjoined the Seabraes Flax Spinning Mill. The area is still known by the name 'Seabraes' with a 'Seabraes Saw Mill' active until recent years.

The establishment had possessed only a limited repair capacity and many jobs were sent to the Scottish Central Railway works at Perth. The Dundee premises were reduced simply to 'engine shed' status on absorption into the SCR in 1863 and by 1883 Dugald Drummond was complaining of the inadequacy of 'the Dundee Engine Shed'. A new one would be required '... on ground west of the present site'.

The new Dundee West shed, opened in 1885, necessarily brought about the abandonment of 'Seabraes'. The area of mud separating it from the tracks into Dundee West station was infilled (Dundee Council had obtained powers for the necessary bulwark etc. in 1868) and given over to mineral sidings as well as the generously laid-out new eight-road engine shed. The new depot, to be precise, stood off a spur, approached from the west at Buckingham Junction box and the turntable as originally provided lay close to the main running lines. A new 70 ft. Cowans Sheldon unit was ordered on 19th June 1906, for the 0–8–0 tender engines and

'J91' 0–6–0T No. 68545 and '3F' 0–6–0T No. 56325, on 13th September 1955. It was afterwards converted for diesels and lavishly appointed with respect to fuelling, lighting and inspection facilities. It closed around 1982 shortly after the authorisation of improvements totalling £¾M.

P. J. Kelley

this was laid in the centre of the yard, requiring a rearrangement of the shed roads.

Dundee shared with Ferryhill a curiously inconsequential status and had only a dozen or so locos in 1922/23. By the end of 1933 the complement stood stubbornly at only 28, made up as follows:

CR 2F 0–6–0
17352 17394 17397 17401

CR 3F 0–6–0
17561 17563 17568 17589 17590 17591
17596 17630

CR 2F 0–6–0T
16173

CR 2P 0–4–4T
15132 15173 15180 15193 15213 15219
15220 15222 15223 15231

CR 0F 0–4–0 ST
16001 16003 16013

LMS 3F 0–6–0T
16413 16414

A decline continued throughout LMS days, leaving only fifteen locos officially allocated on 31st December 1947. The much more active Tay Bridge shed, largely mechanised, lay only a matter of yards from the LMS shed and on Nationalisation it very quickly became clear that 'the LNER' would prevail in the city. Dundee West, 29C since 1935, did not exactly close, but its engines and men were absorbed by the shed 'across the way'. It was very soon serving as an engine store simultaneously proving a useful dispersal place, 'as and when required', for the overcrowded Tay Bridge. As early as 15th January 1948 five ex-LNER locos were stored in its dim interior and in 1950 the *Railway Observer* could note: 'Dundee LMS shed is still in use, no doubt it will be required for some time yet as Tay Bridge shed is most cramped'. (BR later listed it as a sub-shed of Tay Bridge.)

So it was that despite relatively lavish resources, 'Dundee West' saw out the 1950s as a kind of store/stabling point. Its engines, included in the Tay Bridge allocation were represented 'historically' in 1959 by a handful of 5MT 4–6–0s and two or three tanks, lost amid 'V2s', 'B1s' and Pacifics. The under-utilised building proved convenient for the maintenance and repair of diesels (DMUs and shunters) and, suitably refurbished, was thus employed by the summer of 1960. By the following year at least it was responsible for the maintenance of 'all diesel multiple-unit trains and shunters, and some main-line locomotives, in the Dundee District'.

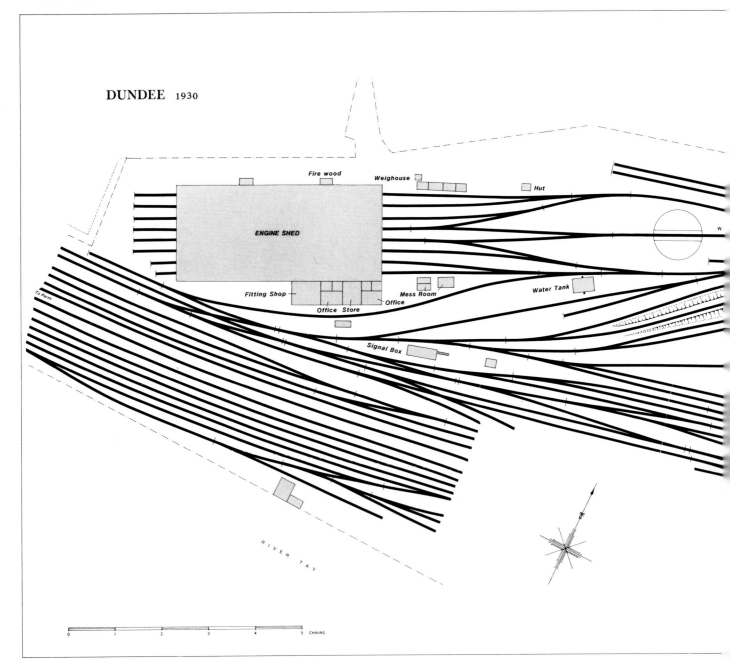

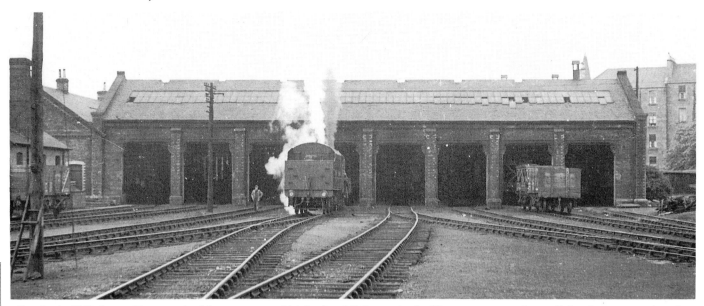

Dundee in 1949. Its workings remained in essence parochial; it played little part in the Glasgow turns apart from relief, and concentrated on the Dundee-Perth locals. Even the dock tanks did not last much beyond 1933. The depot workings were concentrated mainly on the Newtyle line, to Alyth Junction and Blairgowrie and on the Dundee (East)-Forfar line. It also shared with the LNER the Arbroath trains on the Joint Line. Coal was worked from a large depot at Maryfield, to the north of the city on a spur off the Alyth Junction line (the old Dundee and Newtyle).

J. L. Stevenson

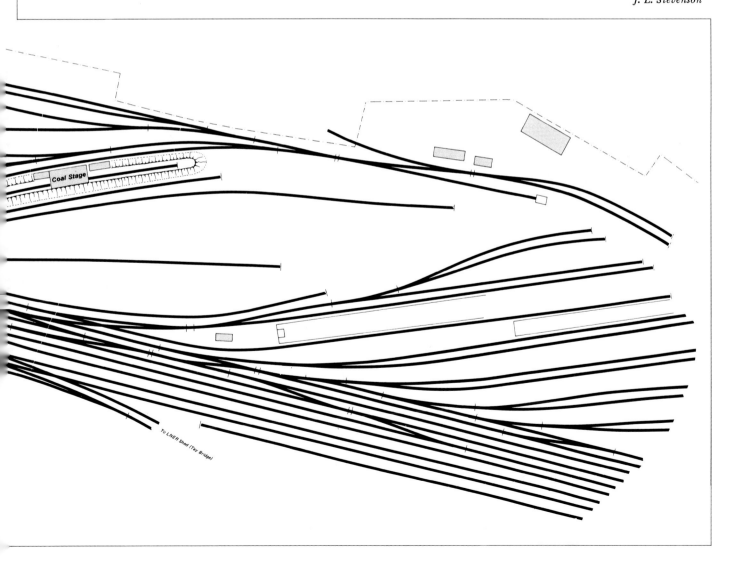

Forfar was a backwater, of a type familiar throughout Britain, a shed where the slow count of years went almost unremarked, a small shed on the edge of a small town. There were hundreds of places like this, the gentle pace of traffic a comfort rather than a warning.   *W. A. Camwell*

FORFAR

A junction on the main Aberdeen road, with lines to Brechin, Arbroath and Dundee, Forfar grew to importance at an early date. An engine shed was in use more or less from the first, by the 1850s a four-road building, south of the station on the opposite side of 'Market Street'. It stood on a spur which at one time led down to the original Arbroath and Forfar Railway terminus of December 1838. An extraordinarily cramped building, access was directly from a small turntable reached both from the east, under a kind of tank house, and from the west, a siding which also skirted a lengthy timber coke stage. The series of drawings for this curious establishment, intended as operational headquarters of the line, are dated 1848 but parts at least seem to have been adapted from earlier, original premises associated with the 1838 terminus. The building, subsequently labelled 'Tank', was in fact a separate 'Working Engine Shed' – a line passed through it onto a 34 ft. turntable and various proposals were laid before the directors for a second building nearby. Access to this was from the opposite side of the turntable and in 1848 plans were prepared for both a two-road and a single-road building, the 'Spare Engine Shed'. This structure provided the basis for the four-road shed mentioned earlier and was largely complete by the 1850s, the

'Working Engine shed' becoming the tank house.

With four routes meeting at Forfar as well as other branch work in the area, these ancient arrangements would quite clearly require replacement and a fine new shed duly opened, built on spare ground to the north of the station and of four roads, like its simple predecessor. Drawings were prepared in 1898 and the new shed, a most attractive building with a fine ornateness of style, came into use on 18th December the following year. A substantial coaling shelter with ramp was erected on the north side of the yard with a turntable, 54 ft. in accordance with CR specifications of the previous year, laid by the eastern entrance. Its diameter was subsequently increased to 56 ft. (apparently in LMS days) by the simple if awkward expedient of laying rails such that they overhung the treadway. By 1948 it was noted that the 'decking boards require renewal'.

The twenty or so locos at Forfar were employed on various minor duties about the district – 0–6–0s for all manner of goods (seed potato traffic was heavy in the autumn) with 0–4–4–Ts and latterly a few 4–4–0s for a vigorous local passenger traffic. This involved a number of outstations, with corresponding paperwork and supervision; in LMS days these variously included Arbroath, Montrose, Brechin, Alyth and Kirriemuir. The shed was coded 29D under Perth in 1935, becoming 63C in BR days, whilst from

November 1959 it was regarded simply as a sub-shed of the main depot at Perth. Forfar was noted over many years for the quite exceptional external condition of its locos but, with branch closures and service reductions, the complement of about twenty was reduced as the 1950s drew on. The following three allocations illustrate the slow change of years:

31st October 1933:
CR 2F 0–6–0
17313, 17376, 17441, 17449, 17450

CR 3F 0–6–0
17654, 17671, 17672

CR 3F 0–6–0T
16323

CR 2P 0–44T
15184, 15190, 15196, 15198, 15212, 15214, 15230, 15232

Total 17

31st December 1947:
CR 3P 4–4–0
14450, 14454, 14486

LMS 'Crab' 2–6–0
2738, 2800, 2801

CR 2F 0–6–0
17324, 17368, 17441

CR 3F 0–6–0
17642

CR 2P 0–4–4T
15160, 15161, 15162, 15172, 15184, 15185, 15190, 15194, 15195, 15198, 15200, 15214, 15230

Total 23

Drummond 4—4—0 No. 1081, allocated LMS No. 14109 but never carried. In the early years, long before the new shed was built, the collection of sheds at Forfar principally served the Aberdeen Railway; here that company took and delivered trains to the Scottish Midland Junction Railway. During the period when traffic was 'pooled', trains worked through from Perth to Aberdeen, with Forfar the base for local traffic worked all along the line.   *G. Coltas*

No. 15230 on 8th June 1936, a Forfar resident over decades.   *W. A. Camwell*

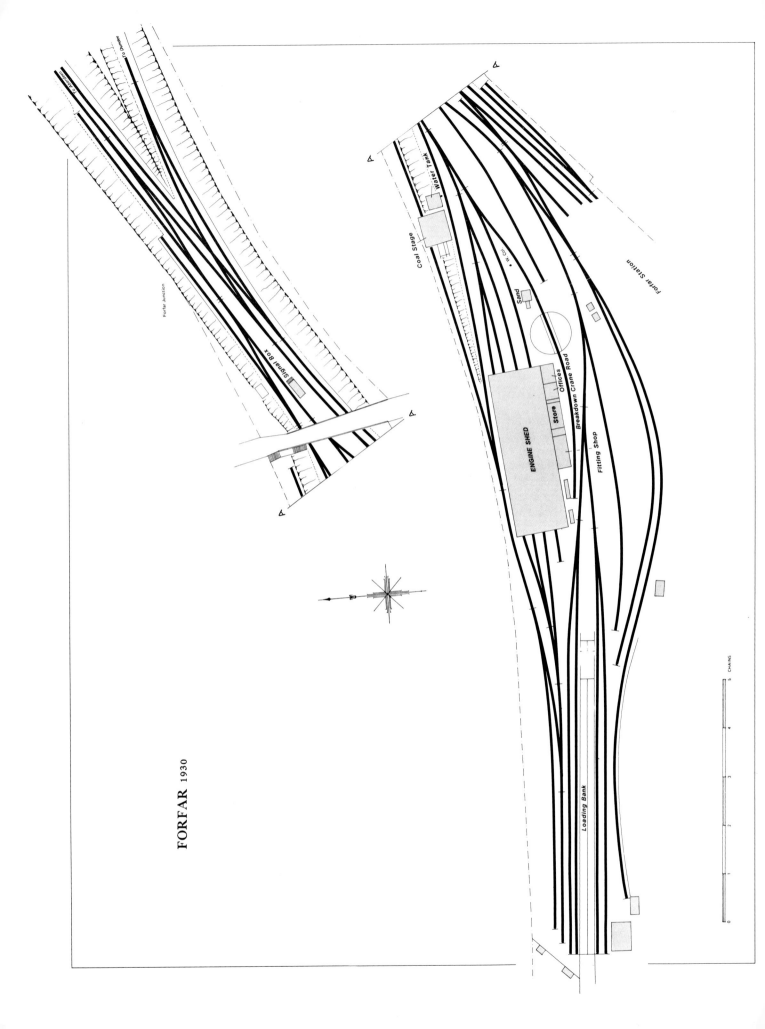

FORFAR 1930

To Glamis
To Dundee
Forfar Junction
Signal Box

Water Tank
Coal Stage
Sand
W.C.
Engine Shed
Store
Offices
Breakdown Crane Road
Fitting Shop
Forfar Station
Loading Bank

0 1 2 3 4 5 CHAINS

Forfar on 26th April 1952.

H. C. Casserley

Ex-LNER 'C16' 4—4—2T No. 67493 at Forfar, on 26th April 1952. Not the least fascination of engine shed working was the inescapable 'human' touches. It is all part of the illusion upon which the passion is grounded, but, however objectively one examines such scenes, it is hard to escape the conclusion that it reveals much (despite the harsh realities) of the attraction of the steam engine. There was always something of the 'steed' — the mythical 'bonds' which are seen between men and machine. It could never be thus with a railcar, for instance.

H. C. Casserley

Forfar on 1st August 1957. At the centre of several routes here was the classic engine shed 'routine', periods of quiescence, an empty yard, interspersed with short periods of clattering activity. Men appeared from nowhere at these times and just as quickly faded from sight.

W. Potter

9th September 1950:
CMS 'Crab' 2–6–0
42738, 42800, 42801.

CR 3P 4–4–0
54450, 54454, 54486

CR 2P 0–4–4T
55136, 55161, 55162, 55169, 55172, 55185, 55193, 55194, 55195, 55200, 55214, 55230

CR 2F 0–6–0
57324, 57368, 57441

Total 21

It is worth noting that in the summer of 1948, and quite probably for a year or so, Forfar had an LMS Compound, No 41176, on loan, assisting the class 5 on the 10 am Glasgow–Aberdeen and 5.30 pm return. The ex-CR 4–4–0s also occasionally performed this duty, generally in emergencies.

Forfar retained a Caledonian atmosphere more or less until closure but by 1959 the only locomotive officially allocated was said to be '0–6–0 No. 57441, built 1896' and therefore older than the shed itself. On 4th February 1961 six ex-CR locomotives were noted, '2F' 0–6–0s Nos. 57324 and 57441 and '2P' 0–4–4Ts Nos. 55126, 55167, 55202 and 55209 – doubtless some at least were in store, The shed finally closed in July 1964.

The shed on 7th September 1953. The nature of its duties made a somewhat rag-tag complement inevitable, based around the 'stiffening' of its three 'Crabs'. In March 1953 the allocation was LMS 4–4–0: 40939; 'Crab 2–6–0: 42738, 42800, 42801; LMS 0–6–0: 44318; CR 4–4–0: 54450, 54454, 54486; CR 0–4–4T: 55161, 55193, 55194, 55198, 55200, 55230; CR 0–6–0: 57368, 57441.

B. Hilton

0—4—4T No. 55209 and 4—4—0 No. 54489 in September 1959. There was an ornate styling in the shed at Forfar, almost Gothic in its intricacy and only really apparent when the building is viewed in its entirety.
Photomatic

4—4—0 No. 54499 in 1959. Closed in 1964, the shed was afterwards extensively used to store engines surplus to requirements or awaiting withdrawal.
Pendon Museum

Grangemouth in 1936. It opened at the height of Caledonian prosperity and power, to tap a rich new source of traffic.

National Railway Museum

'Fouldubs' engine shed; it was precisely situated to deal with goods traffic, including that generated by the docks and the accompanying shunting work. Goods and shunting remained its staple duties and an allocation of 0–6–0Ts and 0–6–0s sufficed. One or two 0–4–4Ts were available for what local passenger duties there were and the 0–6–0s were gradually joined by class 5 4–6–0s and WD 2–8–0s. *W. A. Camwell*

GRANGEMOUTH

The docks on the Forth at Grangemouth were long important to the Caledonian. Reviewing developments in 1897, a company officer could tell the editor of the *Railway Magazine:* 'In 1867 we took over the Forth and Clyde and Monkland canals, and the purchase included Grangemouth Docks on the Firth of Forth. Traffic developed so rapidly that a new dock had to be added in 1882 and traffic has again outstripped the room. More work is proceeding.' The development was intended, 'when new dock and railway are completed' to 'equal 50 miles of sidings'.

Two at least of the great 'Wet Docks' and the Timber Basin were complete by 1862, at which time there is little evidence for a shed – certainly no turntable existed. Whatever, a single road shed did later appear, south of the station on the west side of the line with turntable alongside, tanks, coal stage etc. whilst to the north beyond the Bo'ness Road bridge and alongside the Grangemouth Dock was a further building, labelled 'Engine Shed' on Survey publications of 1896. Assuming this is not a labelling error, then some as yet poorly understood developments had taken place. The Caledonian is believed to have put up the shed (on the west side of the line that is) in 1870 but the records are very uncertain, with authorisation for engine sheds in both 1873 and 1874 and an apparent construction in 1875. Two 0–4–0Ts of 1853/1854 were operated by the Docks in independent days and this complicates the picture further; they may well have been accommodated separately, accounting for a deal of the confusion. In the midst of all this, presumably from the original turntable site,

'Grangemouth Dock Engine Siding' evolved, its turntable enlarged to 70 ft. in 1905.

The situation hardly resolves itself as the nineteenth century wears on, with a new shed for the expanding traffic planned about 1897 to the south at 'Fouldubs.' This was a spaciously laid out six-road straight shed, in contemporary CR style with a single road repair shop (with 40-ton hoist) provided alongside. A contract for dormitories was drawn up on 19th April 1898 and the shed was also equipped with a 70 ft. turntable, a Ransomes Rapier unit bearing the date 1907. Again the sequence of events is out of the ordinary with the depot not coming fully into use until, it would seem, 1907–1908. The new dock, opening in 1906, might well provide the explanation, the depot seeing increasing use as the dock became fully operational. In 1902 there is the inconclusive reference 'Additional lighting for Grangemouth shed, £40. Approved.' and on 5th February 1918 £390 was authorised for 'a small Engine Shed for the Admiralty at Grangemouth Docks ... Costs to be borne by the Government'. This building was to house three LSWR 2–2–0Ts, used to transfer mines within the docks.

The main shed enjoyed from the first a substantial part in Caledonian goods operations. 0–6–0STs (replaced as they wore out by 0–6–0Ts) had shunted the Docks since the mid-1880s and 0–6–0s and 0–6–0Ts characterised the new shed from its opening well into BR days. CR 0–8–0s were frequent visitors on coal trains until 1914, when the Docks were closed to all but Admiralty traffic. There were always two or three 0–4–4Ts for local passenger work, Nos. 15129 and 15142

in October 1933 and Nos. 15119, 15142 and 15238 in December 1947. Standard 0–6–0s had arrived before 1933, with Nos. 4148, 4252 and 4253 present in that year and later on 'Crab' moguls and Stanier 2–8–0s could be found. On 31st December 1947 six of the latter were present, Nos. 8147, 8148, 8149, 8150, 8151 and 8152, with 'Crabs' Nos. 2736 and 2737. By 1950 the '8Fs' had gone, replaced by a number of WD locos, 2–8–0s Nos. 90134, 90219, 90236, 90536 and 90616, and 2–10–0s Nos. 90755, 90757, 90759 and 90765. Further 'Crabs' arrived later in the 'fifties and by 1959 ex-NB engines (no doubt from Polmont), 'J36' and 'J37' 0–6–0s with a 'J88' 0–6–0T, had helped reduce the numbers of ex-CR locos to only ten. By 1965 BR standard locomotives, 4–6–0s and 2–6–0s with 'Black 5s' made redundant elsewhere, and WD 2–8–0s formed the great part of the complement, down now to only thirty engines. Diesel shunters had been in use since the early 1950s and a pair of 'B1' 4–6–0s, Nos. 61401 and 61403, were reportedly allocated in 1961.

Grangemouth was converted with little difficulty to diesel maintenance in 1965, the building was still in fine condition and had required little attention over the years. The water pipes had been replaced in 1939 at a cost of £298 and in June 1946 the 70 ft. turntable had been fitted with a vacuum tractor '... latterly released from Nottingham'. Coded 28C under Motherwell in 1935, and 31D under St Rollox in 1940, Grangemouth ended with steam in 1965 as 65F. It is still in use as a diesel stabling point, having altered little since steam days.

Grangemouth on 7th June 1936. Present were 0–4–4Ts Nos. 15129, 15134, 15142, 15145; 0–6–0Ts Nos. 16152, 16164, 16267, 16271, 16275, 16280, 16299, 16300, 16301, 16375; 0–6–0s Nos. 17239, 17245, 17257, 17264, 17265, 17287, 17324, 17348, 17581, 17587, 17610, 17642, 17661, 17684; 2–6–0s Nos. 17804 (CR), 17825 (GSWR). *W. A. Camwell*

'Fouldubs' shed on 3rd April 1965. It lay in the fork of the Grangemouth line and the Grahamston branch, the two coming together at 'Fouldubs' Junction', where there was a substantial yard. 'Grangemouth', it seems, was the official LMS description. *W. T. Stubbs*

Familiar with diesel shunters since at least the early 'fifites, various main line units began arriving at Grangemouth in the early 1960s. It was converted fully for this use, presumably, in 1965 when steam was finally dispensed with.   *K. Fairey*

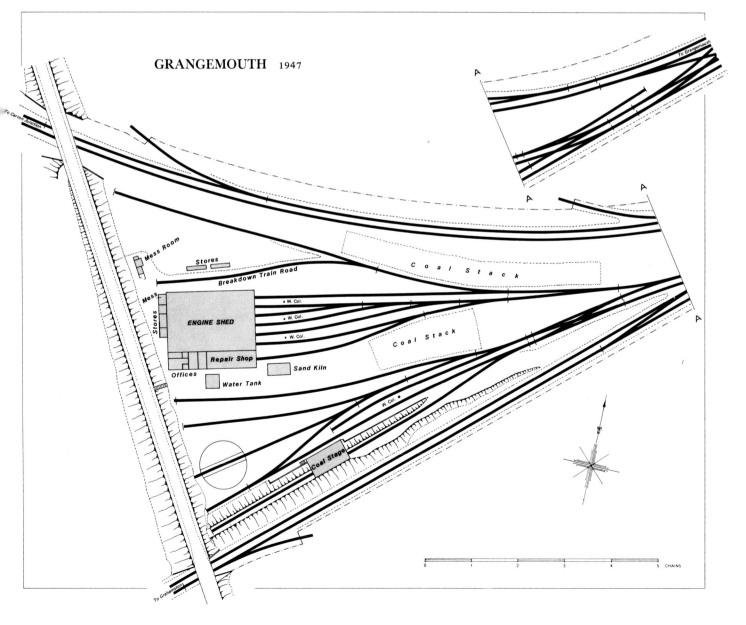

GRANGEMOUTH 1947

GREENOCK LADYBURN

Ladyburn 1929, with original northlight pattern roof. The first depot, as the text below relates, stood by the Glasgow Paisley & Greenock Railway terminus at Cathcart Street; this shed was further expanded (it is thought) on removal of the locomotive 'works'. These years are invariably muddied by a paucity of detail and a complex series of events, which discourages exactitude; in addition to the Cathcart Street collection of buildings, the precise status of which is not clear, an engine shed was also built (according to plans) a short distance away on the south side of the line. It was an extraordinary shed, two roads off a turntable and set at more than 90° from the running line. Other roads came off the turntable and were equipped with pits. The rear of the shed fronted St. John (later John) Street and seems to have come about through an Agreement of 8th June 1852, between the Glasgow Paisley & Greenock Railway and the Caledonian Railway. This arranged for certain ground to be acquired. Minuted complaints later suggest that the shed was indeed built. 'St. John Street' was extant in 1865 but disappeared or went out of use at an unknown date subsequent to this. The gap in the John Street buildings marking its site existed for many years, until at least very recently.

J. F. McEwan

The Glasgow Paisley and Greenock Railway opened in 1841, establishing a locomotive shed adjacent to their works at Greenock. The Caledonian leased the premises in 1846, intending them for new construction but though the works building was enlarged, the shed, it seems, remained unaltered; until 1853 only the GP & G stock seems to have been based there, or at Cook Street, Glasgow. The area around the works was nevertheless becoming extremely congested, such that the Caledonian determined upon a move to the long-delayed new works at St. Rollox. This took place in 1856, the vacated premises then becoming part of the engine shed.

In the 1878 session of Parliament a bill was sent up for extension of the Greenock branch. This failed but is of interest in its reference to a site for a new locomotive depot; no definite details were arrived at unfortunately before the bill fell. An Act was finally obtained in 1884 and, as the line at Greenock (existing) station was to be a little more to the south, it became obvious that the engine shed would have to be moved elsewhere. A site at Bogston, then an unused ground, was first chosen – it had been acquired in or around 1873 in connection with the proposed branch to Port Glasgow harbour. This area was again in mind in 1878, abandoned when the Gourock Extension bill failed. The Gourock Act of 1884 made it essential that the Greenock sheds be moved and, since the new route to Port Glasgow docks had been determined,

it was agreed that 'Ladyburn' be constructed. It seems to have been mid-1885 before the shed came into use for no work was started on the Extension line prior to this date.

Ladyburn was a substantial building, the roads leading through to a turntable at the rear. Its construction reflected the burgeoning passenger and heavy goods traffic on south Clydeside, the shed lying amidst a mass of sidings half a mile or so west of the junction of the Wemyss Bay and Gourock lines. The Wemyss branch in fact passed a few yards to the south of (and above) the shed itself. Greenock (Ladyburn, not unknown in CR

4–6–2T, for Ladyburn's prestigious 'business' workings, on 16th June 1936. The 'Wemyss Bay Pugs' had a not inconsiderable task on these trains; the Bay branch runs past Ladyburn just to the south, rising more than fifty feet above the shed to give a gradient steeper than Beattock.

W. A. Camwell

times, appears to have come increasingly into use in the LMS period, presumably to distinguish the shed from Princes Pier) performed its varied duties unsung but with perfect competence over many decades, in particular the working of the Glasgow-Gourock and Wemyss Bay trains by Polmadie and Ladyburn was extremely efficient with running very smart and fast.

The shed nevertheless attracted little attention over the years and was entirely forgotten with regard to mechanical aids. There was some activity, mainly concentrated between the turn of the century and the period of the First World War, detail alterations which nonetheless improved life at the depot. On 2nd May 1905 a new engine pit was approved at a cost of £132 and the following year £70 was set aside for an additional water column 'from Robroyston'. In 1912 it was recommended that £120 'be spent on a new siding at Greenock Ladyburn shed for the storage of engine ash wagons' and in 1913 £675 was approved for both 'Greenock Station and Ladyburn Engine Shed'. On 12th June 1917 'Electric Supply' was reported laid into the shed, and in July 1920, under the heading 'proposed new water closet accommodation at Ladyburn Engine Shed', £90 was approved for 'new facilities in substitution of the existing dry closet which is an old timber building in a dilapidated condition'. On 18th January 1927 'improved offices' were promised, at a cost of £373.

For many years trains on the Greenock branch (as the CR chose to describe it) were worked by 2–4–0- and 0–4–2 engines; these remained until the Gourock extension opened in June 1889, although a few Drummond 0–6–0s had been used on the faster goods trains. Greenock was a major industrial centre; it supplied almost all the sugar consumed in Scotland and northern England and was similarly pre-eminent in rope work and the production of sail cloth. All this warranted daily goods trains to Edinburgh and Carlisle whilst further workings were necessary (importing a vast tonnage of metal from Lanarkshire) for the shipbuilding and machinery industries. Greenock prior to 1914 was a world centre of shipbuilding and at one stage an 0–8–0 goods engine is known to have been employed on the work. Ladyburn was responsible in the main for local traffic, servicing in addition the engines off incoming special goods. Drummond 5′9″ 4–4–0s were sent there on opening of the line to Gourock, remaining on passenger work for a number of years. Westinghouse-fitted 0–6–0s could also be found on passenger work, first the small Drummond type, then the McIntosh 18½″ engines. Four of the latter's 'Barochan' 4–6–0s regularly worked passenger turns from Ladyburn, until replaced by superheated 30 class 0–6–0s, and at Grouping the shed also had two 'Dunalastair 1' 4–4–0s. The various yards and their workings were labryinthine – dock tanks, home grown 'Pugs' and 'beetlecrushers' as well as Fowler engines – were an abiding feature at the shed and before 1923 0–4–0STs Nos. 1503 and 1505 were regular engines, typically employed at Upper Greenock, where sharp curves combined with a steep ascent made

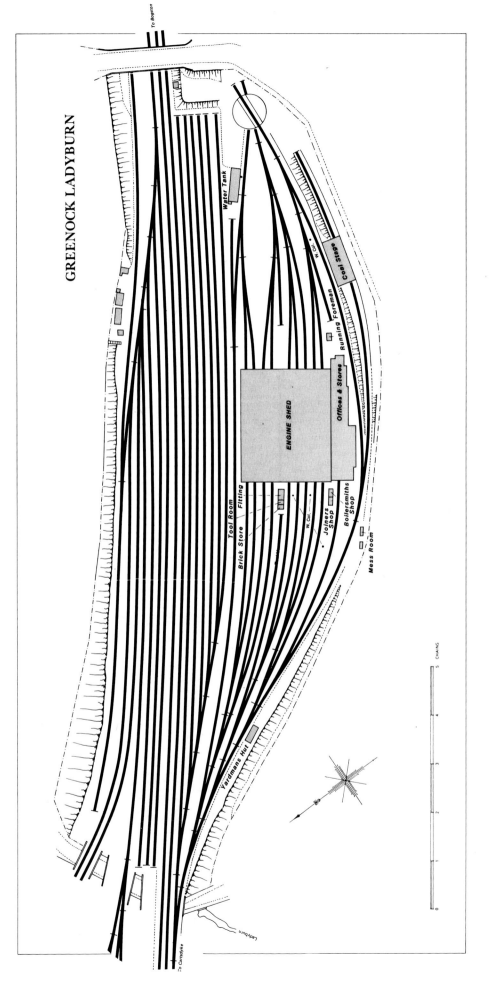

GREENOCK LADYBURN

for a hazardous paper mill shunt. There was also an 0–6–0T employed on more conventional shunting and trip work; collecting wagons from the 'concentration' yards in the area and gathering them together at Cartsdyke.

Despite a relatively spacious layout, Ladyburn could never boast a large allocation. H.J. Campbell Cornwell in *Forty Years of Caledonian Locomotives* has Ladyburn with only twenty-three locomotives in 1921– a pair of 4–4–0s, eight 0–6–0s, five 0–6–0Ts and eight 'others'. The big Pickersgill 4–6–2Ts were later allocated, for the heavy business traffic, with Nos. 15352, 15353, 15354, 15355 and 15356 present in October 1933. The following month, a recognition of the importance of these trains, Ladyburn received No. 2418, one of a number of Fowler 2–6–4Ts sent new to Scotland. Others had gone to Princes Pier, the ex-GSWR shed, but soon found their way to Ladyburn to form a distinctive part of the allocation until the post-war years. In 1945, eight of them, having displaced the CR 4–6–2Ts, were among forty-five engines allocated. About a third of these, including most of the nine CR 4–4–0s, were at Princes Pier, under the supervision of the Ladyburn foreman since about 1930. It had been the practice over many years to send 'demoted' 4–4–0s to Ladyburn, some even finishing their days on goods work. 'Dunalastair' 4–4–0s (the relatively easy grades of the coast line rendered them suitable for the

'Greenock' was a complex of docks and works, from Port Glasgow to Princes Pier and the railway served this great engine of Scottish industry. Much of it was still in evidence in 1962; outside the shed is an immaculately turned out Fairburn 2–6–4T, amongst a number of mineral wagons destined for the shunt to Inchgreen Gas Works, one of the last of Ladyburn's arcane jobs, and closed down in 1964.   *William Sinclair, cty. John Sinclair*

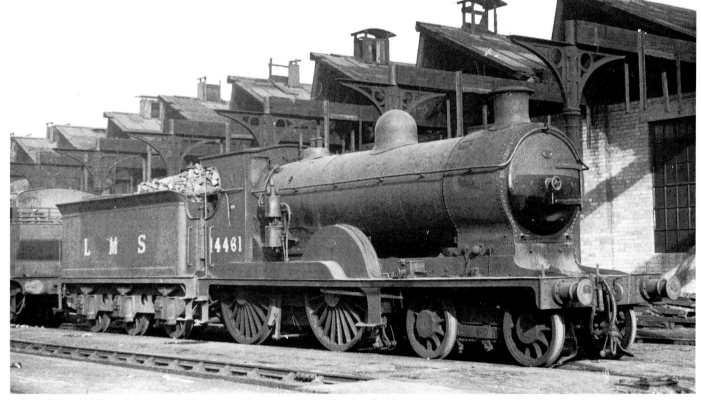

4–4–0 No. 14461 on 5th October 1946. Air raids occurred in 1940 and early 1941, all of them to prove minor in comparison with the events of 5th-7th May 1941, known locally as 'The Blitz' and every bit as horrifying as that suffered in London. Shortly after midnight on Monday, 5th May 1941, an estimated fifty bombers attacked the district, the shed and sidings suffering a number of direct hits. 'Dunalastair IV' No. 14356 ended upside down in a pit where it remained until scrapped a month later. To add to the chaos, a few gunpowder vans (probably for Ross & Marshall Munitions Factory) lying across the main line west of the up sidings exploded. A second attack followed twenty-four hours later, with, it is suggested, up to 250 bombers. 280 people were killed and 1,200 injured, many of them seriously. Work at the depot can not be said to have properly been restored to normal until the 1950s.   *H. C. Casserley*

Ladyburn in September 1954. The shed roads, in happier times, had been numbered from the south side, i.e. that furthest from the main line; the first five were generally reserved for passenger locos, the rest for goods, with No. 10 principally for the shunters. A coal bing was sited between roads 7 & 8 and 9 & 10, facing the water tank, but it was taken up in 1943. The area abounded in obscure shunts and trips and numbers of specialised shunting tanks were a feature of the shed. Perhaps the most exotic was the Overton Paper Mill Branch — the 'Puggie line' — an absurdly graded branch reaching peaks of 1 in 13. A runaway killed a Ladyburn driver in 1907, the loco leaping an embankment and small burn to land in the road.
Photomatic

passenger traffic) present in 1933 had comprised Nos. 14313, 14318, 14322, 14325, 14339, 14345, 14352, 14364 and 14365. Tanks for the docks and works turns in 1945 numbered twelve, distributed between the two sheds: 'Beetlecrusher' 0–6–0T: 16156, 16157, 16163, 16165, 16166, 16173; Fowler Dock Tank: 7167, 7168, 7169; 'Pug': 16030, 16035, 16038. (An L & Y 0–4–0ST was also tried out in the Harbour area at one time.) Despite the sub-shed status of Princes Pier, administered from Ladyburn, there was effectively no rail connection and repairs were carried out at Corkerhill.

At the end of 1946 a 'Wemyss Bay' 4–6–2T staged a brief return, with No. 15355 at Ladyburn before joining the remaining members of the class at Beattock. By 1950 the allocation was as follows:

LMS 4P 4–4–0
41148, 41149, 41182

LMS 4P Fowler 2–6–4T
42400, 42415, 42416, 42417, 42418
42419, 42020, 42421, 42422, 42423

LMS Fairburn 2–6–4T
42175, 42176, 42697

LMS 2F 0–6–0T
47167, 47168

CR 3P 4–4–0
54457

CR 0F 0–4–0ST
56028, 56031, 56035

CR 2F 0–6–0T
56156, 56157, 56163, 56166, 56173

CR 3F 0–6–0T
56288

CR 3F 0–6–0
57552, 57556

The bombed passenger roads were covered in a new lightweight material, using a wall put up by D. McEwing after the bombing on No. 6 road. This left an insubstantial five-road shed, greatly different in character from the old Caledonian building.
K. Fairey

In March 1954, part of a rationalisation of the 2–6–4T disposition, BR had the big Fowler tanks (all ten Scottish examples were by now based at the shed) sent to English depots in exchange for Fairburn engines. By 1959 a couple of 'Crabs' had arrived, Nos. 42740 and 42741, but the allocation thereafter declined, with only a dozen 2–6–4Ts present towards the end.

Ladyburn (the stream, latterly storm drain of that name passed under the shed's western approach) had a northlight pattern roof rather than the traditional transverse roofing and by the end of World War II what remained of the covering was in extremely poor condition. Five roads in the southern half of the shed were entirely bereft of cover

and what remained required all manner of additional support – props, and a new brick wall along the centre of No. 6 road (read south–north). The shed area had received a number of direct hits in the raids of May 1941, one consequence being the withdrawal of CR 4–4–0 No. 14356 in June. In 1958 the patched up roofing was finally condemned and new covering erected over the open part of the shed. The contract was placed with Fleming Bros of Glasgow on 20th June 1958 and the old roofing section dismantled.

Coded 27G by the LMS in 1935 (with Princes Pier officially as sub-shed), Ladyburn became 27B in the wartime alterations and 66D under BR in 1949. It closed in December 1966.

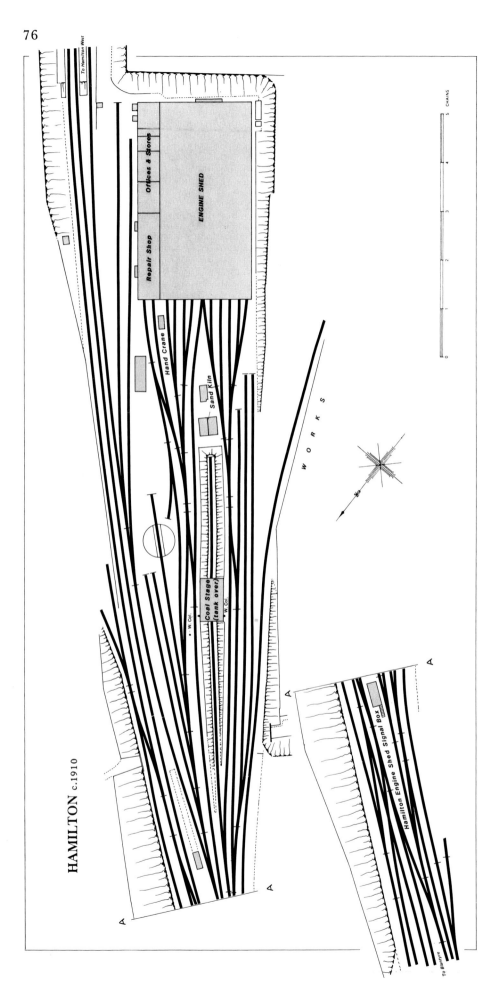

HAMILTON c.1910

Labels within map: To Hamilton West · Offices & Stores · Repair Shop · ENGINE SHED · Hand Crane · Sand Kiln · Coal Stage (tank over) · W. Col. · W. Col. · WORKS · Hamilton Engine Shed Signal Box · To Blantyre · 5 CHAINS

HAMILTON

Hamilton, a coal mining district on the south banks of the Clyde opposite Motherwell, was originally served by a terminus at what was to become 'Hamilton West'. In a cutting fronting Clyde Street the line was later extended through to Hamilton Central and on to Larkhall, Motherwell and so on, but in October of 1860 locomotive facilities at the terminus comprised nothing more than a turntable (less than 20 ft. in diameter) sited opposite the southern extremity of the lengthy single platform.

There are (imperfect) references to a Hamilton engine shed from the opening of the branch in 1849. In that year a small one-road engine 'house' was put up but the following year, with the company's economic future hanging in the balance (the Caledonian was well and truly broke), the engine outbased there was removed. The shed would then have been disused. The line had been built to develop a number of existing pits and, as the workings extended southwards, the line to Strathaven via Quarter was built, opening for minerals in August 1860. A small engine shed now appears to have been erected at Hamilton West, around 1861 in connection with a mineral traffic from the collieries stretching along the line to Quarter.

Coal production grew rapidly around Hamilton; High Blantyre, Quarter, Cadzow and Blantyre were major sites with, more locally, Silvertown, Barncluith, Allanshaw, (even Bent) collieries in operation before the end of the 1880s. It was a lucrative traffic for the Caledonian and it was not long before more suitable locomotive accommodation was warranted. Accordingly a well arranged depot, laid out on a generous scale, was erected, on a site excavated some yards to the north of Hamilton West station. The CR Board placed the contract for a new engine shed 'at Hamilton West' on 15th November 1881 and on 27th March 1883 Drummond asked that a 50 ft. timetable be provided. On 4th August 1885 it was agreed that 'the old Engine Shed at Hamilton West' could be removed 'to Bridgeton', where it would serve as a goods shed. There is a tradition that further bays were added to the new shed within a few years of opening; plausible enough for the Lanarkshire coalfield was reaching its peak, not beginning its decline until around 1914.

The shed, in any event, was ordered in classic Caledonian fashion – two road repair shop backed by offices and workshops on the east side, separate from the ten-road 'running' section. These roads divided in the yard into two parts, (unusually in CR practice) by a claustrophobic brick-built 'tank over' coal stage. The repair shop, two roads yet short, as the establishment at Motherwell, was in brick, but the typically lofty frontage, masking a 40 ton hoist, was faced in timber. The shed roof was composed of traditional longitudinal pitches but much of the frontage (around 40% of the shed) was removed following the sinking of old coal workings. It had first begun to suffer in the 1930s; up

The cavernous wooden building at Hamilton was, like the other Caledonian sheds ordered in this startling fashion, doomed to relatively early demise. Coal sinkings rendered it unsafe; it is not possible to say whether a brick construction might have proved more resistant, but a timber building must presumably have been more susceptible to shifting ground than any more conventional building form. Hamilton concerned itself with the hauling of coal and the shunting thereof, much to the exclusion of all else. Collieries surrounded the district and the Brocketsbrae and Coalburn branches formed conduits to further workings. Sorted and shunted in Ross or Hamilton yards, coal was worked forward, to Glasgow, or across the Clyde to the Motherwell steel works.

H. F. Wheeller Collection

till then only the Craighead Yard had been affected but the ground movement spread, rendering the front part of the shed dangerous. It was removed and a variety of proposals ensued for resisting or closing the depot – an alternative site was not, however, available on railway ground, the continuous decline in the coal trade proving no positive encouragement to action. The Cowans Sheldon turntable remained at 50 ft. for many years, and bore the date 1884.

On 6th September 1910 the shed was supplied with £25-worth of improved piping and three hydrants at the coal bench, 'for the purpose of drenching ashes and keeping down dust' and the following year £55 was 'granted, to improve office accommodation at Hamilton Shed'. In 1922 an unspecified amount was approved for 'new joiners shop at Hamilton shed to replace former wooden example recently demolished.' This, however, was not strictly part of the locomotive department – wagon repairs were carried out at Hamilton, particularly timber work, avoiding a trip to St. Rollox. Hamilton remained essentially a goods engine shed, a stud of 0–6–0s hauling coal mainly to Glasgow or Mossend Yard with 0–6–0Ts for endless shunting and trip work from the scattered collieries. Several of the big 0–8–0Ts of 1903 found their way to the shed and by 1921 the complement was made up of, in the main, 0–6–0s and 0–6–0Ts, with a number of 0–4–4Ts on local passenger work. This concerned the Coalburn, Brocketsbrae and Strathaven branches, the Hamilton–Motherwell–Holytown service, etc., as well

No. 15 166 on 14th June 1935. The number of 0–4–4Ts at Hamilton declined, replaced by more modern types and a collection of unregarded railcars and a 2–4–2T. The latter seemed never in steam and the railcars, when available, worked half a dozen or so trains a day Hamilton-Holytown as well as three daily workings Hamilton-Brocketsbrae. They were 'loathed' by the staff.

H. F. Wheeller Collection

as trains to Glasgow. While most of the latter ran to Glasgow Central – some to Low Level – there was also a service to Buchanan Street via Motherwell, Mossend and Coatbridge.

Withdrawals of the 0–8–0Ts began in 1932 and none were present by 31st November 1933, when the allocation showed little change from Caledonian days; only a single LMS engine was present, standard 0–6–0 No. 4111, the remaining 69 locos (all ex-CR) neatly divided as follows:

CR 2F 0–6–0
17237, 17238, 17239, 17249, 17261, 17281, 17288, 17293, 17299, 17305, 17309, 17336, 17338, 17350, 17354, 17384, 17395, 17398, 17407, 17408, 17410, 17413, 17420

CR 3F 0–6–0
17592, 17664, 17665, 17666, 17667, 17668, 17669, 17678, 17687, 17689

CR 3F 0–6–0T
16230, 16240, 16242, 16243, 16244, 16246, 16247, 16254, 16255, 16256, 16257, 16284,

16286, 16293, 16302, 16309, 16319, 16320, 16321, 16322, 16325, 16371

CR 2P 0–4–4T
15130, 15131, 15139, 15140, 15141, 15146, 15165, 15166, 15167, 15171, 15174, 15175, 15185, 15192

The shed had provided a home over the years for various railcars – Sentinel No. 4148, unsuccessful on the Warlockhead line, was moved to Hamilton in 1933 and the three Leyland diesel railcars built that year, Nos. 29950, 29951 and 29952 were there at one time. A pioneering venture, they were of particular interest, working to Holytown, Strathaven (via Glassford) or Brocketsbrae, latterly, in the words of G. H. Robin, 'very much off and on'. They were withdrawn in 1951.

LMS changes had by the end of 1947 left the shed, paradoxically, with a far more varied complement – three Pickersgill '60' class 4–6–0s and three LMS 'Crabs' dealt with much of the longer distance freight work whilst Stanier 2–6–2Ts replaced the Caledonian 0–4–4Ts, the duties more onerous with heavier carriage stock. The 1947 total of over fifty locomotives, with three railcars, was made up as follows:

CR 4P 4–6–0
14638, 14639, 14648

'Crab' 2–6–0
2735, 2740, 2741

CR 2F 0–6–0
17237, 17242, 17244, 17250, 17260, 17280, 17307, 17382, 17384, 17393, 17395, 17398, 17401, 17407, 17408, 17410, 17420, 17430, 17431

'Crab' No. 42740 on 21st June 1949. Hamilton remained little more than a rather extensive engine yard, and presumably the unpredictability of the ground precluded any rebuilding. Furthermore, the coal traffic was in long term decline and the site increasingly unsuited to changing workings.

H. C. Casserley

CR 3F 0–6–0
17609, 17630, 17663, 17665

LMS 4P 2–6–4T
2217

LNW 1P 2–4–2T
6656

LMS 3P 2–6–2T
150, 151, 152, 153, 154, 158

CR 3F 0–6–0T
16237, 16242, 16255, 16256, 16284, 16286, 16287, 16296, 16303, 16309, 16319, 16320, 16321, 16360, 16362, 16371

CR 2P 0–4–4T
15146

LMS Diesel Railcars
29950, 29951, 29952

The last Pickersgill 4–6–0 to remain in service, No. 54639, was withdrawn from

Hamilton on 29th June 1947, with left to right: 0–6–0 No. 17663, 'Crab' 2–6–0 No. 2878, 0–6–0s Nos. 17407 and 17393, 0–6–0Ts Nos. 16362 and 16242.

G. S. Lloyd

Hamilton on 5th June 1949. At the shed were 0–4–4Ts Nos. 55123 and 55146; 0–6–0Ts Nos. 16255, 16296, 16303, 16319, 16321, 16362, 16371, 56237, 56256, 56286, 56287 and 56320; 0–6–0s Nos. 17236, 17242, 17244, 17250, 17280, 17385, 17401, 17407, 17410, 17609, 57237, 57260, 57307, 57398, 57430, 57431 and 57665; 2–6–2Ts Nos. 40150, 40152, 40153 and 40156; 2–6–4Ts Nos. 42164, 42165 and 42166; 2–6–0s Nos. 2850 and 2880; 4F 0–6–0 No. 44258 and Railcars Nos. 29950, 29951 and 29952. The 2–6–2Ts long worked the fairly frequent and smartly timed trains between Hamilton and Glasgow as well as going up to Coalburn and Strathaven. The bigger 2–6–4Ts came to supplement them on these trains. Perhaps the most intriguing of the shed's jobs was the Hamilton Central station pilot, a dual-fitted 0–6–0T, 16296 or 16303, taking a passenger train to Holytown. Passenger work with these engines was otherwise unknown. *W. A. Camwell*

Hamilton in December 1953 and by the following year Fairburn 2–6–4Ts dominated the local work. BR class 3MT 2–6–0s were in use and WD locos, 2–8–0 and 2–10–0, were available for heavy goods work. In 1959 Hamilton could boast the following complement:

4MT 2–6–4–T
42128, 42129, 42164, 42165, 42166, 42167

'Crab' 2–6–0
42735, 42738, 42746, 42850, 42880

4F 0–6–0
44196

3F 0–60T
47331

CR 3F 0–6–0T
56242, 56256, 56286, 56287, 56296, 56309, 56321, 56360, 56362, 56371

CR 2F 0–6–0
57242, 57244, 57250, 57307, 57321, 57335, 57370, 57384, 57398, 57407, 57431, 57446, 57447

CR 3F 0–6–0
57609, 57630, 57663, 57665

BR 3MT 2–6–0
77005, 77006, 77007

BR 4MT 2–6–4T
80109

WD 2–10–0
90764, 90771, 90772

BR railbuses worked from the shed in the 1950s and on 6th July 1959 'three diesel sets' began operations 'made up of Cravens twin units and two Bristol A.E.C. railbuses. (M79958 and M79959).' By 1960 four roads on the west side were reserved for diesel sets and three railbuses were (again 'off and on') available.

Hamilton was coded 28B in the Motherwell District in 1935 and 27C under Polmadie in the subsequent rearrangements. The BR code from 1949 was 66C. The last four steam locomotives were sent away in November 1962, the *Railway Magazine* early the next year reporting 'Hamilton Shed, Glasgow . . . now completely dieselised.'

'Crab' 2–6–0 No. 42735, on 4th July 1957. In the early days following Nationalisation, NBL 'L1' 2–6–4Ts were run in from Hamilton shed, the duties there considered more appropriate than Eastfield. *H. C. Casserley*

No. 42128 and 57242 on 4th July 1957. Railbuses came to Hamilton in the 1950s and the dreary practice continued of substituting 2F 0–6–0s during their frequent failures. By 1962/3 the depot had been given over entirely to DMUs and shunters and, despite its poor location, around £120,000 was expended in the later 'sixties on updating the improvised set-up of early diesel days. With electrification to Hamilton, its position proved particularly anomalous and it finally closed around 1980, the scene having changed little since steam days. *H. C. Casserley*

4–6–0 No. 14758 and 0–6–0 No. 17615 on 18th September 1926.

B. Mathews Collection

The work of 1915/16 amounted to a careful substitution, in brick, utilising, it would seem, the precise foundation work and pits of the old shed. It was an extraordinary project, 'Kingmoor' emerging from the fabric of 'Etterby', a transmutation that the casual observer passing Etterby Bridge would fail to notice amongst the smoke. The north yard (seen here) was altered at some time between 1899 and 1924 (presumably during the 1915/16 work), reversing the approach roads. Originally they had led in directly from the Glasgow end, but were slewed, engines approaching from the south into dead sidings, to thence reverse into the shed. This at least describes physically access to and from the shed; in practice engines did not arrive willy-nilly and followed predetermined paths.

James Venn Collection

KINGMOOR

The first Caledonian shed at Carlisle was intended, it would seem, as something of a temporary measure. A timber building at the north end of the station, it was replaced on completion of the viaduct approach from the River Caldew by a much more substantial brick building, by tradition known as 'West Walls'. Erected in 1849, once the necessary infilling had taken place, for official purposes it was always referred to simply as 'Carlisle' (as were its successors). The term 'West Walls', however, does from time to time find its way into official records and was certainly in use locally.

The building was divided internally to accommodate separately both Caledonian and Glasgow & South Western locomotives and lay on the east side of the line, uncomfortably close to the Deanery. This gave endless offence, and full ecclesiastical blessing was readily forthcoming when in the early 1870s the CR purposed a move to Etterby, outside the city. The company had come by the necessary land as early as 1857, a move intended to deny the North British easy access to Carlisle; a few sidings had been laid, their purpose to foil a number of NB attempts at compulsory purchase, but the ground was not put to any proper traffic use. This was to prove most fortuitous when in July 1872 the Caledonian finally obtained powers to lay down a set of sidings and erect an engine shed. An enthusiastic supporter was the Dean

of Carlisle, exasperated 'by over 23 years' of smoke and noise from the West Walls shed. The Deanery windows were on a level with the building, described in one complaint as 'two sheds 350 feet long' (corresponding to the two bays), 'open at the top' with the top of the engine chimneys less than two feet below the Dean's windows. In 1859 the problem had been so severe that the Carlisle Summer Assizes had been moved to serve a smoke abatement notice (or the contemporary equivalent thereof) on both the CR and the GSWR.

'Etterby' shed was partly in use by 1876 and was completed in August 1877. The Board had finally agreed the scheme in detail on 25th September 1873 and let the contract, at £18,293, in December. Construction had thus not got properly underway until at least 1874. West Walls was eventually allowed to become more or less derelict; by 1886 there had been a number of further complaints, this time regarding the unkempt nature of the ground about the old shed, and on 1st September the Board agreed to co-operate with the Carlisle City authorities in 'landscaping' the offending area.

Etterby represented a new, spacious development, though it was to suffer, like Polmadie, through the less than permanent nature of its timber construction. It was a great through building, of LNWR 'steam shed' proportions, and lay on the east side of the main line between the River Eden and, almost in mockery, the NBR Edinburgh–Carlisle line. All engines, passenger and

freight, working into the city had of necessity to visit the depot which was accordingly possessed of lavish yard arrangements. On 7th October 1890 'barracks' at Kingmoor were deemed necessary, the plans approved on 18th November and a contract made with Henry Court on 6th January 1891 for £1,359 14s. 7d. The plans were headed 'Kingmoor Contract' the latter appellation now finding increasing favour. The depot was extensively remodelled in the 1890s with the following authorised in August 1895:

Coaling shed and Bank – £830
Permanent Way and Signals – £1700
New Engine Turntable for Etterby Engine Shed – £620.

The latter was put into use in November but on 17th November 1903 a 70 ft. turntable had been ordered 'to be put in', the old one to be 'removed to Guthrie'; it was less than ten years old but such replacements became necessary at various key places in this period. The new bogie tender 4–6–0s made their first appearance in 1903 and 70 ft. tables were required to accommodate their 65 ft. 6 ins. length. On 22nd December 1908 the Carlisle Water Board sought permission to connect their pipe to the CR mains carrying water from the River Eden to Etterby sheds. This was agreed, provided that the authority installed a water meter. By 1915 further alterations were in prospect. Anticipating the rebuilding planned at Polmadie, the shed was constructed anew in brick upon the original site, using pre-existing foundations, flooring

KINGMOOR 1936

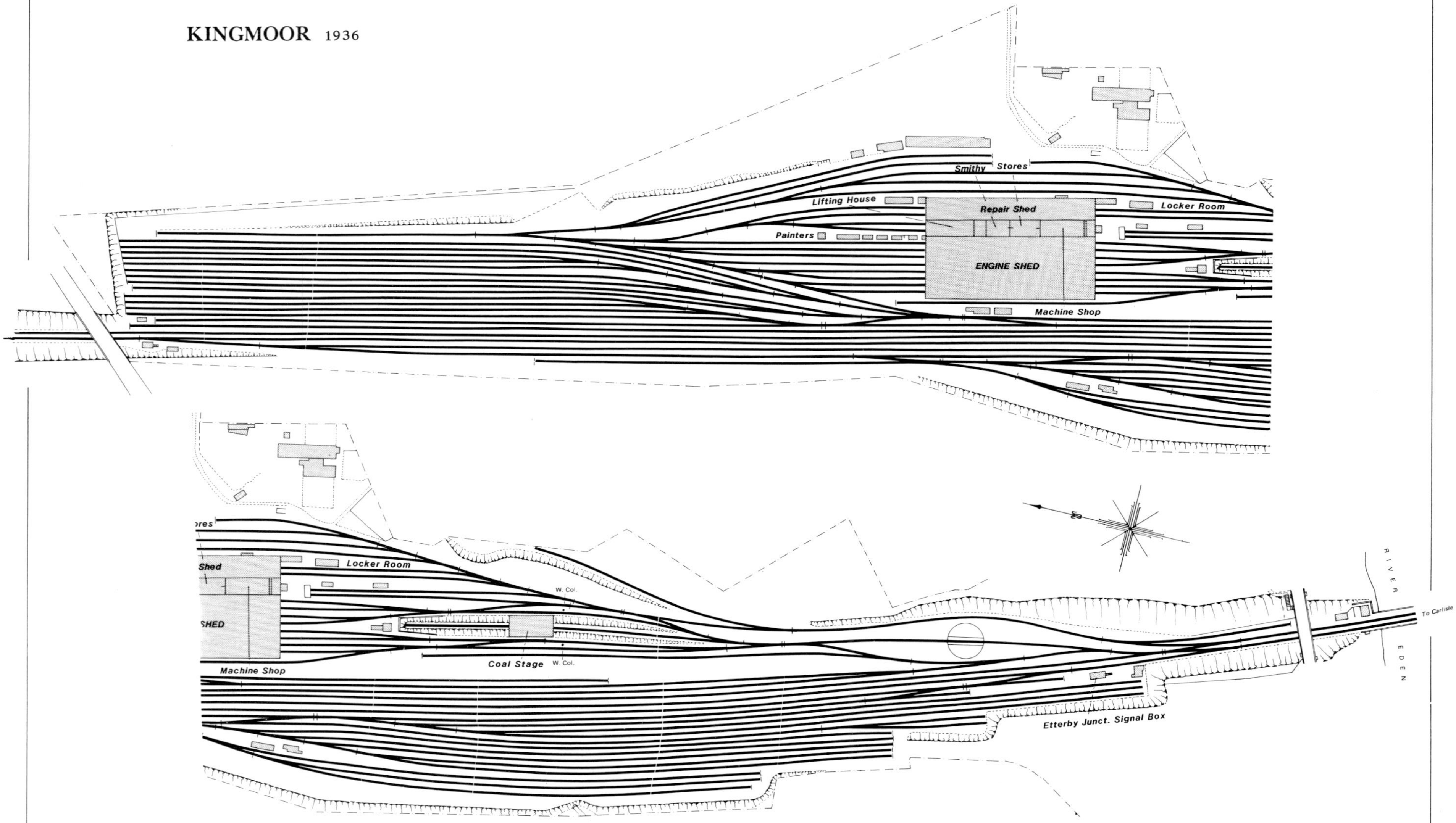

SCALE: 4 chains to 1 inch

To Carlisle

RIVER EDEN

Locker Room

Smithy Stores

Repair Shed

ENGINE SHED

Machine Shop

Lifting House

Painters

Etterby Junct. Signal Box

Coal Stage

W. Col.

W. Col.

Locker Room

Machine Shop

Shed

SHED

res

Kingmoor in June 1936. From around this time (it was set up as the 12A 'concentration' district the previous year) began the changes that were to set Kingmoor firmly apart from the other former Caledonian sheds. It lay in England in any event and increasingly (and inevitably) began to acquire its 'cosmopolitan' air.

W. Potter

and pits: 'Approved. (Approximately) £23,000 for the Renewal of Carlisle Engine Shed . . . to be remade as Balornock . . . Messrs P & W Anderson to carry out the work . . . to be known as Kingmoor'.

The new 'Kingmoor' shed would have opened the following year, or perhaps in 1917, crowning a series of major improvements and prompting all manner of prudent additions. In 1919 a further £1,040 was expended on new electric pumps for the boiler washing out plant, replacing the obsolete locomotive used for this purpose since about 1906. From September 1923 the coal stage began to receive attention, when it was decided that the roof, 'which is too low . . . should be raised'. The offending height was twelve feet above rail level and evidently required to be raised by 16 inches. The estimated cost was £345, giving an annual saving of £300; 'in all about 60 engines per day are coaled at Kingmoor; due to the insufficient height of the coal stage there is a delay of about 10 minutes per engine in coaling.'

Kingmoor retained its importance throughout LMS days; well laid out with little restriction, it moved easily to pre-eminence in Carlisle, absorbing first the former G & SWR engines (stationed at Currock) then aspects of Durran Hill and, in its last years, Upperby. Waverley route duties followed on closure of the former NB shed at Canal in June 1963. Kingmoor was indeed exceptional in the extraordinary diversity of its work; the engines roamed all the routes northwards and west from the city, to Glasgow both on ex-CR and ex-GSW lines, to Stranraer, Edinburgh, Perth, Ayr, Ardrossan (goods) as well as down the Maryport and Carlisle and the Settle lines.

It was beyond the resources of the LMS to concentrate locomotive work at Kingmoor, though moves to that end were reported as

early as 1929–30. The problem remained one of inheritance; disparate yards worked in doggedly pre-Grouping fashion. Apart from changing engines off passenger trains (at the station) it was always the practice to change freight locos at Carlisle. This would occur as a matter of course, trains from the north arriving at Viaduct, Upperby, Dentonholme, Durran Hill yards, or wherever, wagons then being tripped endlessly around Carlisle. Kingmoor, before completion of the New Yard in April 1963, was itself quite small and situated almost entirely on the down side. There were relatively few Anglo-Scottish freights not requiring any shunting and these

in turn were duly re-engined. The constant succession of wagons trundling around Carlisle was overseen by a Goods Lines Committee, with each company providing the requisite engine power. Only in the First World War did CR locomotives run through to Upperby exchange sidings, with a matching LNW working to Kingmoor. Coaling and watering at the 'foreign' depot was quite usual, to avoid disturbance of the goods lines working.

Kingmoor was thus a scene of continuous activity, servicing a stream of visitors as well as its own substantial allocation. Situated in addition at an extremity of the system (oper-

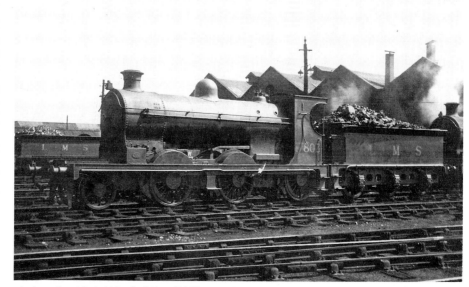

Awkward and hybrid 2—6—0 No. 17803, one of the Caledonian lot, in August of 1935.

H. N. James

ationally in its essentials little altered through to BR days), it was accordingly generously equipped with machinery. A pair of overhead hoists was available, each over two roads, and the LMS added a wheeldrop, connected to a modernised and re-equipped machine shop. Furthermore, the depot was again extensively remodelled, this time under proposals dating from the early part of 1937, the main features being a vast 'No. 1' type coaling plant (see Volume 1) and 'double skip' automated ash disposal arrangements. The old coaling ramp was necessarily eradicated during this thorough-going rearrangement, the work in stark contrast to the ex-LNWR shed at Upperby (again see Volume I), a crumbling ruin where such developments were more than a decade away.

The war, with its operational pressures, saw further change, and, before the 1940s were out, a new office/stores block had appeared at the south end of the shed, separate from the main building, whilst the two terminal bays at the north end of the repair shop had been commandeered for the first 0–6–0 diesel shunters. Kingmoor was the only CR establishment to receive some of the early LMS jackshaft drive diesel shunters. The machine shop separated the main repair roads from the dirt and smoke of the running shed proper and retained to the end additional accommodation on the first floor. This in itself was an unusual feature and a further indication of the level of activity at the depot.

Kingmore itself lay in England, one factor in the creation of its 1935, 12A 'concentration' depot status, head of a Carlisle District with bounds both to the north and south. The resulting District was uniquely cosmopolitan, containing depots of Caledonian, LNWR, Midland, G & SW and Furness origin. Its complement was thus more thoroughly 'LMS' in nature, at an earlier date than was perhaps the case at other major depots.

As one of the principal sheds, located at the southern end of the main line, Kingmoor had ever played host to the Caledonian's top link express engines, from the two large 6 ft. 6 in. 4–6–0s of the '49' class and the five similar 'Cardean' engines of 1903–1906 to the celebrated series of McIntosh 'Dunalastair' 4–4–0s. Two of the first batch of superheated 4–4–0s, Nos. 134 and 135, were sent new to Kingmoor in 1911 followed by others; similarly, when the Pickersgill '60' class were introduced, Nos. 62 and 63 arrived new, in 1917. Finally, they were joined by two of the imposing 3-cylinder '956' engines, Nos. 957 and 958 of 1921. Goods and shunting turns to and from and within Carlisle were, of course, legion, attended by a host of 0–6–0s and fussing tanks. The north end Citadel station pilot was traditionally a Kingmoor 0–6–0T.

The first change of note after Grouping was the arrival of the ex-Glasgow and South Western engines from Currock, closed in 1924. The event pleased neither of the erstwhile rivals, but the GSWR line rosters were duly assimilated into the Kingmoor workings. In 1925 twenty new Compound 4–4–0s

South end of Kingmoor, 11th February 1949.   *J. L. Stevenson*

arrived for the principal duties over both the northern routes and found some favour through a more economical coal consumption. By 1933 the 'top link' included two 'Royal Scot' 4–6–0s, Nos. 6155, *The Lancer* and 6156 *South Wales Borderer*; the complement of '4P' Compound 4–4–0s had risen to twenty-four but the CR continued to be well represented. The two 3-cylinder 4–6–0s were still resident, as LMS Nos. 14801 and 14802, with three '60' class and nine similar engines built in 1925/6, all mainly engaged on goods work. Ten McIntosh and Pickersgill 4–4–0s were employed on local and pilot work but possibly the most interesting occupants were the five CR '3F' 2–6–0s, Nos. 17800–17804, which were sent new to Kingmoor in 1912 and spent their lives there. Accompanying them were all but one of Drummond's '4F' locos for the GSWR, Nos. 17820–17829, dating from 1915. The classes were similar, being in effect little more than 0–6–0s with a pony truck and inside cylinders, 'primitive' moguls of doubtful advantage. Two GSWR 0–6–2Ts worked alongside the CR tanks and 'Jumbo' 0–6–0s on the local goods and shunting turns.

In 1936 Durranhill ex-Midland shed was closed and its allocation divided between Upperby and Kingmoor. This brought more '4F' 0–6–0s and Midland line workings with Leeds engines appearing for servicing. The Stanier era swept away the majority of the CR engines and by Nationalisation a wholly different situation existed. At the end of 1947 no CR passenger or goods tender engines remained at all, with the exception of a solitary Pickersgill 0–6–0, No. 17653, clinging on throughout the 'fifties. Three LMS '2P' and six '4P' 4–4–0s were still there with sixteen '4F' 0–6–0s, more than thirty Horwich moguls, nearly fifty class '5' 4–6–0s and sixteen 'Jubilees', Nos. 5564 *New South Wales*, 5577 *Bengal*, 5579 *Punjab*, 5580 *Burma*, 5581 *Bihar and Orissa*, 5582 *Central Provinces*, 5713

Renown, 5714 *Revenge*, 5715 *Invincible*, 5716 *Swiftsure*, 5727 *Inflexible*, 5728 *Defiance*, 5729 *Furious*, 5730 *Ocean*, 5731 *Perseverance* and 5732 *Sanspareil*. Fourteen ex-CR 0–6–0Ts nevertheless remained on the Kingmoor complement (total 147) and the last surviving ex-GSWR engine, 0–6–2T No. 16905, did not succumb until April 1948. Five diesel electric shunters, which first arrived in 1942, Nos. 7111, 7112, 7113, 7114 and 7115, were at work in the neighbouring yards. Two WD 2–10–0s. Nos. 73798 and 73799 were working from Kingmoor at this time but the depot, along with much of Scotland, was largely denied the new '8F' 2–8–0s. By July 1946 up to a dozen were present but by 1950 only five remained, Nos. 48321, 48464, 48472, 48536 and 48612, along with further WD locos, 2–10–0s Nos. 90751, 90763, 90767, 90769, 90773 and 90774, and 2–8–0s Nos. 90464 and 90505. Due to its strategic position, the period of BR steam operation at Kingmoor was more than usually interesting. From 1952, half of the 'Clan' Pacifics were at the shed and in May 1953 some of the CR 0–6–0Ts were displaced by Midland '3F' 0–6–0s, Nos. 43241, 43301, 43351, 43622, 43636, and 43678 for yard shunting and transfer trips; the six surviving CR tanks, Nos. 56235, 56322, 56333, 56340, 56373 and 56374, were not withdrawn until October/November 1959.

Kingmoor became increasingly a haven of steam power, redundancy elsewhere bringing an influx of types previously little in evidence. In the early 'sixties the shed was host to several 'Princess' and 'Duchess' Pacifics prior to withdrawal in 1962–1964, and at the other end of the scale three ex-Midland 0–6–0Ts were available for shed and station pilot duties at various times during 1963/64 – Nos. 47211, 47230 and 47236. The 'Crab' 2–6–0s and 0–6–0s gradually disappeared and by the mid-sixties a number of the surviving rebuilt 'Patriot', 'Royal Scot', and

The shed from the Etterby Road bridge. Kingmoor was outside the city, it still is, and lay amidst open ground. There was a 'barracks' for staff dating from the 1890s and a 'Kingmoor Terrace' yards from the shed, thoughtfully erected by the Caledonian close to an open brick field.

H. C. Casserley

Kingmoor was, in effect, as far as the Caledonian went; after that the flow of traffic depended upon shunting, transfers, signal hold-ups and further shunting before the whole lot could be got away south. In this respect Carlisle was an impediment to traffic, whatever its attraction and allure as a great railway centre. Carlisle, with its years of Joint Committees, agreements, counts, adjudications, arbitrations, cussedness and frustration, proved a dead weight of demarcation, vested interest, and sheer physical barriers such that freight train working could never be properly reformed, more or less until it was too late. Practice doggedly followed pre-Group habit — thus the old GSWR shed could be closed and absorbed by Kingmoor, for its workings led north. The LMS could not close Durran Hill ex-Midland shed until the 1930s and even then had to re-open it. Upperby only expired at the end of steam and that had been thoroughly rebuilt by BR.

Photomatic

Kingmoor came to represent, through chance, the 'standard' ideals of the early 1950s, a few large classes bolstered by increasing numbers of BR engines. This is in part illusory, for at Kingmoor and other places the proper 'mix' only began to be achieved on an ebb tide of withdrawal and loss but the picture is still there, how the engine stock would look in the mid-1970s 'when the numbers of steam engines might probably be expected to decline significantly'. *R. J. Essery*

Perhaps the oddest sensation to be felt at a busy engine shed was the alarmingly abrupt transition from deafening clamour to relative silence. The long walk down the side of the building was sealed off from the noise and smoke, the only sound the reassuring crunch of cinders underfoot. *R. J. Essery*

Quiescent mood at Kingmoor. *R. J. Essery*

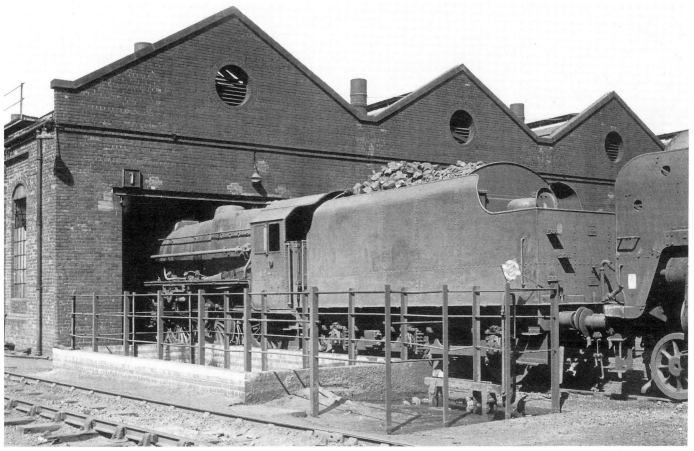

Any movement across the ends of a place like Kingmoor was difficult and could be hazardous; one quickly learned to think in linear fashion. This was an enormous disadvantage of straight sheds; despite painstaking attention to 'Not to be Moved' boards and an obsessive interest in tightly screwed down handbrakes, anyone twisting his way across inside motion was never entirely free of the worm of worry. It was always possible that engines could be thrust along by the merest jolt, a nagging sense of vulnerability made monstrous by night. *R. J. Essery*

Above: The Kingmoor 'No. 1' type coaler clanked and crashed its way to the end, a typical 'landmark' site visible from the Etterby Road and beyond in almost any conditions.
J. F. Henderson

Right: The coaling plant on 11th March 1967. Despite prodigious, painful effort involved in their manufacture and erection, the great concrete coalers, once the engines they served had gone, were outstandingly useless. Shed buildings might possibly find a further purpose but the coalers, despite their bunker-like construction and the fact that their specific design included the more or less continuous processing of hundreds of tons of coal, were deemed an insurance risk, liable to collapse if a trespassing child bounced its ball on the side. Retention would have involved a certain 'maintenance watch' and it could not really be otherwise, but it was an irony to observe the almost obsessive extirpation of the plants across Britain. They frequently baffled the demolition experts (BR, knowingly, sub-contracted the work) and most districts had incidents reported in their local papers, of the extremes of effort required to reduce these towering blockhouses. The British demolition trade cut its teeth on coalers put up on the LMS and LNER, preparing it ideally for the removal of further vast swathes of British industry.

J. F. Henderson

Kingmoor on 29th April 1967.

D. F. Tee

Kingmoor was of particular interest in the last years for the numbers of engines which found their way there as other duties fell to dieselisation; thus LMS Pacifics had a spell at Kingmoor in the 1960s. The allocation prior to this had been notable for its great emphasis on 'Crabs', the Class 5 and 'Jubilees' and 'Clans' which were more or less equivalent. 8F 2—8—0s only latterly became available in any numbers; they were everywhere south of Carlisle, some coalfield sheds eventually using them to the exclusion of all else. They were never put to extensive use in Scotland, where the Class 5 4—6—0 was used in many roles that in England would be customarily handed over to an '8F'. There is no real conclusion possible from this; there was no shortage of coal trains in Scotland after all. Kingmoor had eight by 1953 which was probably quite a high figure for a 'Scottish' shed. It may be that with so many long and steep gradients (across the whole of the LMS in Scotland) loads had to be limited in the *downhill* direction and therefore 4—6—0s or 'Crabs' could deal satisfactorily with these *uphill* as well as being more versatile for any other duties, such as Gleneagles-Crieff.   *R. J. Essery*

Steam locomotive repairs for well over a century took place often, at best, in half light, though raised rails, illuminated pits and fluorescent lighting could have been provided with the greatest facility, from the 1940s and even the 1930s. It was partly because the sheds had always 'got by' and almost thrived in adversity — at Kingmoor new crank pins were fitted simply by jacking, off a convenient part of the shed wall.   *R. J. Essery*

'Jubilee' 4–6–0s could be found at the shed. The depot was to be the last refuge also for the 'Britannia' 4–6–2s, no less than 48 of the 55 built finishing their careers at Kingmoor between 1965 and 1967. The shed in its last years dealt almost exclusively with freight. ('9F' 2–10–0s were much in evidence toward the end) but as late as 1965 the allocation was still well over 100 engines, the majority the redoubtable class '5s'.

With steam rapidly running down and Upperby closing in December 1966, King-

moor was to become the last steam shed in the border city. It had been coded 12A in 1935, the obvious choice to head the Carlisle District, but in the early years, as far as 'organisation' affected the LMS sheds, it had remained firmly 'Scottish'. The 1935 rearrangement placed it in the English Western Division, a move dictated by an obscure legal requirement. For the same reason the divisional boundary was set at the border, at Gretna Junction. The outstations at Kirtlebridge and Brayton had long dis-

appeared by the next code change; King-moor passed to the Scottish Region in 1949 as 68A, reverting to 12A from February 1958 and remaining thus until closure. Steam working on the Scottish Region ceased in May 1967 (though in January no less than 89 steam locomotives were observed at the shed) and a new diesel depot was coming increasingly into use. Kingmoor finally closed on 1st January 1968 and the site subsequently entirely cleared.

Though it must needs have been repaired and renewed over the years, the 70 ft Caledonian turntable of 1903 apparently sufficed for LMS and BR requirements. There were no problems of space at Kingmoor and the 'table was well sited for the 1930s mechanised servicing procedures.

J. F. Henderson

0—4—4T No. 15103 at Loch Tay on 28th July 1931. There was no run-round loop at Killin (village) and to reposition the engine at the outgoing head of the train the empty carriages would be propelled up the gradient to the Dochart bridge, uncoupled and held by the guard's brake until the train engine was inside the goods yard at Killin. The brakes were then released and the train descended by gravity to beyond Killin station where the engine coupled up to the train. It was ideal in the days of the Westinghouse brake but latterly such stock became scarce and handbrakes were used. The engine could run round at Loch Tay in conventional fashion though this service ended on 9th September 1939.   *H. C. Casserley*

LOCH TAY/KILLIN

The Killin Railway opened from a remote exchange platform at Killin Junction on the Callander and Oban line, through to the north shore of Loch Tay in 1886. A timber-built shed was erected from the first at the very extremity of the branch, by Loch Tay station, remaining in use even after closure to passengers of the section from Killin onwards to the Loch shore. The service connected with steamers on the Loch and in any case ran in summer only. It was abandoned on the outbreak of war.

The shed, provided with a water column but next to nothing in the way of coal supplies, housed the branch engine, an 0—4—4T over very many years outstationed from Stirling. Before this the line had enjoyed the distinction of two specially built engines, 0—4—2Ts Nos. 1262 and 1263 of 1885. Increasingly inadequate, after about five years they had been replaced by the inevitable 0—4—4Ts. The 'Killin Tanks' (the 0—4—0ST design with a pair of trailing wheels) were afterwards employed on sundry shunting tasks; 1262 never received its LMS number, 15000, but 1263, as 15001, eventually found itself at Inverness, working the Harbour and Canal Basin.

The Drummond ('IP') tanks were afterwards on the branch; Nos. 1229 and 1175 were in use on alternate-weeks in 1915, whilst in 1916 the changeover from Stirling shed was being effected fortnightly. No. 1229 (LMS No. 15105) was known to be still at work in June 1925 and No. 15103 (formerly 1177) was there in the summer of 1931. A pair of the tanks had formed the complement in 1921, around which time (when No. 1179

was withdrawn) McIntosh 0—4—4Ts began to appear: '2P' engines, like 15222, were in use over many years – as 55222 it was still at work in May 1856. No. 55145 'of 63B' was reported 'the regular engine' in 1950 and occasionally in latter years an 0—6—0 would turn up, No. 57246 of a time.

The CR tanks remained until the 1960s and from 1962 BR standard 2-6-4Ts were

provided. The big tanks entirely dwarfed the tiny shed, in its turn obscured by undergrowth and overhanging boughs. 80092, ill at ease in its rural surroundings, could be found there, for example, in 1964, and 80028 was employed in June 1965. Loch Tay was a last steam outpost on the Oban line, the bigger engines possible only through a relaying with heavier rails carried out at a late

The shed at Loch Tay on 10th October 1934; the line, effectively, terminated inside the engine shed.   *W. A. Camwell*

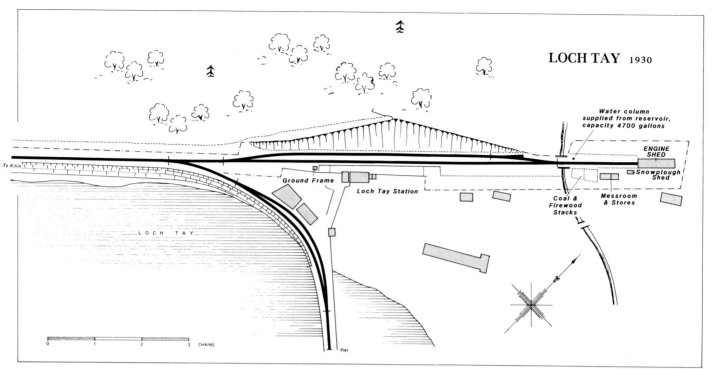

No. 15103 on 28th July 1931. The pier lay close by, known originally as Loch Tay (Killin Pier); when passengers were taken on it only one coach was used, the engine setting it back and running round on what was possibly the shortest rounding loop in the country. Water came from a tank set in the hillside above and also served houses nearby.

H. C. Casserley

By 1956 many of the trees had been lost through a hydro-electric project close by and the charming setting destroyed; much of it grew back but the atmosphere was never recreated.   *J. L. Stevenson*

Stirling '2F' 0—6—0 No. 57339. Taking an engine down to the shed was akin to leading a horse or cow to a forgotten corner of a rather benignly neglected garden.   *W. A. Brown*

Coaling took place latterly from a wagon parked on the Loch Tay run-round loop. Prior to this the wagon had been parked outside the shed, ideally placed with respect to the water column (see page 93). The later arrangement presumably did not render it essential for the engine to be bunker first. *E. Wilmshurst*

date, eliminating the remaining flat-bottomed rail.

The little shed, hugging the wooded slopes above the Loch, was more or less destroyed in 1917, evidenced by the following minute: 'Killin Railway. Loch Tay engine shed burnt down on 24th October 1917. Should be rebuilt, current price £560, pre-war price £280 ... difference will be a special charge against the government, that is, the expenditure by the Co. will be £280. This sum, however, will stand to be reduced to £160, inasmuch as the old shed was insured for £120, which sum has been received from the insurers ...'. 'Get the work Done' was the instruction and the new shed, timber-built on a low brick wall, was duly re-erected. Its title, 'Killin' or 'Loch Tay' seems never to have been absolutely settled, though in truth its precise location was indeed by the shore of the Loch. 'Loch Tay', logically enough, has indeed been the more accepted label, though 'Killin (Loch Tay)' appears consistently in latter-day engine diagrams. The shed closed on 4th October 1965.

Right: 2–6–4Ts sent out in the last year or two waited out the time between trips at the shed in time-honoured fashion; much of the vegetation had grown back and the big tanks, standing apparently unattended amidst weeds and scrub gave every impression of having been abandoned some months before.

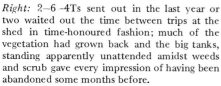

B. t'Till, *James Rose*

MOTHERWELL

Whatever architectural merit Motherwell possessed had long dimmed to disappearing point, in an unlovely environment of iron works, collieries and spoil heaps — waste 'bings'. It existed to serve the coalfield and the metal forges, most of the traffic centring on the giant Mossend yard to the north, on the far side of the Edinburgh-Glasgow line.
J. L. Stevenson

A uniquely ornate style was arrived at for the great shed at Motherwell, a lengthy through building in the centre of the iron-making and coal mining district, with land first purchased on 17th February 1858. The CR Board had found that the mineral traffic from the Lesmahagow coalfield was far exceeding expectations; the existing shed at Gartsherrie (Coatbridge) taxed, it would appear (along with South Side), by the extremes of light mileage required. The new shed, Motherwell, opened in March 1866 and by December 1870 (it was reported) no less than twenty locomotives were continually employed on the 'Lesmahagow line' – a further ten indeed 'could easily be put to use'. These engines would have been of the 0–4–2 mineral type, with passenger duties first worked by Motherwell in the mid-1880s. Amongst a mass of mineral work – from the Ross Yard to Glasgow, iron from the Motherwell area works, there was fruit (in season) from Lanark, Braidwood and Carluke as well as a substantial milk traffic, both from these areas and from around Auchenheath. Later, the shed may well have been extended: '30th November 1897: Proposed alterations to the south of the Engine Sheds and provision of new offices Bothy and Lamp Room, estimate £11,000. Approved.'

The Motherwell shed came to be something of a contrast to subsequent buildings of similar size, the sheds from the years of consolidation and wealth. Its appearance was firmly of an earlier age, wholly different from those buildings erected in the Caledonian's maturity. It recalled the first essays in its ornateness and later products appeared in comparison relatively plain, almost utilitarian, affairs.

The turntable lay, inconveniently, on a short spur at the southern end of the depot and was enlarged, continuing to occupy the same site, at intervals over the years. A 70 ft. 'table was approved on 10th January 1906 at a cost of £1,400, but by 1915 was (not for the first time) 'out of use due to coal sinkings.' The Caledonian was plagued by this problem in the Motherwell district and was constantly consulted by local pit owners, required by law to notify the railway when workings approached within 40 ft., the mineral rights usually having been purchased with the line. This was not the case with goods lines, but the biggest problem remained ancient shallow workings unrecorded and long-forgotten. There was fortunately a triangular complex of lines a short distance to the north, where the line from Motherwell passed under the CR Edinburgh–Glasgow route and engines could conveniently be turned here, especially as many of the workings centred on the nearby Mossend Sidings. The Motherwell turntable was later put into good order and was eventually fitted with vacuum tractor. This would have been provided by the LMS in the 1930s, though in the early years of that decade the 'table had suffered yet again from

subsidence. In 1912 McIntosh had written suggesting 'that the coaling bench now in use at Motherwell can only accommodate one locomotive and should be lengthened by 28 ft. so as to accommodate two.' This was approved at a cost of £170. The depot had two coal stages, one at each end, and it is not clear which one was involved, for they seemed more or less identical.

For years a substantial dormitory block was a feature at Motherwell, a singularly ill-sited haven wreathed in smoke and spoil heaps the only outlook. A 'horror,' its provision was determined on 25th March 1919: 'In connection with the recent introduction of the eight hour day ... great many additional men drafted into the Motherwell District. By reason of the present scarcity of houses it is impossible there for men to obtain lodgings. In consequence ... have suffered ... much inconvenience and discomfort. Propose a Dormitory for about 90 men, to provide lodging room in the vicinity of the Engine Shed at Motherwell ... The accommodation would be for the use of unmarried men only.' Costs were estimated at £9,500, with the proviso 'accommodation will be partly second hand purchased from the government in Gretna.' (This probably meant beds, etc.)

Various minor improvements had, in fact, been made around this period, following the Great War. In September 1918 electric lighting was approved, replacing gas at a cost of

£1,785; the pre-war price was estimated at £920, the difference to be made up as 'a special charge against the Government'. In February 1920 alterations to the smoke troughs costing £270 were authorised, 'to allow the modern type of Engines to be stabled'. The shed received some further attention in 1923, trivial in nature but of interest. In May £110 was approved for 'Renewal and modifications of floor in the oil store.' The whole building was to be replaced, substituted by 'the "Bowser" system of oil storage.' Later, in June, 'Motherwell Locomotive Dept. Football Club' asked for some form of accommodation (the oil store would no doubt have been considered too noxious even by the authorities) but their request was 'Declined, there being no hut available'. At the same meeting water supply was discussed, particularly with regard to Mossend Yard, the largest in Scotland.

The Motherwell allocation, approaching 100 in CR days (and considerably greater by 1947), overwhelmingly comprised 0–6–0s and tanks on goods/shunting work. The shed lay at the heart of a vast goods and mineral complex and was accordingly of great importance to the Caledonian's commercial well-being, concerning itself with freight almost to the exclusion of all else. A number of the CR 0–8–0s were employed there and six 0–8–0Ts, Nos. 492–497, were specially built at the turn of the century for heavy coal work over the (locally) steep grades. In the course of normal working all the engines would find themselves regularly at Mossend: 'June 12th 1923. Mossend Water Supply. Is insufficient, used by over 90 locos per day. Is pumped from the Clyde at Motherwell but owing to the larger 'draw-off' in that district not much reaches the tank at Mossend'. New 8 inch pipes were approved, costing £1,450 and laid to a plan dating from August 1921. The saving in 'engine time' was estimated at £2,000 *per annum*.

Life at Motherwell went on unrelieved in great part by any modern aids. The ancient wooden coal stages were ruinous by the 'sixties though the shed roof had new cladding applied at intervals. Motherwell was charged with the full range of repair work for its hard-pressed locos – the necessary machinery was available for lifting, tyre turning and axlebox boring and the usual 30-ton hoist was provided, in an undersized two road 'repair shop' at the north end of the shed. This was entirely inadequate for the allocation and large portions of the running shed were necessarily given over to repair work. The old sand kiln was removed from its central position within the shed and rebuilt in the north yard and a second 30-ton hoist was erected in the shed itself, on the easternmost road.

LMS influence at Motherwell, as at many of the Caledonian sheds, was not apparent for a considerable period and after ten years the new order was represented only by five '4F' 0–6–0s. At that time, October 1933, three 4–4–0s of the saturated Dunalastair classes, Nos. 14329, 14341 and 14360, remained for local work to Glasgow (along with the 0–4–4Ts) whilst fifty CR 0–6–0s were

Bings loomed everywhere at Motherwell, the whole area settling and shifting as waste from the ground piled ever higher round about. The shed was of an ancient lineage, built for its time on a grand scale and had seen a succession of iron and steel works grow up close by, only to fail and disappear. The Parkneuk Iron Works stood alongside the shed and close by that was the enormous Motherwell Iron and Steel Works. It had all gone by 1910, covered in spoil heaps and the engine shed carried on doggedly, increasingly hedged about with waste. *H. C. Casserley*

available for goods work. The big 0–8–0s had all gone by 1929 but three of the 0–8–0Ts, Nos. 16950, 16952 and 16955, were still present, the last surviving to 1939. Stanier class '5s' subsequently became familiar and during the 1940s a number of '8F' 2–8–0s were allocated, including, briefly in 1942, several of the WD examples with Westinghouse brakes. In 1947 seven were present. The '4Fs' were never established in any numbers and only two, both original Midland Railway examples, Nos. 3884 and 4011, remained at the end of that year. The former, as No. 43884, was the only representative in 1950 and was still at Motherwell (along with 43883) as late as 1961. In their latter days many of the Pickersgill 60 class 4–6–0s found their way to the shed and became a familiar sight working to Carlisle etc on freights. By 1945 eighteen of them were on the complement but were swept away in the post-war influx of class '5s,' WD 2–8–0s and 2–10–0s; all had gone by 1953. In the following year the allocation totalled 104, including five standard class '4MT' 2–6–0s and thirteen WD 2–10–0s. Despite the modern types, five Pickersgill 4–4–0s remained for local work; they were gradually withdrawn but No. 54465 survived into 1962, reduced to ballast jobs and one of the last active members of the class.

The following allocations illustrate the differences over many years of LMS operation. The increase reflects a recovery in traffic levels from a Depression low to the eve of a post-war boom:

31st October 1933:
CR 2P 4–4–0
14329, 14341, 14360.

LMS 4F 0–6–0
4110, 4112, 4113, 4114, 4147

CR 2F 0–6–0
17230, 17231, 17232, 17235, 17241, 17256, 17267, 17270, 17272, 17273, 17278, 17280, 17284, 17291, 17302, 17325, 17326, 17327, 17332, 17335, 17337, 17342, 17344, 17359, 17363, 17378, 17382, 17403, 17405, 17406, 17416, 17417, 17418, 17419, 17435, 17437, 17462

CR 3F 0–6–0
17572, 17575, 17581, 17582, 17584, 17588, 17593, 17606, 17634, 17636, 17653, 17674, 17688

CR 4F 0–8–0T
16950, 16952, 16955

CR 3F 0–6–0T
16241, 16245, 16258, 16264, 16265, 16266, 16267, 16268, 16269, 16270, 16275, 16276, 16277, 16278, 16281, 16285, 16334, 16338, 16340, 16356, 16357, 16358, 16376

CR 2P 0–4–4T
15128, 15133, 15134, 15144, 15145, 15187, 15191, 15211.
Total – 92

31st December 1947:
LMS 5 4–6–0
4791, 4792, 5007, 5008, 5012, 5016, 5018, 5120, 5121, 5453, 5461, 5462, 5483, 5488, 5496, 5497, 5498, 5499

LMS/CR 4P 4–6–0
14631, 14634, 14635, 14636, 14637, 14640, 14641, 14642, 14643, 14645, 14646, 14647, 14649, 14650, 14651, 14652, 14653, 14654.

CR 3P 4–4–0
14441, 14453, 14460, 14462, 14464, 14465, 14498, 14506.

LMS 8F 2–8–0
8156, 8183, 8184, 8185, 8186, 8187, 8188

LMS 4F 0–6–0
3884, 4011

CR 2F 0–6–0
17231, 17247, 17256, 17267, 17270, 17272, 17273, 17278, 17289, 17290, 17291, 17299,

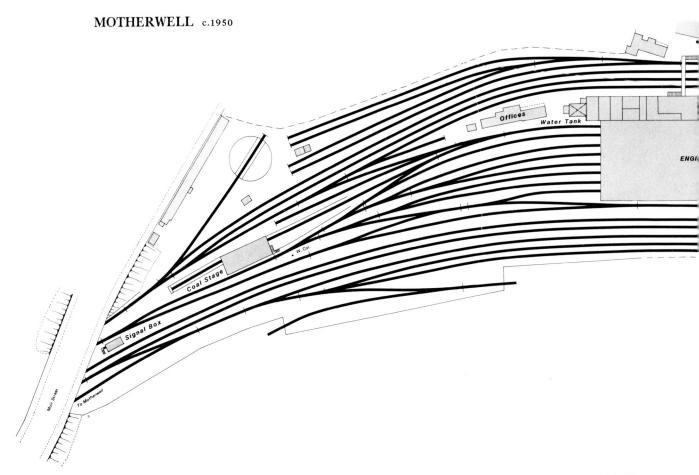

MOTHERWELL c.1950

The dismal south coal stage at Motherwell, on 28th August 1961.

K. Fairey

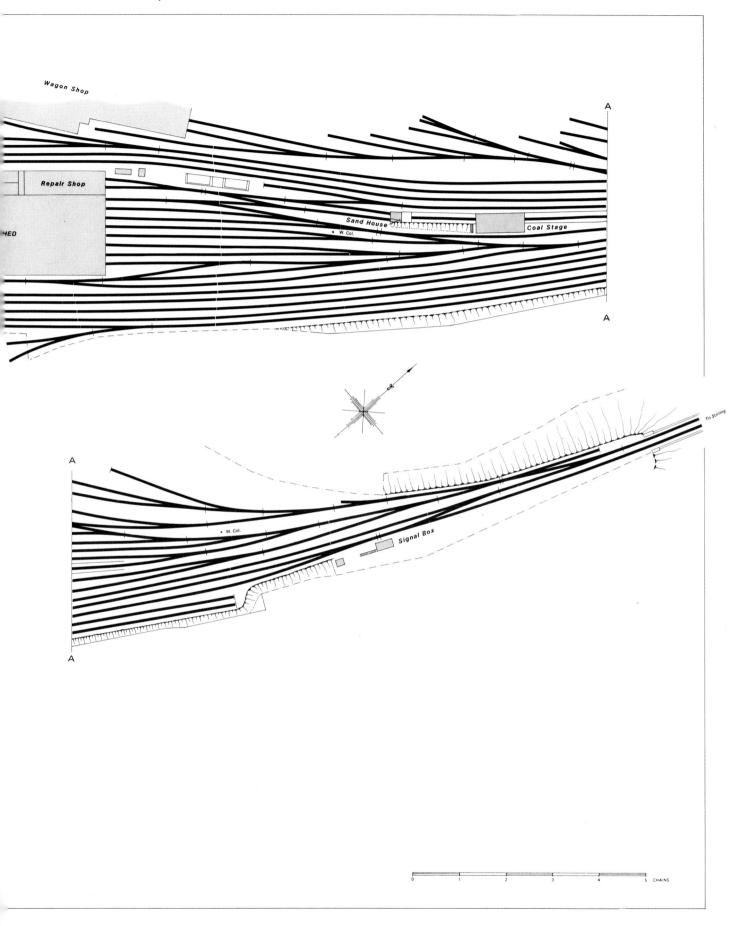

Wagon Shop

Repair Shop

HED

A

Sand House   Coal Stage

• W. Col.

A

A

• W. Col.

Signal Box

To Stirling

A

0   1   2   3   4   5 CHAINS

Very little was done at Motherwell to lighten the burden of shifting this awesome quantity of coal; the depot had over a hundred locomotives, on profitable coal working, as well as Glasgow passenger services, but the servicing arrangements remained more or less unaltered from Caledonian days. In this respect it was presumably simply a matter of chance. Depots could only be modernised at a certain rate and any not seen to by about 1959 had, essentially, to get on with it.

H. I. Cameron

17301, 17303, 17308, 17313, 17325, 17326,
17327, 17328, 17332, 17342, 17344, 17358,
17363, 17377, 17403, 17404, 17406, 17413,
17414, 17415, 17416, 17417, 17418, 17419,
17435, 17437, 17461, 17462

CR 3F 0–6–0
17588, 17593, 17595, 17599, 17606, 17638,
17666, 17668, 17681, 17582, 17584

LMS 3 2–6–2T
159, 200

CR 2F 0–6–0T
16155

CR 3F 0–6–0T
16241, 16245, 16247, 16258, 16264, 16265,
16268, 16269, 16270, 16271, 16276, 16277,
16281, 16285, 16334, 16335, 16337, 16338,
16345, 16356, 16357, 16358

CR 2P 0–4–4T
15134, 15138, 15188, 15191.

CR 0F 0–4–0ST
16028, 16029, 16031.
Total 136

350 h.p. diesel shunters (four of them) were at Motherwell by early 1956 and by the mid-sixties there were only twenty or so steam locomotives, BR standards and ex-LMS 4–6–0s, active at the depot. Despite this low number, Motherwell soldiered on with steam until its official extinction on the Scottish Region in May 1967. A 'concentration' depot, 28A since 1935, it had been placed under Polmadie and coded 66B in 1949. The building remained in use after the removal of steam, a signing-on point for crews and a stable for dwindling numbers of diesel locomotives. Part is now given over to wagon repairs but the locomotive repair shop has been refurbished and new pits provided on two of the yard roads.

Motherwell in June 1963. Engine sheds exert a fascination and an interest in inverse proportion to the aesthetic poverty of the immediate surroundings; the place was steeped in the ancient bond of coal, steel and the railway and it is no real surprise that a Motherwell driver should will his ashes scattered over the site, a request duly carried out by six fellow drivers (*Rail News* February 1986). *E. Wilmshurst*

Motherwell in September 1955 with 4–6–0 No. 45029. Into the 1950s the great part of the coal was still shifted by ex-Caledonian 0–6–0s.

Photomatic

The goods station spur left the main line some hundreds of yards before it ran into the quay and station, relatively secluded, nestling in the fork in a quiet location,
L & GRP, cty. David & Charles

OBAN

The shed at Oban opened with the line in 1880, a timber building tucked into the fork by the main line and the goods station spur. A wooden coaling canopy was at first provided on the west side of the yard, covering one of the shed roads and served by a separate siding off the turntable. The layout was revised in LMS days; a 'Stranraer' type coaler was installed on the turntable approach road and the former coaler and its siding abandoned and removed. A 60 ft. turntable was also substituted for the 50 ft. unit, an alteration associated with the new coaling arrangements.

Principal among the Oban complement over very many years was a stud of passenger engines, six or more 4–4–0s or 4–6–0s traditionally known as 'Oban bogies'; when the line had first opened throughout, however, the shed housed the specially-built 2–4–2Ts. They performed with a conspicuous lack of success, the main fault lying in the design of radial truck; these were not to Webb's patent or any other recognised design but had been put together by the manufacturers for export. 0–4–2s of the 1878/1881 series provided some kind of 'stop gap' until Brittain could have ten small 4–4–0s brought out by Dübs in 1882.

With the Oban & Callander turntables more suited to the 2–4–2Ts, the new 4–4–0

Building the shed at Oban in 1880.   *Scottish Records Office*

design of necessity suffered a certain shortening; four wheel tenders were perforce used and turntable diameter continued to dictate engine type until two new units, 50 ft. and 60 ft., were ordered from Cowans Sheldon in 1901, for Oban and Callander respectively. This enabled the '55' class 4–6–0s, Nos. 51–59 (LMS Nos. 14600–14608) to be put to use from 1902. 'Oban bogies' in their turn, they did not completely oust the 4–4–0s, four of which remained at Oban in 1914. Pickersgill new 'Oban bogies', Nos. 191–198 (LMS Nos. 14619–14626) appeared in December 1922 but performances were not encouraging

Clan Mackinnon in August 1937.   *W. A. Camwell Collection*

A siding led off alongside the gasworks, near to the junction of the goods spur and main line, which over the years seemed to prove useful for stored locomotives. On 12th June 1927 there was Caledonian 0–6–0 No. 200, No. 14601 and at least one other engine.   *H. C. Casserley*

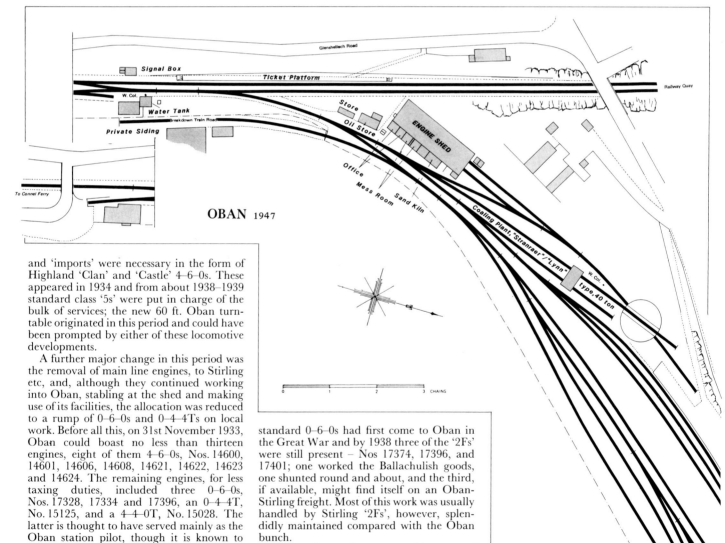

OBAN 1947

and 'imports' were necessary in the form of Highland 'Clan' and 'Castle' 4–6–0s. These appeared in 1934 and from about 1938–1939 standard class '5s' were put in charge of the bulk of services; the new 60 ft. Oban turntable originated in this period and could have been prompted by either of these locomotive developments.

A further major change in this period was the removal of main line engines, to Stirling etc, and, although they continued working into Oban, stabling at the shed and making use of its facilities, the allocation was reduced to a rump of 0–6–0s and 0–4–4Ts on local work. Before all this, on 31st November 1933, Oban could boast no less than thirteen engines, eight of them 4–6–0s, Nos. 14600, 14601, 14606, 14608, 14621, 14622, 14623 and 14624. The remaining engines, for less taxing duties, included three 0–6–0s, Nos. 17328, 17334 and 17396, an 0–4–4T, No. 15125, and a 4–4–0T, No. 15028. The latter is thought to have served mainly as the Oban station pilot, though it is known to have ventured at least to Connel Ferry – withdrawn in September 1936, it was replaced by No 15025, in turn withdrawn as the last of the class two years later. The

standard 0–6–0s had first come to Oban in the Great War and by 1938 three of the '2Fs' were still present – Nos 17374, 17396, and 17401; one worked the Ballachulish goods, one shunted round and about, and the third, if available, might find itself on an Oban-Stirling freight. Most of this work was usually handled by Stirling '2Fs', however, splendidly maintained compared with the Oban bunch.

Five engines only were working out of Oban at the end of 1947: 0–6–0s Nos. 17396 and 17411 and 0–4–4Ts Nos 15187, 15215 and 15263. The shed became a redoubt for these once ubiquitous CR tanks, withdrawn engines replaced by others until July 1962 when the last residents, Nos. 55204, 55217 (withdrawn immediately) and 55260 were 'removed to Perth'.

The long expensive haul of loco coal to Oban made the line eminently suitable for diesel working and the shed closed, accordingly early, in 1962. Despite this, it had not escaped a complex series of code changes – in 1935 it was listed 29E under Perth but the 1940 rearrangements left it 31C under St. Rollox. Under BR Oban was at first 63E, again in the Perth district, recoded 63D from April 1955 and 63C from November 1959.

Diesels were well established by early 1962 and by the summer only two steam engines remained in use, related '2MT' moguls Nos. 46460 and 78052. No. 46468 was at work as late as May but seems to have been employed on little more than pilot and shunting work. In that summer Stanier class '5' 4–6–0s still turned up on passenger workings due to a shortage of diesel power but steam seems finally to have been extinguished by the autumn. By early 1963 both shed roads had been lifted, though the turntable and coaler remained 'serviceable'. Fuel tank wagons were stabled on the old coal wagon road.

Much of the steam work at Oban had gone by the early part of 1961. Nos. 55226, 55195, 55230 and 55238 were all out of use on 13th May, with 55124 (left) in steam.   *M. Mensing*

No. 55263, off the 6.57 a.m. ex-Ballachulish, in 1961. Removal of 'Oban Bogies' to Stirling left the shed with a complement of tanks and one or two 0–6–0s for local work though the main line engines, of course, continued to make use of the depot.   *M. Mensing*

BIRD'S EYE VIEW OF PERTH FROM ABOVE THE EDINBURGH ROAD.

5109.

Self-explanatory postcard of a time when Scotland was as remote and inaccessible to most people as Africa.

PERTH

Perth was secured as a Caledonian stronghold at an early date, though the North British were suffered a discreet presence. The Dundee Perth and Aberdeen Junction Railway had arrived on the far bank of the Tay, outside the city in 1847 (the Edinburgh Perth and Dundee, destined to become part of the North British, appeared in the following year), erecting a station at Princes Street in 1849. The Scottish Midland Junction had come in 1848, together with the Scottish Central, the latter soon to establish a dominance in the city.

Within this short period all the companies provided themselves with locomotive accommodation of a more or less substantial nature. The Edinburgh Perth and Dundee occupied a modest two-road establishment by St. Leonard's Bridge, south of the main station, whilst the 'Dundee and Perth' satisfied itself with similarly modest but eccentrically arranged premises near to their Princes Street station. The building stood immediately to the west of Princes Street, separated from the station and its platform by a bridge over the street itself. This extraordinary brick building covered three running tracks as well as three stabling roads. Pillars separated the two sections, the 'shed' proper reached either by a 34 ft. turntable at the western end or a pair of small 'tables in the building itself. The Scottish Central took charge of this company in 1862, opening a proper connection (there was one of sorts already, used for post vans and excursions) and creating the Dundee platforms at Perth. These first opened in April of 1863 with the 'Dundee and Perth' shed demolished not long thereafter.

The Scottish Midland Junction, more familiar as the Scottish North Eastern Railway, established their locomotive premises near to the station by the Glasgow Road Bridge. Here at the north end of Perth station was an end-on junction made with the Scottish Central, the Midland Junction serving as link between the latter and the Aberdeen Railway. The amalgamation of the two, the Midland Junction and the Aberdeen, in 1856 brought about the Scottish North Eastern, which in turn came into the Caledonian fold in 1866. Engines would then (presumably) have moved to the larger Central shed. It is not clear whether this was accomplished immediately but, in the event it was not long before the building had been sold to the Highland Railway.

The Scottish Central was a major component of the Caledonian, pre-eminent in the city and responsible for a major shed and works to the south, where the main line passed under the Edinburgh Road. The site developed rapidly, the works by the 1850s equipped with turntables, traversers and all the heavy equipment required for a full range of repairs; the shed for the period, was also on a generous scale. It lay on the far side of the Edinburgh road, on the west side of the line, a site perpetuated by the LMS and BR which saw well over a hundred years of unin-

Unlike England, in Scotland many of the great cities fell to one railway company over that of its rival, an outcome of the country's different circumstances of landscape, politics and economics. In Manchester, Liverpool or Leeds and many other centres, the diversity of companies vying for the traffic could be confusing, but in Scotland the dominance of one over the other, if far from absolute, was a striking thing. At Perth, elements of the Highlands mingled uneasily with 'the south' and, though the Highland Railway were suffered a presence for work to the dimly perceived far north, the North British crept into the city almost invisibly. Perth became firmly a Caledonian province, the last before the debated land before Aberdeen; the shed was put up by the Scottish Central Railway in the 1850s, of a size remarkable for the period. Early buildings such as Perth provided a constructional model for the majority of engine sheds in Scotland, of whatever company; lofty, yet massively built, many endured far beyond any English contemporaries.

J. F. McEwan

terrupted use. The company had at first made do with a small wooden shed, inadequate from the start, as early as May 1850. Harrison, the plant superintendent, was arguing that ... 'the Perth Engine Sheds ... should be of brick in lieu of timber one erected for the opening of the line ... timber ... too inflammable'. A new shed would, he averred, allow 'outside hands' to work under cover, for the old building could serve as part of the carriage and wagon workshops – 'Much time is lost when the weather is poor'.

The unfortunate Harrison (he left in 1853, replaced by Alexander Allan from Crewe) does not seem to have got very far for in 1851 he is found asking the Caledonian to undertake repairs to SCR engines ' ... for there is no accommodation to accomplish this work'. The Caledonian refused, having problems of its own, and in August 1854 tenders were finally put out for 'stone or brick' engine sheds at Perth – two weeks later, however, the tenders are referred to as 'Engine Shop'. Allan had, by about 1853, seen to the establishment of the works, on the east side of the line north of the Edinburgh Road Bridge and had indeed taken up residence nearby, at Bellevue House. Purchased in 1852, to 'be adjacent to the proposed works', it became the traditional residence of the Perth Locomotive Foreman. The tenders of 1854 almost certainly refer to the new engine shed, on or close to the original timber building – on a scale without rival in the city, it was built at first with seven roads and was initially single-ended, entry being from the north. Stone-built and quite definitely in use before the close of the 1850s, it was accordingly long possessed of an ancient, rambling look. Of generous proportions, it was much

expanded and improved in the remaining part of the nineteenth century, the building, some 200 ft. in length and about 140 ft. wide, being largely converted into a through shed. The site was simultaneously greatly expanded with the addition of a lengthy, curving coal ramp, with shelter, on the west side. The old 45 ft. turntable had been 'removed to Montrose' in November 1885 and a 50 ft. example put in, repositioned close to its later LMS site. By 1915 it had been enlarged again, to 70 ft.

Drummond ended Perth works' role as a heavy repair centre, restricting it, after anxious discussions between directors and townsfolk, to running repairs beyond the capabilities of the shed but not really warranting a trip to St. Rollox. Political considerations within the company also dictated certain restrictions on coach and wagon work but Perth was allowed to continue boiler repairs, to circumscribed limits. The value of machinery at Perth shops in 1917 still exceeded by many times that in use at the shed. Further restrictions came with LMS rule, however, and by the summer of 1929 all locomotive work had disappeared, leaving a residue of stock repairs – 'Perth. This shop, which has been re-organised since the locomotive work was removed from the old buildings, deals, and will continue to deal, with the wagon repairs in an area extending to Aberdeen, Dundee, etc.' Orders for the 'loco Department Perth', 'to be closed and work transferred to St. Rollox' had first appeared in October 1926, 'alterations to commence in the new year'.

Affairs at Perth pursued a faltering course through early LMS days, the CR & Highland sheds operating in unsatisfactory fashion as Perth 'South' and 'North' respectively. Neither was fit to take the entire locomotive fleet for the city, with the primitive ex-Caledonian facilities matched at the old Highland shed. 'Perth' was thus destined for inclusion in the LMS Modernisations of the 1930s, the scope of the particular scheme conveniently widened to include a new, much larger shed building. Adequate running repair facilities, for the complements of both the Perth sheds, could be provided – the Caledonian site possessed an abundance of room and the 'North' shed could be quietly dispensed with. New turntable, coaling plant, etc. were included in the project, one of the most extensive carried out under the scheme of reform in the motive power department. The new shed, in brick, steel and corrugated sheeting – a corporate product by now familiar the length of the country – opened 'on 14th May 1938'. It had been built to the rear of the old shed, effectively a single-ended building though some roads did extend through as sidings for 'stopped' engines, awaiting parts, or whatever. As it neared completion, what remained of the old shed was removed – making way for the great 'No. 1' coaling tower and new 70 ft. articulated 'table (built by Cowans Sheldon and dating from 1936).

The area in which the depot lay had long come to be known as 'Friarton' and the name could be heard, locally at least, in reference to the shed itself. The opening date of 14th May 1938 is a more or less 'official' one, passed down over the years; it probably refers to the point at which the transfer of locomotives (and/or men) from the old Highland

shed was complete. In July 1937 the new building was to all appearances complete, 'full of engines', with everything working – the 'North', ex-HR, shed was also still 'very much in business'. It has been suggested (and it is indeed likely enough) that staffing negotiations might well have delayed the changeover.

Perth was a depot of advanced design, well equipped for over a hundred locomotives; a modern LMS development, Caledonian features were nevertheless perpetuated – two-

road repair works to one side, separated from the 'running shed' by the various shops and stores, joiners, machinists, exactly as at Kingmoor and Polmadie. This investment was of particular worth in view of Perth's strategic importance, astride the main line with workings to Aberdeen, Dundee, Glasgow, Edinburgh, Carlisle and Inverness. In CR days its importance was reflected in the allocation of the first superheated 4–4–0s, from 1910. The great part of express work at Perth was entrusted to 4–4–0s, supplemented only by

'Crab' moguls, 2905 and 2970 in July 1935.   *G. S. Lloyd*

0–6–0 at Perth. They had, of course, long been common at the shed but by 1947 numbers were drastically reduced. The Stanier 4–6–0s could handle any of the 3F duties whilst a number of Midland-derived 4F 0–6–0s were also made available for goods work.   *H. N. James*

The coaler at Perth, a giant 'No. 1' structure, served a large part of the engines operating in this area of Scotland; the shed had a number of outstations and workings from far afield were re-engined, or terminated, at Perth. The erection of the new shed came after the coaling plant and removal of the old building enabled the final disposition of lines along 'service-sequence' principles.

W. Potter

LMS Compound 4–4–0s, in the late 1920s. Nevertheless examples of Pickersgill 4–6–0s, built in 1917–21, had also appeared when new and the shed retained a wide variety of CR types well into the 1930s. The most interesting resident at that time perhaps was the celebrated single No 123, pottering about on locals as LMS No 14010. It was taken out of traffic in 1935 and its subsequent restoration (in 1957) for use on specials recalled the handsome Caledonian blue livery.

By the beginning of 1934 five Compound 4–4–0s ostensibly made up the Perth 'toplink' stud but no less than nineteen of the CR superheated engines powered the great bulk of passenger trains. It was a substantial number with some examples remaining until the early 1960s. Before the great influx of Stanier 4–6–0s the 'mixed traffic' engines comprised five LMS 'Crab' 2–6–0s, accompanied by five Pickersgill '60' class 4–6–0s, together with one of the first two Mc-Intosh 4–6–0s built in 1903, No 14750 seeing out its last days. There were also in 1934 four of the McIntosh 5′ 9″ 'Express goods' 4–6–0s of 1913, Nos. 17910, 17911, 17912 and 17913; they completed a varied assemblage, soon to be swamped by the all-embracing class '5s'.

Two of the old Lambie 4–4–0Ts finished their long careers, as at other locations, as station pilots. The complete allocation of January 1934 was as follows:

LMS 4P 4–4–0
921, 922, 923, 924, 939
LMS 'Crab' 2–6–0
13205, 13206, 13207, 13208, 13209

CR 1P 4–2–2
14010
CR 3P 4–4–0
14440, 14441, 14442, 14447, 14448, 14452, 14453, 14467, 14468, 14469, 14470, 14479, 14480, 14494, 14495, 14496, 14503, 14504, 14505
LMS/CR 4P 4–6–0
14638, 14646, 14647, 14648
CR 4P 4–6–0
14655, 14750
CR 1P 4–4–0T
15024, 15027
CR 2P 0–4–4T
15159, 15160, 15168,15208, 15209, 15216
CR 3F 0–6–0T
16328, 16331, 16348, 16352
CR 2F 0–6–0
17415, 17442, 17453, 17454, 17455, 17457
CR 3F 0–6–0
17562, 17577, 17598, 17599, 17602, 17604, 17605, 17616, 17631, 17658, 17663, 17675, 17676
CR 3F 4–6–0
17910, 17911, 17912, 17913

The Stanier era saw a rapid displacement of the compounds and CR engines from the most important passenger and freight work, with Perth coming to particular notice for the great numbers of class '5' 4–6–0s present. The large scale production of '8F' 2–8–0s in the 1940s saw seventeen of the class at Perth by 1945 but the class '5s' were found increasingly suited to almost any task on offer. The 2–8–0s subsequently went south to English depots and by 1947 the class '5' complement had risen to no less than sixty, an extraordinary total. One of the few Scottish sheds to maintain a stud of '4F' 0–6–0s, Perth retained several local duties, permanent way trains etc, into the 1960s. The complete allocation, on 31st December 1947 was:

4P 4–4–0
921, 922, 923, 924, 938, 939, 1099, 1125
4F 0–6–0
4193, 4196, 4251, 4258, 4314, 4322, 4328
Class 5 4–6–0
4768, 4769, 4770, 4796, 4797, 4885, 4924, 4925, 4958, 4959, 4960, 4961, 4972, 4973, 4974, 4975, 4976, 4977, 5010, 5011, 5036, 5085, 5086, 5087, 5125, 5161, 5162, 5163, 5164, 5165, 5166, 5167, 5170, 5171, 5172, 5173, 5174, 5175, 5213, 5357, 5365, 5366, 5389, 5452, 5456, 5457, 5458, 5459, 5460, 5463, 5464, 5465, 5466, 5467, 5469, 5470, 5472, 5473, 5474, 5475
CR 3P 4–4–0
14447, 14448, 14458, 14459, 14467, 14469, 14476, 14489, 14499, 14500, 14501, 14502, 14503
CR 2F 0–6–0
17397, 17449, 17473
CR 3F 0–6–0T
16246, 16290, 16328, 16331, 16347, 16352, 16353
CR 2P 0–4–4T
15144, 15171, 15175, 15176, 15208, 15209, 15213, 15216, 15218

The old Highland Railway shed had, of course, 'closed' in 1938 but it was subsequently put to further use as an engine store. No less than twenty were there in 1939 but by 1956 the building was largely derelict. Since then one half has been demolished, but the section nearest the running lines is once more in use, as a store. The old North British shed was also taken over following Nationalisation – engines came to the LMS depot in 1949, after the coaling bench was gutted by fire and soon the engines and men had been entirely absorbed. This building, too, is still in existence and in 1949 had brought two 'Shire' 4–4–0s to the LMS shed, Nos. 62714 *Perthshire* and 62725 *Invernesshire*. They were succeeded by two ex-NBR 'Glens', Nos. 62470 *Glen Roy* and 62484 *Glen Lyon*, a pair still at work in 1959. WD 2–8–0s and 'Jubilee' 4–6–0s were present at least as early as 1950, and as BR days wore on, various 2–6–4Ts and BR classes were put to use. The last '4P' 4–4–0s 'north of Glasgow' were at Perth in 1956, No. 40938 on Dundee locals and No. 40939 in store 'with a damaged buffer beam'. Both were withdrawn later in the year.

The Caledonian engines declined only slowly in these years, the 4–4–0s finding useful employment on all manner of passenger duties in the district. One was subshedded at Crieff and several more at Blair Atholl (ex-HR) for banking to Dalnaspidal and the local passenger service to Perth. Five were there in 1950, by 1954 partially displaced by a pair of 2–6–4Ts. Five of the 'bogies' nevertheless, survived into the sixties, Nos 54485, 54486, 54489, 54494 and 54500. Nos 54485 and 54486 were specially cleaned and attended to in May 1960, for filming purposes and together were rostered on the 6.47 a.m. to Inverness. They constituted a remarkable spectacle, a swan-song amongst the Highland grades, and afterwards continued on local passenger and pick-up work to Blair Atholl, along with No. 54489. All were out of use by the end of 1961. Diesels had replaced CR 0–4–4Ts on station pilot duties by this time but the class lingered on at Perth, principally used on the Aberfeldy branch. The line was dieselised in 1962, 0–4–4Ts in the last years having included Nos. 55173 and 55217.

BR class '5s', Nos. 73005–73009, came new to Perth in 1952, adding further variety to an already cosmopolitan place. Perth had long played host to a wealth of visiting engines, from as far afield as Crewe North and Aberdeen, and Pacifics 'Royal Scots' and (latterly) ex-LNER 'A2s' and 'A4s' were common sights. By 1965 the allocation had been reduced to only 29 engines, class '5s' except for four BR 2–6–4Ts. 29A since 1935, becoming 63A in the Scottish Region, Perth closed with the elimination of steam in Scotland, in May 1967, and was soon afterwards demolished.

The old shed remained in place as the new building was erected close by. At the last it was in poor shape, suffering some damage, it is thought, prior to demolition.   *W. A. Camwell Collection*

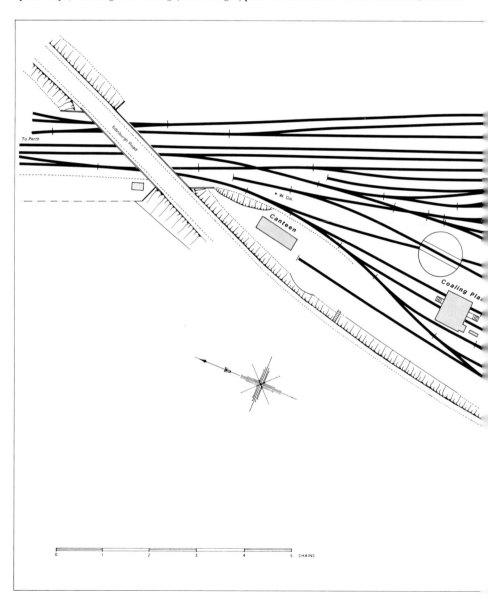

The renewed shed became once more principally a single-ended depot, the lines at 'the back' a convenient place for engines out of use. The LMS 4—4—0s had a long if undistinguished career at Perth and were never highly regarded. Two at least, 40921 (*left*) and 40939, were stored on 26th April 1952, the latter, as 939, having come new, ex-Derby, in November 1933 (*SLS Journal*, January 1933). *H. C. Casserley*

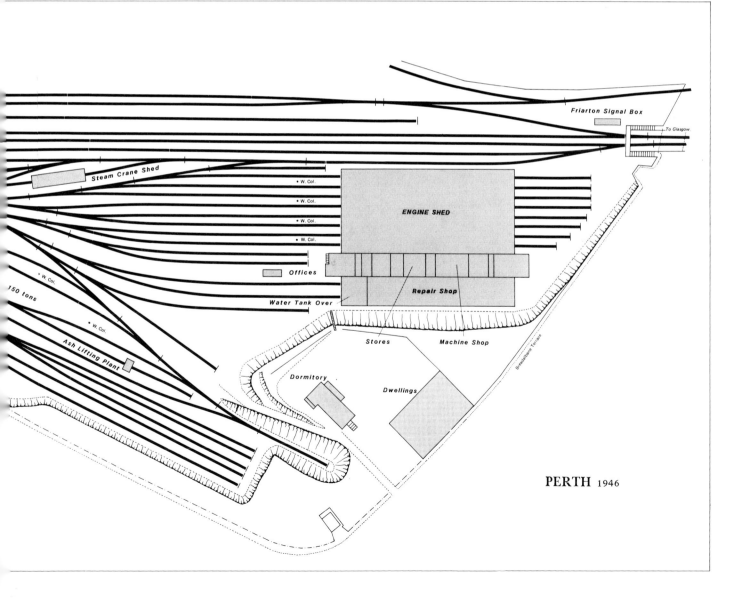

PERTH 1946

Perth on 5th July 1966. Steam numbers were in sharp decline by this time and the monstrous coaler was under-used. It had played an important role over the years and its existence had allowed a more efficient use of the LMS Pacifics, working through to Perth. The Western Division assumed responsibility for all the principal Scottish-English services, the engines working to Perth to attain greater daily mileages, 'instead of loitering around sheds awaiting the return trip south'. *K. Fairey*

At Perth elements contained within the LMS Running Department modernisation programme came together more effectively, possibly, than anywhere else on the railway. The depot had been completely renewed, re-equipped, and servicing had been mechanised and the locomotive complement updated with a concentration of modern effective types. Much has been made of the Class '5' fleet at Perth — it was indeed a strategic 'injection' which transformed work across the District, and beyond.   *G. B. McArthur*

No. 54482, along with other stored or irregularly employed locos, and the conveniently stowed snowplough.   *D. Banks*

The great shed 'at Rutherglen', opening around 1875, an enormous timber structure doomed to rapid decay and an early demise.

POLMADIE

The Polmadie shed was vast, and, despite its eccentric construction, in size it rivalled or overshadowed the largest depots of the English companies. It derived from a series of proposals, mostly thwarted by problems of land acquisition; that of 1870 would have placed the new shed at South Side and brought about an entirely different building, 'the same as at Motherwell'.

National Railway Museum

At least two engine sheds had been in use in the south part of Glasgow prior to the foundation of the great sheds at Polmadie. The first stood at South Side station and dates, it would appear, from opening in 1848. It was a small affair, capable of holding no more than four locomotives and equipped with a turntable of some 30 ft. diameter. Traffic was meagre; a few trains to Hamilton and a twice-daily connection to and from Motherwell for the English traffic, growing by about 1857 to warrant moving the shed. About that year a new building, in brick with three roads some 165 ft. in length, was put up amidst the brickfields of Govan. In the shadow of the giant 'Southern Necropolis', it continued to be described as 'South Side' in official records.

This part of 'Glasgow' was to undergo industrial change at its fiercest and the development destined to wholly transform the district was quickening apace even as the 1857 'South Side' shed received its finishing touches. Before the end of the 1860s the Board had agreed that a further move was desirable and on 24th June 1870 an approach was made to the owner of the desired site, William Dixon and Co, whose blast furnaces stood only yards from South Side station. It was not possible to agree terms but two years later the CR was compelled to approach Dixon once more. This time it was possible to come to an agreement, one of the conditions being that neither the iron company's level crossing over Polmadie Road nor its private line suffer any 'disturbance'. This line ran along the top of an old quarry, used by Dixon to dispose of unwanted furnace slag. With the iron company in agreement, the CR Board decided on 25th September 1873 to go ahead

with the scheme and seek tenders accordingly. Thus on 30th December a price of £12,750 was accepted for the new 'South Side' shed, 'at Rutherglen'. There follows a series of references to the new shed, with the description 'Polmadie' increasingly in evidence:

- 17th November 1874. Rutherglen and Carlisle Engine sheds to be insured.
- 1st December 1874. Hand fire pumps ordered for both sheds.
- 29th December 1874. New signalbox at Rutherglen shed to be known as Polmadie.
- 16th September 1875. Shed now definitely described as 'Polmadie' retained for all later minutes and reports.

From the references available, the shed might well have been in use by July 1875 and by September it figures greatly, implying that the building was largely complete. This new Polmadie depot was a cavernous building, fourteen running roads with two-road repair shop-timber construction on a startling scale.

Timber was unfortunately a material ill-suited to these cathedral proportions: the damp and fume had soon taken hold, the shifting movements growing more alarming with every winter gale. A 1920 proposal for rebuilding of the shed had been ordered 'held over' in the light of imminent developments, but the new project was finally got under way towards the end of 1923. The new brick shed was thus an LMS product, though built on wholly Caledonian principles; of particular note and recalling the ancient LNW–CR links, it incorporated a novel mechanical coaler, reminiscent of the innovatory plant at Crewe. The story is contained in the following notes:

Nov. 20 1923

Glasgow Polmadie Engine Sheds. Proposed Reconstruction

Reported that Polmadie Engine Shed which is very old and structurally done, requires to be reconstructed. Its capacity is measured by about 70 engines, but inasmuch as part of the shed is used for engine repair purposes, it really provides accommodation for only about 50 engines, whereas accommodation for double that number would not be too much. As well as the engine shed, there is also a wagon repair shop at Polmadie. The Deputy General Manager recommends that the engine shed should be entirely reconstructed to such extent as to accommodate about 70 engines, that the relative workshops etc, accommodation should be provided, and that mechanical coaling plant should be installed: and further recommends that substitute wagon repair shop accommodation should be provided at Motherwell, instead of Polmadie: as indicated on the plan, dated 3/10/23. The estimated cost of the work is about £112,240. A small area of land, shown edged purple on the plans, and extending in area to about 1780 sq. yards, is required in connection with the reconstruction of the engine shed. The land belongs to Messrs. William Dixon, Limited, who state that they do not see their way to part with it, as it is required in connection with their blast furnaces. Having regard to that, it has been arranged to make application for statutory powers to acquire the land in the Provisional Order about to be deposited by the company.

Get the work done.

Nov. 29th 1923

Glasgow: Reconstruction of Polmadie Engine Shed and Provision of Wagon Repair Shop. Motherwell

Submitted minute No. 574 of the Traffic and Works Committee of the Scottish Local Com-

'Royal Scots' at Polmadie, October 1927. The shed ran successive generations of engines engaged on the principal English workings. The early years of the LMS were not happy, with Compounds chronically underpowered for the West Coast trains on the Carlisle road, and double-heading with a variety of engines was resorted to. Things would have gone ill if the new 'Royal Scot' 4–6–0s had proved disappointing but, becoming available from the autumn of 1927, the new engines began to prove their worth.   *J. Scott*

6129 *Comet* in 1929.   *J. Hooper Collection*

mittee of the 20th instant recommending that owing to lack of sufficient accommodation the Polmadie Engine Shed, Glasgow, be reconstructed to accommodate 70 engines and that the relative workshop accommodation be provided, together with the installation of mechanical coaling plant; in addition it was proposed to provide wagon repair shop accommodation in place of the existing wagon repair shop at Polmadie, the total estimated cost of the work being £112,240. In connection with the reconstruction of the engine shed, it was necessary to purchase an area of land, about 1780 square yards, belonging to Messrs Wm Dixon, L^td, but as the firm required the land for their own purposes, arrangements had been made for statutory powers to be applied for, for the acquisition of the land. Approved and ordered, that the question of the construction of a wagon repair shop at Motherwell be referred to the Rolling Stock Committee and, subject to their approval, the expenditure be recommended to the general purposes committee.

March 27th 1924

William Dixon, Limited. Reconstruction of Polmadie Engine Shed, London Midland and Scottish Railway Provisional Order. Land (1890 square yards) at Polmadie.

Referring to Minute No. 574 of 20th November 1923, reported result of recent negotiations with Messrs. Moncrieff Warren Paterson and Company, Law Agents for Messrs. William Dixon, Limited, and submitted for instructions the terms proposed for settlement as undernoted, viz.,

(1) That the land to be acquired by the Company will be restricted to the area extending to 1890 square yards or thereby shown edged purple on the Engineer's plan, dated 11th January last;

(2) That the price of the foresaid area of land shall be 10/- per square yard is equal to £945;

(3) That the Company will not interfere with Messrs Dixon's level crossing at Polmadie Road and that they will alter and reinstate the railway sidings belonging to Messrs. Dixon as shown on the foresaid plan; and

(4) That Messrs. Dixon will withdraw their opposition to the Company's Provisional Order.

Approved.

Despite the Engineer's desire for increased accommodation, the covered area of the new shed was really little more than that of its timber predecessor. The shops, however, were extended, fitted with two 35-ton overhead cranes, and the adjacent stores/machine shops refurbished. The old arrangement of transverse rails, whereby wheels could be hauled across the front of the shops to the shed itself, was done away with. The new coaler replaced a ramp affair with shelter, and the turntable remained in place at the rear of the shed at the western corner, by the Polmadie Road entrance. Other alterations, water tanks, etc. dated from 1898: 'Engineers Department Western Division – Polmadie – Proposed two extra tanks 20,000 gallons each, cost £750 (1st March) ... proposed alteration of sidings to admit of more room being provided. £150 (4th October 1898)'. Again the command 'Get the Work Done'.

Considerable change was still in prospect at Polmadie, even after the full-scale renewal

Coaling at Polmadie had been from a simple ramp and shelter affair — 'a coaling station' — of limited capacity and awkwardly sited with respect to the engine yard. It divided around the coaler with the northern part especially remote from the turntable. It is not known if this effective division was intentional, reflecting maybe the separation of goods/passenger engines. The new mechanical coaling plant stood close to the site of the old stage and, whilst it effected an economy in staffing levels, it in turn was less than ideally sited for the working of the depot.

National Railway Museum

The Polmadie coaler in August 1936, with Wemyss Bay tank No. 15358. The yard remained awkwardly arranged and there might well have been problems involved in the taking of water. The Caledonian Working Timetable carries the instruction: 'WATERING OF ENGINES AT POLMADIE, ROSS JUNCT., MOTHERWELL, STRATHAVEN JUNCT. &C. No engine must leave Motherwell, Shieldmuir, Holytown Junction, Mossend, Ross Junction, nor Strathaven Junction without having a FULL supply of water in the Tender, except in cases when to go to the column or tank would cause more than ordinary delay to the traffic. It is most important that all Engines returning to Polmadie be fully supplied with water before leaving the following places:- Benhar, Ross Junction, Motherwell, Mossend, Shieldmuir, Holytown Junction, Barrhead, General Terminus, West Street, Bridgeton, and Baillieston, in order to save time in taking water at Polmadie and this must be strictly adhered to, except in cases when to do so would cause detention. Drivers of Goods and Mineral Trains to water at Omoa, instead of Holytown.'   *N. E. Preedy Collection*

6147 *Courier* in 1932. Stanier Pacifics subsequently formed the main express power but 'Royal Scots' remained on much of the most important passenger work. 'Jubilees' proved overloaded, within their steaming capabilities, for the long inclines between Rutherglen and Craigenhill, Carstairs and the Summit southbound, and Beattock and Carstairs to Craigenhill northbound. The class appeared to be consistently short of steam when working hard and were declared to suffer from too soft a blast.

G. Coltas

4—4—0 No. 14346 in 1932.

J. F. McEwan

Wemyss Bay tanks, 15358 and 15360. As Harvey relates, the work at Polmadie comprised passenger work out of Central, freight and local services. The latter came to be worked by an army of 2–6–4Ts, LMS engines complemented by the BR version. These big straight sheds demanded considerable skill on the part of the shed men, under the running foreman. As near as possible engines had to be in their order of 'going out', and late arrivals and any number of problems meant that some shunting and re-ordering of the lines of engines was usually necessary. It was easy to forget which roads at Polmadie had been foreshortened, bringing about the Polmadie condition, 'the wee bit squeeze up'. As with the 'tight crossing', this could involve unusual force, the expected buffer-locking escalating to the virtual demolition of one 2–6–4T bunker by the smokebox of its neighbour.   *Collection R. J. Essery*

'60' class 4–6–0 No. 14650. At one point in the yard incoming and outgoing movements converged and it was not unknown for minor collisions to occur. This was the phenomenon known as a 'tight crossing', often resulting in bent buffer beams and buckled steps. The foreman fitter would be called out to a 'tight crossing'; it was masterly understatement and he was appalled to find on one occasion two 2–6–4Ts on their sides.
A. G. Ellis

The new shed was put up in an area already marred by some of the crudest early industries; there was an iron works nearby and the land about was soon pockmarked with open, gasping clay pits, brick works, more iron works, saw mills and collieries. Great sidings grew up – the 'Polmadie Mineral Depot' and vast chemical works belched forth into a cauldron of fire and smoke. Railwaymen, as industrial workers everywhere, lived locally in an area now regarded as little short of malodorous. The Gorbals, still a byword for what is seen as urban awfulness (now sanitized as 'deprivation'), was close by Polmadie shed.

National Railway Museum

of the early 'twenties; The depot retained in many respects a primitive layout which demanded reform in accordance with LMS 'service-sequence' notions. The detailed and expensive re-equipment necessary for the depot's modernisation did not take place until the 1940s, finally precipitated by wartime traffic pressures, though the turntable had been enlarged as early as 1934. A Cowans Sheldon 70 ft. unit had been received in that year, with some additional detail recorded on 16th October:

> 'Mechanical and Electrical Engineering Committee. (Scotland) Replacement of engine turntable, and sand drying kiln at Polmadie. Estimate £3692 of 12th December 1933, now increased to £3926, viz:
> 1. Additional Gearing for Turntable £100
>   ...
> 2. Additional "Kelbus" drier   ...   £116
> 3. Altered electric light poles   ...   £18
>   ——
>   £234

This 'table occupied the same site as the old Caledonian 51 ft. unit, an apparently inconvenient location chosen deliberately nonetheless, to allow engines from the Shawfield Yards to turn and take water and be briskly away without encroaching on the shed lines. The new servicing arrangements, however, demanded a different site, closer to the coaling and ash disposal equipment and

The turntable by Polmadie Road was increased in size from 51 ft to 70 ft about 1934. Turning arrangements at Polmadie had always been out of the ordinary; the 'table was placed for the convenience of engines off the interminable trains in the 'mineral depot' yards rather than strictly for the working of the depot. Engines which had come down to the Shawfield yards were able to slip in, turn, and be away without cluttering the shed roads. Furthermore, since at least 1906 it had been the practice to turn larger 4—6—0s on the Bridge Street-Shields Road-Gushetfaulds triangle, with smaller engines using the Rutherglen station triangle or putting in a trip on the Cathcart circle. All this was regular everyday practice enshrined in the working procedures, and an explanation for the late survival of the 51 ft turntable. The new 70 ft unit went in at the same site. traditional practice being largely maintained but, with an increased flexibility, larger engines, did not *have* to resort to the triangles.   *W. Potter and R. J. Essery Collection*

accordingly a second Cowans Sheldon 70 ft. 'table appeared in the mid-1940s. The exact date is confused somewhat, the whole exercise delayed by the wartime steel shortage; it was rationed at 1939 levels and supplied subject to strict priorities – railways came seventh or eighth in the 'pecking order' and firms like Cowans Sheldon had necessarily to obtain it wherever and whenever they could.

The modernisation of such a major depot, carried out late and incorporating the latest thinking, was the subject of a detailed professional discourse and appraisal. Mr. R. F. Harvey, Vice-President of the Institution of Locomotive Engineers and Chief Officer (Motive Power) on the Railway Executive, delivered a paper in February 1951 outlining the work, and doubtless Polmadie proved a considerable influence on subsequent BR practice. The developments were first published in 1948, with a detailed description in the *Railway Gazette*:

Polmadie Motive Power Depot, Scottish Region

Recent introduction of new coaling and ash-handling plant

The recent modernisation of the Motive Power Depot at Polmadie, in the southern outskirts of Glasgow, brings it into the first rank of up-to-date depots on British Railways. Among the notable features of the equipment are the coaling plant and the ash-handling plant. The latter is the only one of its type in the country, if not in Europe.

The locomotive coaling plant is of the container hoist type of 400 tons capacity, it has three bunkers, one holding 100 tons of Grade I coal, suitable for express passenger train working, another of 100 tons capacity for Grade II coal, suitable for local passenger and fast freight trains, and one holding 200 tons of Grade III coal for shunting and trip engines. The main structure and bunkers are of reinforced concrete, and the bunkers are lined inside with steel plating, to resist breakage and abrasion by the coal. The steel lining enables the coal to flow freely from the bunkers.

The coal wagons are placed in position by a locomotive, and three electric capstans are installed for feeding the wagons to and from the coaling plant. Mineral wagons of all types from 8 to 20 tons capacity can be handled by the plant. In dry weather, the coal is sprayed with water before it is tipped.

Coaling Plant

When a wagon has been placed centrally on the tippler table, the first movement cants its side into contact with a long retaining beam on the tippler, and the friction against the beam prevents the wagon moving out of position. As the wagon and table are revolved in a side tipping direction, a loaded sustaining beam comes into contact with the top of the wagon, and remains in position until the side of the wagon is at an angle of from 45 to 50 deg. The coal from the wagon is tipped into a steel container alongside, and the empty wagon is returned to ground level. The next full wagon is brought forward by electric capstan, and pushes the empty wagon clear.

The container has a capacity of 22 tons, so that the contents of two small wagons, or one large wagon, can be dealt with before hoisting. The coaling plant is operated from a main control cabin adjacent to the tippler, and it is possible for the operator to select which bunker shall receive the coal from the loaded container. This choice is governed by the grade of coal, and the amount in the bunkers.

Queen Elizabeth on 19th June 1937.   *H. C. Casserley*

6104 *Scottish Borderer* on 27th October 1945.   *H. C. Casserley*

The loaded container is hoisted by wire ropes until it is stopped by an upward limit switch. A travelling carriage is used to traverse the container over the tops of the bunkers, and when the predetermined bunker is reached, an electrically operated mechanism comes into contact with a bottom door on the container, which allows the coal to fall into the bunker. The container carriage is then traversed back to the opening above the tippler, and the container is lowered to ground level, ready for the next charge of coal from the wagon tippler.

Assuming the coal bunkers charged to capacity, the arrangement provides for locomotives to receive any of the three grades of coal, according to the type of engine and duty. The coal is fed out of the bunker outlets by jigger feeders, which are operated from control cabins situated on the platforms between the engine coaling roads. The jiggers are electrically driven, and are capable of supplying coal to the engines at a rate of 60 to 120 tons per hour.

On No. 1 road, nearest the wagon tippler, Grade I coal can be obtained; Grade III coal is available on No. 2 road; and on No. 3 road a cross jigger feeder is provided from the centre bunker, as well as the feeder from the bunker above that road, so that engines have the choice of Grade II or III coal as required.

Ash Disposal

The locomotive ash-handling plant consists of four parallel ash pits, each 190 ft. long. The floor of each pit is provided with steel grids made from second-hand rails, and these allow the ashes to fall through into two reinforced concrete hoppers, which extend the full length of the pits.

The hoppers lead the ashes into a trough filled with water, where they are quenched immediately, and then removed by two 36 in. continuous conveyor belts, submerged in the water trough. These belts extend the full length of the ash pits, and are electrically-driven to travel at a speed of 11 ft. per minute. The ashes

Polmadie on 4th November 1947. Harvey's papers of 1948 and 1951 illuminate the principles involved in the reorganisation of the shed. Every development at Polmadie seemed to be out of the ordinary in some respect and the 1940s modernisation was no exception. It was spread out over several years, no doubt a circumstance of the war, and the equipment was not 'standard' in the sense that it conformed strictly with previous practice. The conveyor-belt equipped ash plant was the most obvious departure from usual LMS (or rather, contractors') principles and this may be the reason for the considerable 'airing' in the technical press. It is not known if the effectiveness of the Polmadie installations was ever measured against the more conventional plants (see *LMS Engine Sheds, passim*) built subsequently by the LMR at Crewe, for instance, and elsewhere on British Railways. Final attention to the trackwork is recorded as taking place in May 1948, leaving only a few weeks of tidying-up.

British Railways

from the main belts are deposited on to a cross travel belt 24 in. wide, situated at the end of the pits, and running at right angles to the main belt. This belt can be operated at speeds of 40, 80 and 120 ft. per minute, according to demand. The ash from this belt is deposited on to an incline conveyor belt 24 in. wide, which carries it to a height of 50 ft. above rail level, where it is discharged into a reinforced concrete bunker of 50 tons capacity. This bunker straddles a siding on which are marshalled wagons for transporting the ash from the bunker. These empty coal wagons are drawn from the empty coal wagons discharged from the coaling plant. The outlets from the ash bunker are controlled manually by chain and sprocket wheels from a platform above ground level.

R. F. Harvey's paper was in turn reported in 1951 in following fashion:

Remodelling of Polmadie Depot

Mr. Harvey said that Polmadie provided a great deal of locomotive power for passenger working from Glasgow Central, including Anglo-Scottish expresses, for freight working to Carlisle, and for local services. Before the formation of the four main-line railways on January 1, 1923, there was also a smaller depot at Eglinton Street, which was subsequently closed for other than coaling, watering, and ash facilities for servicing locomotives employed on local working, an arrangement which relieved Glasgow Central passenger station; the shed buildings were taken over for the maintenance of motor vehicles.

The present shed at Polmadie was built in 1924 and the layout of the locomotive yard was not in keeping with modern practice, while the disposal sequence of operations also left much to be desired. In June, 1940*, with the introduction of the standard arrangement of the L.M.S.R. to form locomotive districts, Polmadie became the parent depot, and supplied power to the district, and also dealt with the repair and examination of its own locomotives, and locomotives from the smaller depots, the repairs to which could not be completed within 48 hr. To meet the heavy demands for locomotive power it was decided, in 1941, to modernise Polmadie Depot. There was, Mr. Harvey said, very heavy wartime traffic both to and from the west coast of Scotland. The locomotive building programme had to be curtailed, and it was increasingly necessary to improve locomotive availability.

* Originally, of course, 1935.

The original layout covered an area of nine acres, compared with 15 acres for the new layout, which provided for a complete re-arrangement of the yard together with the installation of new coaling plant, ash disposal, and watering facilities, all of which were re-sited in what was, under the old layout, the Shawfield yard traffic sidings, most of which were given up because of changed traffic conditions, one of them the discontinuance of sectionising private owner wagons. Preparation pits of precast concrete sections are provided on the 14 roads outside the shed, and the surrounding area paved; fluorescent lighting is sunk into the pit walls. Three coaling roads were included in the new layout, the individual coal hoppers each handling different grades of coal required for various services; cross feed is arranged between two of the hoppers and water spraying facilities are provided.

The ashplant disposal is of the submerged belt type delivering into an overhead bunker, and comprises four ashpits, each 190 ft. long. There are two submerged belt installations, one between each pair of pits, discharging on to a

The repair shop on 19th June 1949, with 4–4–0 No. 41143. David L. Smith, in an extraordinarily detailed article in the SLS *Journal* of October 1962, recounts the story of the Compounds coming to Scotland, 1143 one of fifteen at Kingmoor for 'Caledonian' work, five others being allotted to the former GSWR. They evidently compared favourably with CR engines. Nos. 900-909 came new to Polmadie in April 1927, running in on Gourock trains, the crews having 'a rather curious summer'. Smith recalls the engines having an easy task on the Carlisle road, double-heading with 230 tons per engine.
H. C. Casserley

belt conveyor across the pits, which in turn delivers ashes to the rising belt conveyor and thence to the overhead bunker. The ash hopper straddles the track and discharges into wagons; facilities are provided for slaking ashes.

Remodelling of the existing signal arrangements was also necessary and the number of levers was increased from 64 to 84. Regarding financial justification, Mr. Harvey said that the scheme involved an expenditure of £181,681, the total savings visualised being £25,336, which, after allowing for interest on capital and increased annual expenditure, showed a saving of 13.9 per cent.

By virtue of its great size, and the generously equipped repair shop (the 'back shed' was second only to St. Rollox and was capable of almost anything short of new construction), Polmadie was the main depot of the Caledonian. Anyone appointed the post of foreman (the major CR depots were in the charge of a Locomotive Foreman) was being groomed for success, and was acknowledged as destined for higher things.

The workings were extremely varied and complex – passenger work to the south, to Edinburgh and to Gourock/Wemyss Bay was shared, for instance, with Kingmoor, Dalry Road and Ladyburn; Polmadie engines in addition worked passenger trains on the Cathcart Circle, to Neilston, Uplawmoor, Ardrossan and East Kilbride, together with all manner of goods and coal. The latter generally involved a takeover from Motherwell and Hamilton engines, in turn bringing trains from the outer colliery areas; in addition, there was goods work connected with the docks on the south side of the Clyde and traffic like shipyard steel, a 'conditional' working which arrived at the Polmadie yards at odd times of the day to be disposed of to the shipyard concerned by first thing in the morning. Much of Polmadie's goods and

mineral work was 'conditional' in this sense, connected with a vast and varied heavy industry, subject to myriad economic and commercial vagaries. In the course of a week a goods or mineral driver could find himself never repeating a run.

31st December 1933

LMS 4P 4–4–0
900, 901, 902, 903, 904, 905, 906, 907, 908, 909, 1083, 1084

LMS 4P 2–6–4T
2415, 2416, 2417, 2418, 2419

LMS 'Royal Scot' 4–6–0
6102 *Black Watch*, 6103 *Royal Scots Fusilier*, 6104 *Scottish Borderer*, 6105 *Cameron Highlander*, 6106 *Gordon Highlander*, 6107 *Argyll & Sutherland Highlander*, 6108 *Seaforth Highlander*, 6115 *Scots Guardsman*

LMS 'Crab' 2–6–0
13210, 13211

CR 2P 4–4–0
14346, 14351, 14356

CR 3P 4–4–0
14436, 14443, 14466, 14475, 14476

CR 4P 4–6–0
14518, 14630, 14637, 14651

CR 1P 4–4–0T
15025

CR 1P 0–4–4T
15153

CR 2P 0–4–4T
15170, 15177, 15179, 15183, 15186, 15189, 15197, 15201, 15207, 15228, 15264, 15265, 15266, 15267, 15268

CR 4P 4–6–2T
15350, 15351, 15357, 15358, 15359, 15360, 15361

CR 0–4–0ST
16027, 16035

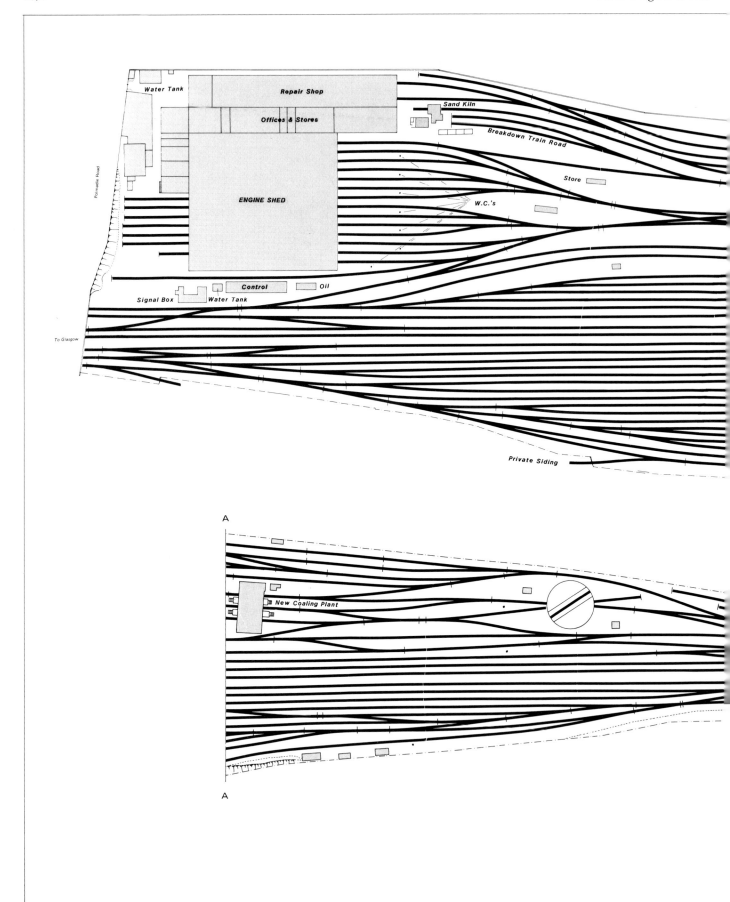

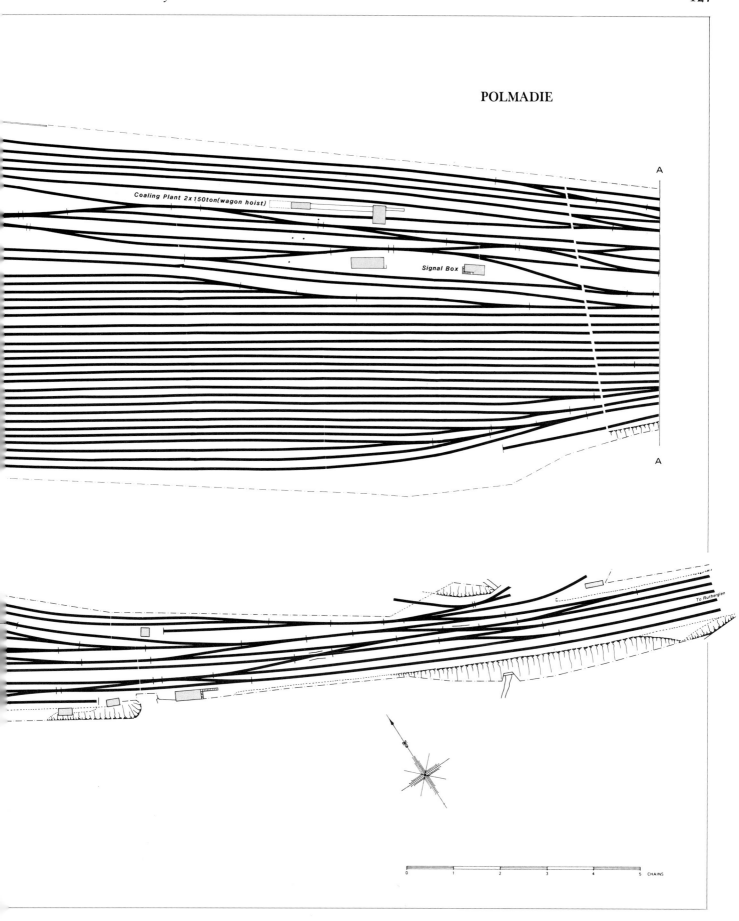

POLMADIE

Coaling Plant 2×150ton(wagon hoist)

Signal Box

A

A

To Rutherglen

0 1 2 3 4 5 CHAINS

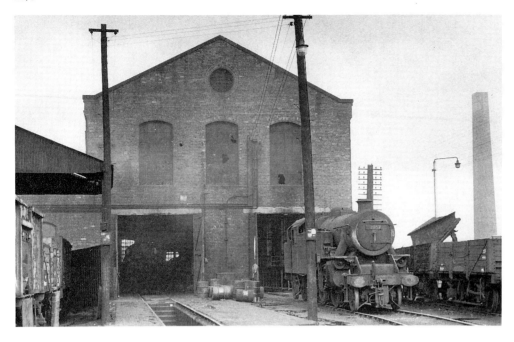

The great shop at Polmadie, unmistakably Scottish in its antecedents. No. 42057, 20th August 1962. The shed was demolished to make way for a carriage depot but the Polmadie repair shop remains in use, refurbished for coach work.   *K. Fairey*

CR 2F 0–6–0T
16153, 16154, 16155, 16159, 16172

CR 3F 0–6–0T
16237, 16239, 16259, 16260, 16261, 16263, 16287, 16294, 16296, 16304, 16305, 16306, 16307, 16311, 16314, 16315, 16316, 16317, 16318, 16324, 16336, 16342, 16343, 16346, 16347, 16353, 16354, 16355, 16367, 16373, 16374

LMS 3F 0–6–0T
16419

CR 4F 0–8–0T
16953

CR 2F 0–6–0
17268, 17275, 17279, 17292, 17296, 17315, 17317, 17319, 17320, 17321, 17345, 17347, 17361, 17267, 17369, 17370, 17373, 17388, 17414, 17433, 17434, 17443, 17444, 17445, 17446, 17447, 17448, 17459, 17463, 17464, 17465

CR 3F 0–6–0
17550, 17553, 17555, 17564, 17615, 17646, 17647, 17690, 17692
                                        TOTAL 144

31st December 1947
LMS 7P 4–6–2
6220 *Coronation*, 6221 *Queen Elizabeth*, 6222 *Queen Mary*, 6223 *Princess Alice*, 6224 *Princess Alexandra*, 6230 *Duchess of Buccleuch*, 6231 *Duchess of Atholl*, 6232 *Duchess of Montrose*, 6242 *City of Glasgow*

LMS 5 4–6–0
4793, 4794, 4978, 4979, 4980, 5309, 5484, 5485, 5486, 5487

LMS 'Jubilee' 4–6–0
5583 *Assam*, 5584 *North West Frontier*, 5691 *Orion*, 5692 *Cyclops*

LMS 'Royal Scot' 4–6–0
6102 *Black Watch*, 6104 *Scottish Borderer*, 6105 *Cameron Highlander*, 6107 *Argyll & Sutherland Highlander*, 6143 *The South Staffordshire Regiment*

LMS 4P 4–4–0
916, 1131

LMS 4P 2–6–4T
2200, 2201, 2202, 2203, 2204, 2205, 2206, 2207, 2208, 2211, 2213, 2214, 2215, 2216, 2238, 2239, 2240, 2241, 2242, 2243, 2244, 2245, 2246, 2247,

2274, 2688, 2689, 2690, 2691, 2692, 2693, 2694, 2695, 2696, 2698, 2699

LMS 4F 0–6–0
4234, 4281

LMS 3F 0–6–0T
7331, 7332, 7536, 7537, 7540

CR 2F 0–6–0T
16153, 16159, 16160, 16162, 16167, 16172

CR 3F 0–6–0T
16239, 16244, 16260, 16261, 16263, 16280, 16292, 16294, 16295, 16298, 16304, 16305, 16306, 16307, 16308, 16314, 16318, 16322, 16324, 16342, 16346, 16349

CR 2P 0–4–4T
15116, 15123, 15127, 15141, 15167, 15170, 15179, 15183, 15197, 15201, 15207, 15221, 15224, 15228, 15265, 15267, 15268

CR 2F 0–6–0
17239, 17268, 17275, 17292, 17310, 17316, 17317, 17319, 17320, 17321, 17330, 17335, 17347, 17360, 17361, 17365, 17367, 17370, 17381, 17387, 17388, 17389, 17412, 17432, 17433, 17436, 17439, 17443, 17444, 17446, 17447, 17448, 17459, 17464, 17465, 17467

CR 3F 0–6–0
17555, 17564, 17581, 17619, 17632, 17641, 17661, 17690
                                        TOTAL 162

Polmadie was possessed of the entire range of CR engines, from the big passenger and mixed traffic 4–6–0s, 4–4–0s and large and small 0–6–0s to a host of tanks on local goods, shunting and passenger work. Engines of particular interest were the Pickersgill 'Wemyss Bay' 4–6–2Ts, Nos 944–955 (LMS 15350–15361), built for the Clyde Coast and Greenock trains, the '104' class Cathcart Circle 0–4–4Ts with 4′6″ driving wheels and the 'pugs' and 'beetlecrushers' on dock work.

The most immediate manifestation of the Grouping was the arrival in 1924 of a batch of Compound 4–4–0s. Intended for the Carlisle road, they were received less than enthusiastically, resented as a Derby diktat. Despite a fleeting fame in 1927 on the newly inaugurated 'Royal Scot' as far as Carnforth (before 'Royal Scot' 4–6–0s were available),

they would accomplish little without resorting to double-heading. After the new 4–6–0s became available in numbers, they drifted away, mainly to the ex-GSW section – those remaining at Polmadie found employment mainly on the Edinburgh line or on locals to Carlisle.

By 1933 the earlier Dunalastair 4–4–0s were represented only by Nos 14346, 14351, and 14356, and the superheated 4–4–0s by Nos. 14436, 14443, 14466, 14475 and 14476. Only two CR-built 4–6–0s remained, No. 14618 of the inside cylinder '908' class and No. 14651 of the Pickersgill '60' class; they were accompanied by two of the 1925 LMS engines. A solitary 'Cathcart' tank No. 15153 and a Lambie 4–4–0T remained of the smaller passenger tanks, though larger 0–4–4Ts remained, as well as seven of the 'Wemyss Bay' tanks. However, in November 1933 a batch of new Fowler 2–6–4Ts were sent to the Northern Division, Nos 2415, 2416 and 2417 being allocated to Polmadie, welcome additions on the heavier passenger work. The Compounds remained in principle top link alternatives to the eight 'Royal Scot' 4–6–0s until the Stanier era, when firstly 'Princess Royal' Pacifics (1934–1936) and then (in 1940) 'Duchess' 4–6–2s appeared for the heaviest duties. Nos 6220–6224, 6230–6232 and 6242 were resident over many years. A handful of 'Jubilees' came along (with a few class '5s') forming, with the 'Royal Scots', the staple express power well into Nationalisation. The 'Jubilees' were 'a poor lot', earning an unenviable reputation for losing time on the Liverpool and Manchester trains.

Polmadie lacked an adequate stud of modern 2–6–4Ts for suburban work, a situation alleviated somewhat by November 1945 with the arrival of ten of the new Fairburn engines. Over the ensuing months more examples were delivered new, so that by the end of 1947 there were no less than thirty-six of them at Polmadie, allowing the last of the 4–6–2Ts to be transferred away for banking duties. The last of the 4–4–0s were also disposed of but the many small tanks and 0–6–0s soldiered on into the 'fifties and beyond.

BR 'Clan' Pacifics arriving in 1952 replaced the 4–6–0s on the Liverpool and Manchester workings but in truth were little better; the 'Britannia' 4–6–2s, the 'Firth' engines Nos 70050–70054, were quite a different matter, coming to Polmadie in 1954. Together with BR class '5MTs', Nos 73055–73064, for instance, they were extremely well received.

As the 1950s progressed the allocation grew increasingly 'standard'; ex-CR locos were disposed of and BR engines became increasingly in evidence. The stock of 'Coronation' Pacifics and 'Royal Scot' 4–6–0s (many of them extremely long-term residents) remained much as it always had been, but the 'Jubilees' and 'Black 5s' had departed by the late 'fifties. In 1959 the allocation stood at nearly two hundred, a total which included over forty 2–6–4Ts (both LMS and BR) 'Britannia' and 'Clan' Pacifics, BR 4–6–0s and moguls and WD goods engines. There were over sixty CR engines still at Polmadie, and a handful of ex-LNER 0–6–0s had also found their way to the shed. Late arrivals were ex-WD Stanier 2–8–0s, Nos 48773, 48774, and 48775, put to use long after most of the class had departed Scotland.

The early 1960s saw a rapid decline of steam power – the 'Royal Scots' and Stanier Pacifics were withdrawn in 1962–1963 along with the remaining ex-CR locos, and as early as 1963 four roads were reported 'screened off ... and fuel tanks built'. Nine 350 h.p. shunters had been at work since at least April 1956 and new diesels were delivered throughout the early 1960s. The first 900 h.p. Clayton Bo Bo, No. D8500 (unsuccessful yet characteristic Polmadie inhabitants for several years), was put new into traffic at Polmadie on 10th September 1962. By 1965 there were only thirty steam locomotives at the shed, compared with no less than ninety-five diesels; remarkable amongst the survivors, however, were three ex-LNER Pacifics, Nos 60512 *Steady Aim*, 60522 *Straight Deal* and 60535 *Hornets Beauty*. They seem to have been sent to Polmadie primarily to 'see out mileage' before withdrawal – no one quite knew what to do with them and they languished for much of the time, out of action at the rear of the shed. They did sally forth on occasion, however, in substitution for failed diesels – *Straight Deal* accompanied class '5' No. 44887 one night out of St Enoch on the St. Pancras sleeper as far as Leeds, and another of the trio took over an Inverness–Glasgow (Low Level) relief at Perth.

Steam activity ceased in May 1967, with, it would appear, 2–6–4Ts No. 80116 as Glasgow Central pilot and 42274 on the 17.03 from Gourock on Friday, 28th May. Steam visits from Carlisle continued throughout the following summer and after many years as a diesel depot Polmadie has only latterly been closed and demolished. The shed had been coded 27A in 1935, being less affected by subsequent changes than many depots. It was given the code 66A in 1949, retaining it until closure.

The LMS Pacifics and their workings were well documented and closely observed over many years. At the last, however, there seem to have been little of the unexpected roamings, transfers and swan-songs which seemed to dog the last days of the LNER classes. They lingered in variously obscure roles, often far from their original lines, in contrast to the LMS examples, which seem to have disappeared in relatively peremptory fashion. 60152 *Holyrood* had been at Polmadie in 1953 and at the end other Pacifics turned up to 'see out mileage'. This is a fascinating and little recorded adjunct to the end of steam on BR and brought many fascinating transfers, ephemera, unfortunately, seldom recorded in detail. Left to right: 60527 *Sun Chariot*, 60535 *Hornet's Beauty* and 60512 *Steady Aim*.   *D. J. Montgomery*

Class 3MT 2–6–0 No. 77008. These little moguls were not a success, in that only very few were built; it was difficult to find the right duties for them and they suffered from the old problem of unfamiliarity. New types were best received when sent to sheds in numbers, and it was no accident that large concentrations of 'Black 5s' went to Scotland, the Northern Division involving certain political sensitivity within the LMS. Scottish crews (most LMS men, for that) came to swear by the 'Black 5' and 'the classic Class 5 4–6–0', whether in LMS or BR guise, must be seen 'all round' as the most successful British locomotive development. Other standards which came to Scotland were accepted more or less with alacrity – the 2–6–4Ts were put to great good use at Polmadie and the BR class '5MTs', as at St. Rollox, were equally successful. Nos. 73055-73064 came to Polmadie and were long familiar on passenger trains to Gourock and Wemyss Bay, to Edinburgh and to Carlisle with freights and reliefs.   *B. Morrison*

SEAFIELD

The shed at Seafield is one of the most curious to be encountered in this series. It was opened in 1902, part of a breathtakingly speculative scheme designed to entice Leith dock traffic away from the North British Railway. Christened the Leith New Lines project, at vast expense a line was taken from the Caledonian's branch at Newhaven across the centre of Leith to the east side where extensive yards were established. The two-road brick engine shed, with generous coal ramp and a 60 ft. Cowans Sheldon turntable, was built at the eastern extremity of the site, overlooking the sea at 'Marine Esplanade'.

The scheme was not a success and, if the shed was put into use at all, within a couple of years or so it was standing empty and abandoned. Thus 'mothballed' it came to the attention of the North British; their South Leith traffic continued in nothing but the best of health and its own servicing point, turntable etc. was found increasingly wanting. It stood nearby (and survived along with Seafield itself, well into BR days) where the CR line crossed over the NB and was very much in need of additional accommodation. The Caledonian were accordingly approached in the summer of 1912 and were persuaded to lease the depot to the old rival, the very advantageous terms obtained by the North British doing little to ease the CR's humiliation.

A comprehensive agreement covering the Dock traffic was arrived at in November 1912, the Caledonian holding little hope for any restorative effect upon its own slender share of the workings. The following extract makes clear the conditions under which the shed would pass to the new occupant:

Fifth. The North British Company shall, in respect of the said fixed tolls and minimum as aforesaid, be entitled to run over and use the Branch Railway with and for empty wagons, including not only wagons which have been run over the Branch Railway or part of it with traffic but also wagons which when loaded or partly loaded have reached South Leith by the North British Company's own railways, and such use with and for empty wagons shall include such storage of empty wagons as is reasonably incidental to the working of the traffic. The North British Company shall also be entitled to use free of any toll charge or other payment the lines upon the areas coloured pink and grey upon the plan for wagons with locomotive coal or other locomotive stores carried by the North British Company to or from the Locomotive Depot after-mentioned.

Sixth. The use, to which the North British Company shall by this Agreement be entitled of the locomotive depot, including shed, coaling stage and other accommodation and conveniences connected therewith, and the necessary access lines thereto, all situated on the ground coloured grey on the plan, shall be exclusive, except in the case of the turntable of which the Caledonian Company shall have joint use with the North British Company. In respect of such use conferred upon the North British Company by this article the North British Company shall pay to the Caledonian Company the sum or rent of two hundred

'Lieth Docks' engine shed on 20th September 1935. The New Lines project, for all its great expense, was a commercial flop and in a sense the Seafield engine shed was a memorial to that failure. The subsequent deal to let the building to the North British, an open-ended agreement to fit it out to their satisfaction, was, as McIntosh ruefully noted, 'a poor bargain'.   *W. A. Camwell*

pounds sterling per annum as at 31st December in each year for the year preceding over and above the payments provided for in Article Second hereof. The Caledonian Company shall be responsible for the said locomotive depot being maintained in good condition and properly equipped and maintained in the matter of arrangements for getting in a supply of water, and shall also be responsible for the provision and maintenance of all gas and water piping and lamps and other necessary or reasonable requirements being provided for the lighting of the rails and sidings present or future upon the area coloured pink. The water columns on and connected with the Branch Railway shall be allocated between the Companies as may be agreed or determined by arbitration, and each Company shall pay for its own water supply. The North British Company shall pay the cost of lighting the subjects in respect of which the annual rent of £200 above mentioned is payable.

The North British were not prepared to take up residence until the shed was restored in every detail and this led to further correspondence. McIntosh to his General Manager:

23rd December 1913.
Donald A. Matheson, Esq.,
  General Manager.

Dear Sir,
  Running Powers to North British Company
  over part of Caledonian Company's South
  Leith Branch, &c.

Further to my letter of 18th instant.
  I caused one of my Inspectors to visit the Locomotive and Coal Sheds at Leith, and he reports that during the time the shed has been shut up, there has been considerable damage done. There are six lamps required for gas brackets and 47 panes of glass in shed, also 16 panes of glass for bothy and sand kiln; water pipe in bothy is in need of repair and a water

meter will require to be put in and connection cut off from the tank at Seafield Gate.
  I presume the Engineer's Department will attend to these matters.
  My Inspector also reports that there are no coal boxes, and that two hosebags are wanted for water columns and two washing out bags for hydrants in the shed, but as this is moveable equipment of the shed, I shall be glad to know if this Company will be responsible for supplying these articles, and the subsequent maintenance of same.

Yours truly,

McIntosh frowned upon the Leith dealings and had written to Matheson only a few days previously: 'I am sorry to see that by the Agreement... the Caledonian Company is to be responsible for the depot being maintained and properly equipped, as I am afraid it may turn out a poor bargain for this Company to equip the shed to the satisfaction of the North British Co. for £200 per year.'

There was a long delay before the NBR took possession of Seafield, witnessed by this final letter from Matheson:

William Pickersgill Esq.,
  Locomotive Superintendent.

The Caledonian Railway Company

General Manager's Office
302 Buchanan Street
Glasgow
16th March 1916.

Dear Sir,
  Leith, Engine Shed, Seafield.

As you are aware in terms of Article Sixth of Agreement between the Company and the North British Company of April 1912 the North British Company are to have use of the Locomotive Depot at Seafield, Leith.
  The North British Company have not so far used the Depot but they are now making

It is not clear if the NB ever made use of the shed, despite the years of obfuscation. The £20 for 'hydrants' in 1917 seems to indicate some activity at the shed but relations between the companies at local level were never harmonious. The North British seems to have made a final exit after the First World War. It only properly opened in the next war, and remained an active and busy depot. On 2nd May 1948 there were fifteen LNER engines there: 4462, 4486, 4533, 4538, 4547, 4566, 4576, 4594, 4605, 4606, 4607, 4614, 5251, 5298 and 5919. *W. A. Camwell*

arrangements to do so, and have asked that certain repairs should be executed.

In a telegram which I have received from Mr. Jackson to-day he says: 'Presume you are arranging to supply twelve boxes suitable for coal stage at South Leith to enable us to coal our engines there'.

I send you herewith a print of the Agreement of April 1912 and shall be glad to know whether you think it falls to the Company to provide coal boxes.

Yours faithfully,
Donald A. Matheson,

A realisation had dawned by now that traffic was generally at a peak and the 1912 agreement effectively dampened competition between the CR and the NB.

In 1917 £20 was authorised for 'new hydrants' at 'Seafield Shed' accompanied by the note 'The North British have sole use of this shed at £200 p.a.' Despite all this, it remains uncertain whether or not the North British ever got round to working engines off Seafield, though they are said to have used it briefly during the Great War, to store engines awaiting repair. Certainly the turntable was in regular use, by Lothian coal engines. By 1935 it was mouldering quietly away, with no indication of any use at all for decades. The 1912 Agreement had effectively been abandoned – the LMS was certainly not looking after its 'necessary or reasonable requirements' and the LNER was not using it. It is amusing to speculate that the fears

No. 4602 on 2nd May 1948. *W. A. Camwell*

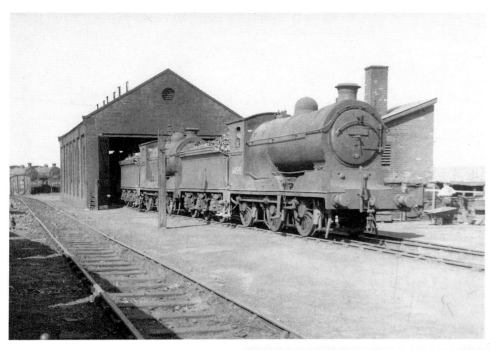

0–6–0s Nos. 64599 and 64577 on 31st
August 1952.   *D. F. Tee*

expressed by McIntosh proved in the event
groundless – maybe the £200 p.a. was duly
handed over, forgotten, through the bureau-
cratic machine. If so, by 1939 the shed would
have been largely paid for, St. Rollox having
the last laugh after all.

Whatever had happened to the leasing
agreement the shed did come into use,
arranged by the Railway Executive and
financed by the Government, during the
Second World War; with St. Margaret's
depot suffering severe overcrowding, the
LNER took to outstationing a number of
freight locos at Seafield and in this guise, a
bustling, crowded depot, it served throughout BR days until closure on 13th october
1962.

It is unlikely that the shed was actually
sold to the LNER – the transfer can really
be regarded as another example of wartime
LMS/LNER co-operation, like the coaling of
Bletchley engines at Cambridge ex-GE. In
this fashion is Seafield, for the purposes of this
series at least, bracketed with other sheds
'open at 1947' though stricter classifications
might, of course, be made. Ultimately, in a
sense, it might be possible to argue that as a
Caledonian shed Seafield didn't exist at all;
nevertheless it is an interesting story and,
without doubt, an unusual one. It was indis-
putably 'open' on Nationalisation (up to
twenty ex-LNER locos were found on one
visit in 1948) and it is thus included here. In
1952 the allocation comprised some fifteen
ex-NBR and LNER 0–6–0s from St. Margaret's and, only a year before final closure
the following were noted at the shed:

'J37'
64555, 64594, 64601, 64607

'J39'
64725

'J36'
65327, 65334, 65344

'J38'
65912, 65918

Seafield shed on 13th September 1953. The shed staff and crews were all from St. Margaret's
though it is not clear if any, or all, were permanently based there, or if men booked on/off at the
main shed.   *B. Hilton*

Seafield on 13th September 1953. There was no fixed allocation, the main purpose being to
relieve the dreadful congestion at the main shed, St. Margaret's. The South Lieth ex-NBR locomotive yard was very close by and also remained in use in BR days; Seafield shed, however,
proved particularly useful for the 0–6–0s working thus, originating from Meadows Yard
(between South Lieth and Portobello) and from South Lieth itself.   *B. Hilton*

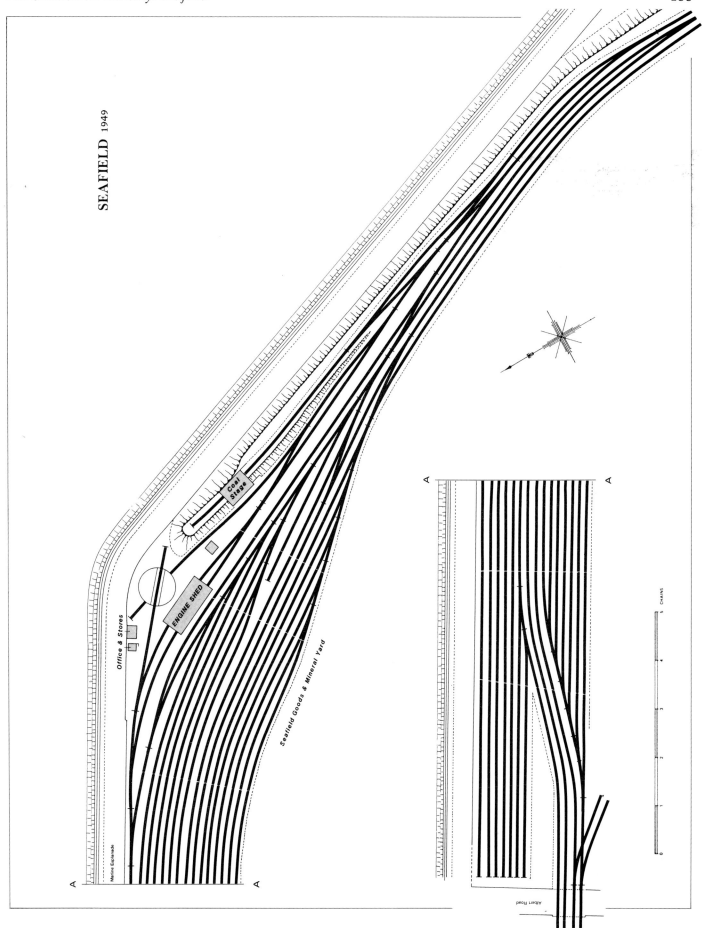

SEAFIELD 1949

Coal Stage

ENGINE SHED

Office & Stores

Marine Esplanade

Seafield Goods & Mineral Yard

Albert Road

CHAINS
0 1 2 3 4 5

STIRLING

Stirling shed was an ancient construction, its massive walls and low roof leaving it squat and primitive of aspect, wholly at variance with later Caledonian practice.   *J. Robertson*

Stirling shed, a characteristically massive yet decorative stone building, was designed for the Scottish Central Railway in 1850. Of four roads, it retained fine arched entrances throughout LMS days and was distinguished by a continuing series of proposals and alterations, both enacted and abandoned. It replaced a broken down timber shed, by repute a hastily put-together leftover from the construction period, in existence in March 1848 and said to have stood at the southern end of the station platforms.

The Scottish Central gave some considerable thought to its new engine shed at Stirling and three drawings were submitted in 1850. the site available was somewhat restricted, to the south of the station opposite a brick and tile works and near to a road, 'The Craigs'. The building, ranging from 142–125 ft. × 65 ft. with smithy and store attached, was disposed variously around this site for the consideration of the Board, which finally elected for 'Drawing No. 1', a single-ended shed at the southernmost extremity of the strip of land. 'Drawing No. 2' would have been a through building in the middle of what became the yard, whilst 'Drawing No. 3' was a 'mirror image' of 'Drawing No. 1', single-ended and at the north end of the site, its entrances facing south. The water tank and coke stage underwent similar juggling, the 'Tank House' ending up near to the end of a lengthy headshunt, which for some fifty or so years was the means of access to the shed. The coke stage stood between

the running lines and the shed yard and the plans of 1850 included a 50 ft. turntable, huge for its time, situated on the far extremity of the headshunt. Puzzlingly, it is absent from Ordnance Survey records of 1863, a cartographic error may be. Stirling shed thus emerges from a confusing array of proposals

and possibilities, only to retreat into relative obscurity. Nothing at all changed for over twenty years but by at least the mid-1890s the shed area had been completely remodelled. By 1896 it had been found possible to extend the restricted site southwards across 'The Craigs', dispensing with the rail over-

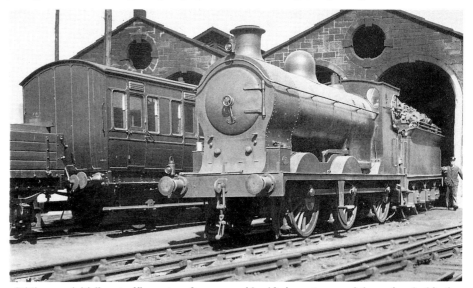

Stirling was initially a traffic centre of some considerable importance and the engine shed in the 1850s was on a scale commensurate with the grand designs of the Scottish Central. With merger and expansion of lines, its importance declined and by the 1930s it lay in relative obscurity.

H. N. James

bridge. The truncated portion of the road became 'Springfield Place' a cul-de-sac ending hard by a new and re-positioned 50 ft. turntable. The site of the old headshunt was obscured by a new, more direct, exit to the running lines, a new sand kiln and mess appeared by the shed and stores offices and new water tank were erected by the turntable. At the same time Stirling was converted into a through shed, recalling the old 'Drawing No. 2' of 1850. The building was indeed provided from the first with arches at its southern 'terminal' end and the tracks had only to be led through onto the main line near the bridge, carrying 'The Craigs' successor, 'Kerse Road'. Very much later, between 1947 and 1953 the southern end of the shed required rebuilding and the arches were dispensed with. By 1909 a new coal stage with ramp had been built in the north part of the yard; in that year £10 was expended on a 'new water pipe and slacker [!] at the coal stage, Stirling, Cost £10.'

Stirling thoroughly merited the attention it received in Caledonian days and but for site difficulties might well have been expanded further. The forty or so locos on its complement at the Grouping were engaged principally on goods and passenger work of a primary nature, the shed occupying a position at the gateway to the Oban line, with which it was mainly concerned. Stirling locomotives did not play a great part in main line work on other routes, though its crews were involved in a fair amount of remanning. The shed did provide for a considerable local traffic, to Glasgow and Edinburgh as well as a Stirling–Larbert–Edinburgh turn which often included through coaches from Oban.

Shunting engines were necessary whilst its repair facilities (a hoist had been provided at an early date) attended a number of engines outstationed (by the Great War period) at Alloa, Callander, Denny and Killin. Over half of Stirling's locos were 0–6–0s at Grouping and the shed retained an extremely marked 'Caledonian' air well into BR days. On 31st January 1934 the complement still included three of the '55' class 4–6–0s, Nos. 14603, 14604 and 14607, introduced in 1902 specifically for the Oban line in succession to the 4–4–0 'Oban Bogies' built by Brittain twenty years before. The Dunalastair 4–4–0s were available for passenger work, including all four of the 'Dunalastair II' rebuilds. Two surviving Drummond 0–4–4Ts, Nos. 15103 and 15104, were also there, accompanied by two standard McIntosh tanks, the complete list reading:

CR 4P 4–6–0
14603, 14604, 14607

CR 2P 'Dunalastair II' 4–4–0
14326, 14327, 14328, 14332, 14336

CR 2P 'Dunalastair III' 4–4–0
14342

CR 3P 'Dunalastair II' Rebuilt 4–4–0
14430, 14431, 14432, 14433

CR 2F 0–6–0
17242, 17243, 17244, 17246, 17250, 17252, 17253, 17276, 17308, 17339, 17340, 17391, 17402, 17423, 17424, 17425, 17461, 17466, 17467, 17468

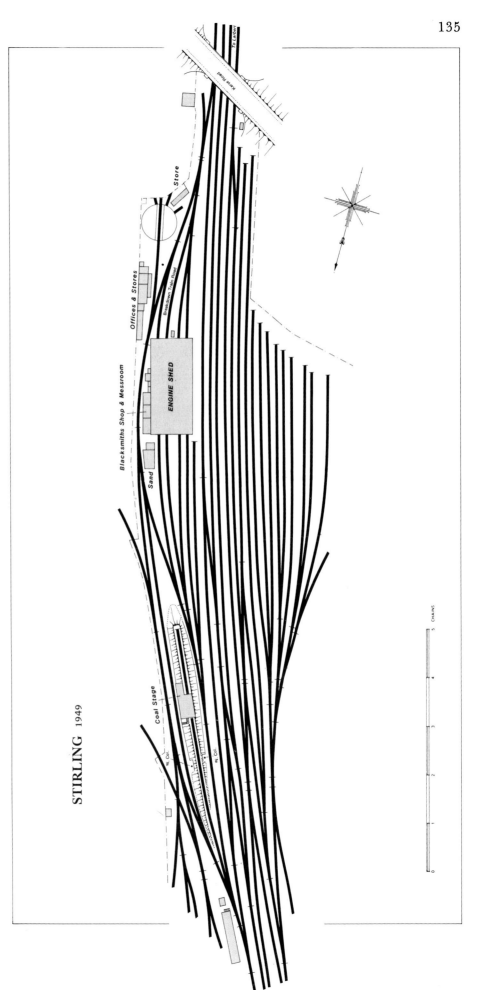

STIRLING 1949

Stirling on 23rd July 1947.

D. F. Tee

CR 3F Pickersgill 0–6–0
17650, 17660, 17661, 17673

CR 3F 0–6–0T
16236, 16292, 16335

CR 1P 0–4–4T
15103, 15104

CR 2P 0–4–4T
15202, 15210

The '2F' 0–6–0s worked much of the freight on the Oban line and in the summer it was common to see them on pilot duties. There were two Highland 'Clans' at Stirling between 1934 and 1939, Nos. 14762 and 14765, usually employed on the 5.45 a.m. Stirling–Oban (which included through sleeping cars from Euston), or the summer only 5.10 a.m. The combination of '2F' and 'Clan' was found to be extremely effective. 1939 saw the advent of the class '5' 4–6–0s on such duties but responsibility for power provision largely passed to Balornock.

The shed by 1923 was cramped and in poor condition, its facilities elderly and inadequate. The LMS did nothing to improve the building itself but was moved to take some measures to ease conditions at the depot. They hardly amounted to much, a new ash pit ordered in December 1928 at a cost of £243 and in 1938 a 'new wooden tank, columns and piping £2,418.' There was a 30-ton hoist in the yard at Stirling, noticeable in photographs of the early 1930s but it seems to have disappeared after about 1940 when its 'displacement' was authorised. Heavy repair work was transferred to Perth (and

Ex-GN 4–4–0 at Stirling, doubtless a resident of the LNER shed. As 'Shore Road' it became a 'sub shed' of Stirling LMS, differentiated in the 1950s as 'Stirling South'.   *W. A. Camwell*

The work at Stirling became more or less local in nature, 0–6–0s and small tanks sufficing for most of the duties, bolstered latterly by one or two 2–6–4Ts and a few class 5 4–6–0s for main line jobs.

B. Hilton

Scottish coal 'benches' were primitive and lightly built, in contrast both to the shed buildings themselves and to English tradition, where frequently considerable care went into the provision of a high, brick-built stage. Most of the 'benches' that survived into BR days seemed in imminent danger of collapse.

J. F. McEwan

Stirling in September 1954. A handful of LMS 4—4—0s spent some years in obscurity around Stirling. David L. Smith notes the arrival of Nos. 900-924 in the late 1920s, the latter going initially to Aberdeen. The distribution, he wryly points out, gave cause for wonder that the LMS authorities 'had ever seen any of the Scottish locomotive depots except as names in a timetable!' The old turntable was put out of use in the preliminary rebuilding work of the 1950s; Stirling got the old Polmadie 70 ft 'table but the new roundhouse never materialised — 'from the running man's point of view it is a great pity that so many of these schemes failed to come to fruition'.

Photomatic

Balornock in the event of overcrowding) in connection with that shed's 'concentration' status of 1935 (see Volume 1).

For many years a football pitch had lain immediately to the east of the shed but by the beginning of the BR period this ground, or part of it, at least, became available, and in 1951 preliminary work (first planned by the LMS) began on a fine new roundhouse, partly utilising this site. A new 70 ft. turntable, second-hand from Polmadie and driven by vacuum tractor, was laid out, with two access roads, but work ceased on completion of the office block and machine shop. All that could then be done was to fill in the old 50 ft. turntable pit, a stock siding being led across it.

Stirling became a 'garage' of Perth, coded 29B in 1935, its only 'sub' being at Loch Tay. It served as 31B under St. Rollox from 1940, ending up after the post-1948 confusion as 63B, again part of the Perth District, with the ex-NBR Shore Road as an additional sub-shed. The allocation was around 35 engines; in 1954 it comprised one Compound 4–4–0, two LMS 2–6–4Ts, five MR/LMS '4F' 0–6–0s, four class '5' 4–6–0s, three CR 0–4–4Ts, one of which was out at Killin, five CR '3F' 0–6–0Ts and twelve CR 0–6–0s. Shore Road was closed on 16th September 1957 and its allocation of around a dozen ex-NB/LNE types, transferred to the main shed, labelled for convenience in BR days 'Stirling South'. There was a further

recoding, 65J, from April 1960, under the ex-NBR shed at Eastfield.

Diesel shunters were well in evidence at Stirling by the late 1950s and main line diesels, NBL and BRCW Type 2s had ousted steam by the summer of 1966. (It was 'closed to steam' on 13th June.) The previous year its allocation had fallen to only ten locos, six steam and four diesel, the latter housed for a while at the depot until a signing on point was established at the station.

Stirling in July 1952. The south gable end had been altered shortly before, making for a slightly less claustrophobic, if dull, building.
J. F. McEwan

No. 80060 on the old Polmadie 'table, 22nd August 1962. The Stirling locos were ousted by BCRW engines of the D5300 series and the unlamented NBL D6100 locos, which wilted very early on. What jobs remained were eventually covered by Grangemouth and the site is now cleared and partly sold off.
H. N. James

The industrial belt on the north bank of the Clyde was a relatively late development and in the 1890s Yoker was simply a village skirted by two rival railway lines. With the Rothesay Dock came rival branch lines to serve it, sidings, doublings and new roads. By 1934 Yoker was a strange district, people and housing somehow slotted in like afterthoughts in a confusing landscape of docks, railways and yards.

W. A. Camwell Collection

YOKER

Apparently referred to as 'Clydebank' in earlier years, Yoker shed opened around March 1907. It was designed as an outstation of Dawsholm and at first had only a pair of 0–4–0STs, to work the 'Whiteinch Tramway'. This line made its way through the streets, on private ground and served the various shipyards and engine works alongside. The shed also turned and serviced 0–6–0s, both those working traffic connected with the tramway and those with goods beyond Stobcross (now Finnieston) and Clydebank.

Yoker was obviously built in expectation of traffic on the opening of Rothesay Dock in April 1907. The allocation was then strengthened with 0–6–0Ts from Dawsholm, and the shed later became a stable for 0–6–0s, handling everything from iron ore to esparto grass trains, from the new dock. Rothesay provided a great part of Yoker's work, the outward traffic (particularly coal) not beginning to decline until after the Second World War. The engines, four of them in 1922, were changed only at fairly irregular intervals but visited Dawsholm frequently for repairs and washout. Yoker was very roughly contemporaneous with Dumbarton, having a like appearance and similar layout. The turntable differed in being of 60 ft. diameter (despite being a second-hand Cowans Sheldon unit, 'of 1887'.)

The building of the shed had been contracted to Lawson & Co. in January 1907 for the Caledonian had a habit almost of establishing an engine shed adjacent to such big new developments. This had served them well at Grangemouth but had proved a bit embarrassing at Seafield. Lawson's contract was 'confirmed' on 1st March 1907, at £1,891 1s. 4d. and on 3rd March it was ordered that 'incandescent burners . . . be fitted . . . in lieu of open gas flame'. *W. A. Camwell*

56250 and 56344 at Yoker. *R. J. Essery Collection*

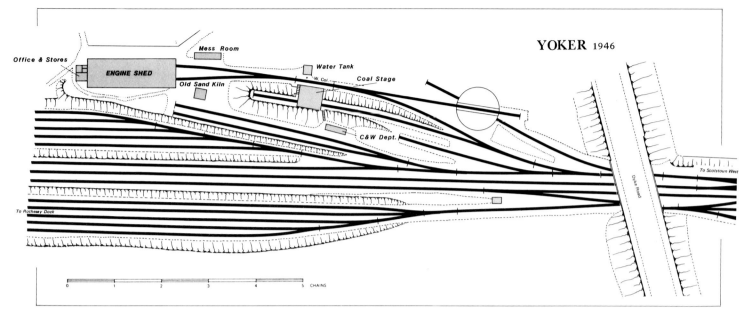

Yoker remained a sub-shed throughout LMS days, with, by 1949, a normal complement of a dozen engines, a '2F' 0–6–0 (tripping from Scotstown Yard to the decrepit and subsidence-afflicted Robroyston Yard), five '3F' 0–6–0Ts, four '2F' 0–6–0Ts and a pair of 0–4–0STs. In that year BR saw fit to code the shed, although the pattern of operations seems to have remained unaltered – repair work was still the responsibility of Dawsholm. As '65G' the shed's allocation had risen in 1950 to thirteen, 0–4–0STs Nos. 56030 and 56039, 0–6–0Ts Nos. 56158, 56161, 56168, 56170, 56238, 56250, 56297, 56315 and 56339, a '2F' 0–6–0 No. 57259, and an ex-NBR 'Y9' tank, 0–4–0ST No. 68112. On 19th August 1951 the shed contained 0–4–0STs Nos. 56030 and 56031, 0–6–0Ts Nos. 56170 and 56339, 0–6–0s Nos. 57346 and 57394 and ex-Great Eastern 0–6–0T No. 68551.

Hidden and remote, in the midst of a confusion of lines and yards, Yoker attracted little attention in LMS days but redundant materials from the 'coaling bench' at Airdrie were made available for improvements in the early 1940s, at a cost of £260. In October 1946 new mess room and stores in pre-cast concrete were authorised. By 1956 0–6–0 diesel shunters were supplementing the steam engines, reduced to three only by 1959. The shed itself was reported 'closed' in January 1964 but a signing-on point remained in use and diesel operation continued from 'Yoker'. On the last Thursday in July 1964, for instance, the Dawsholm records reveal several D8000 Type 1 diesels to have been at work in the vicinity, D8100, D8101, D8110 etc. with shunters D3386, D3899 and smaller examples like D2771. There was a regular ballast working, on Wednesdays or Thursdays, normally entrusted to an 0–6–0 diesel. On the closure of Dawsholm some seventy drivers and firemen 'were attached to a new booking on point at Yoker (LNER)'. This was in fact Yoker Yard, an ex-NBR/LNER establishment now more or less abandoned but earmarked for a new EMU depot.

The shed had a remote quality unusual in a city; tender engines were serviced there but it was notable for its clutch of dock tanks. At certain times all of them would be out at work with the shed apparently deserted. G. H. Robin in *The Railway Magazine* of January 1959, 'The Lanarkshire & Dumbartonshire Railway', describes 'some half dozen engines, formerly 0–6–0 tanks but now being replaced by diesel shunters, are used on three shifts.'

H. C. Casserley

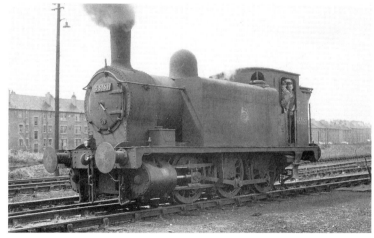

'Beetlecrusher' out at work in the Yoker yards, June 1958.

Tony Wright

No. 16010, the Airdrie 'pug'.   *W. H. Whitworth*

SHEDS CLOSED PRIOR TO 1947

AIRDRIE

The original shed serving the CR terminus at Airdrie, opened on 19th April 1886, was a wooden building of two roads, with 42 ft. turntable and open coal stage alongside. An extension of the shed was ordered on 5th October 1897, at a cost of £200 but only two years later, on 21st November 1899, the building was entirely burnt down, the cause of the disaster being 'officially unknown'. On 6th February 1900 the CR Engineers Department, Western Division, pondered its successor – the 'New Engine Shed, Airdrie', to 'accomodate 12 Engines to replace the shed destroyed by fire'. An estimate of £3,300 was approved and the new shed, enlarged to three roads and doubled in length, duly appeared, occupying part of the old site and utilising the old pits. The contract had been approved on 1st May 1900 and the shed opened in November. A more substantial coaling stage was now provided, on a modest earth ramp, but the old turntable was dispensed with. Airdrie's dozen or so locos were in any case all tanks, 4–4–0Ts and 0–4–4Ts for the passenger service with 0–6–0Ts and 0–4–0STs on goods and shunting work, and a triangle lay close at hand. In September 1906 further improvements were under consideration: 'Airdrie; proposed extension of coaling bench accommodation and covering over the same; also the erection of a sand kiln. Estimate £350. Approved'. On closure, in LMS days, part of this covering found its way to Yoker at a cost of £260.

Airdrie, an outstation of Dawsholm both in Caledonian and LMS days, remained home to a handful of 0–4–4Ts, 0–6–0Ts and 0–4–0STs, finally closing on 11th September 1939.

ALLOA

The Caledonian, in combative mood, arrived in the town itself in 1885, having taken over the local Alloa Railway and its impressive swing bridge over the Forth. (The Caledonian already owned the goods line to 'South Alloa' across the Forth from Alloa itself.) A connection between the Caledonian and the North British was made in October 1889 and, although the latter had erected their own two-road stone shed, with 40 ft. turntable, at least as early as 1865, the CR does not seem to have sought accommodation.

By 1902 the Caledonian decided that they, too, needed premises of a permanent nature and £860 was authorised for 'an Engine shed and siding at North Alloa'. The following year the tender of one J.J. & P. McLachlan was accepted, at £696/8/3½. A drawing exists (see p. 167) but little more is known of this shed other than the fact that it stood in the Caledonian goods yard, some distance from Alloa station near to the north bank of the Forth. It was demolished by 1935, after which it is assumed, an LMS engine was no longer outbased in the town. Stirling had always been the main shed, providing in

1922, for instance, a 4–4–0, No. 1195 (LMS No. 14112), replaced in 1923 by No. 14114.

ALYTH

A shed was provided at Alyth from August 1861. It lay on the north side of the station, a robust, well-proportioned building in brick – on a visit in 1950, after the shed's closure, a correspondent of the *Railway Observer* could still find it impressive: 'An excellent brick-built shed with room for two locos still stands at Alyth and contained a brake van'.

A turntable was added after opening, 40 ft in diameter, and ordered replaced after many years by a redundant 'table from 'Perth North'. In April 1913 this unit had been 'sent to Alyth', 'to replace a very old one'. It is not clear if this substitution was indeed carried out – the Perth 'table is recorded as 40 ft whilst Alyth is shown later having a 42 ft turntable. It would in any case have been as old, if not older, than the Alyth example; surviving into BR days, its builder's plate enabled the year of manufacture to be registered as 1862. On examination in 1952 it was noted that the original Cowans Sheldon 'table had been 40 ft, and had been extended to 42 ft, at 'an unknown date'.

There does not seem to have been a coal stage at Alyth, the operation relying simply on open wagons. The locomotives involved in latter years included 'an 0–4–4T or two' supplied by Forfar. This certainly appears to

Alyth (*top*) on 29th September 1935 and (*bottom*) on 2nd May 1950, with 0—4—4T No. 55194. Little ostensibly changed after closure, engines taking water on the shed road.

W. A. Camwell

Site of Baillieston, 1937. The shed's origins seem linked with the Monkland Canal section of the Forth & Clyde Navigation, for this concern had an engine shed in the vicinity of Nackerty in 1860. This may have developed into the CR Baillieston of the 1870s.   *W. A. Camwell*

have been the practice from at least 1917 but in 1900 'and on for many years' Alyth had been an outstation of Dundee; in all probability this had been the case since the 1860s/1870s.

The shed was reportedly closed (this very fine building ... which became redundant as services were reduced') as early as 3rd January 1942; after which engines stood on the approach road to take water. This practice apparently ceased on withdrawal of the passenger service in July 1951 but the shed still stood, trackless, at least as late as 1960.

ARDROSSAN

A four-road, northlight pattern shed built in brick, Ardrossan was completed by the contractors, Robert McAlpine in September 1888, the Caledonian being relative latecomers in the town. The turntable, 42 ft. in diameter, was delivered from Cowans Sheldon in that year and was enlarged after about 1900, to 51 ft. 4 ins. The shed was an outstation of Polmadie in CR days but passenger traffic did not fully live up to the company's hopes; it comprised mainly imported iron ore and esparto grass, with passenger receipts poor, excepting the Arran steamer. Drummond 0–6–0s were used on the goods and mineral trains and the 4–4–0 *Eglinton* was often put on the boat trains – the Earl of Eglinton owned most of the Ardrossan Harbour capital. Local trains were generally

hauled by the Connor 4–4–0 'Dundee Bogies' and after 1903 a Polmadie 0–8–0 was used on the ore trains which went to Coatbridge and Motherwell. 0–4–4Ts and 0–4–2s used on the Irvine branch were later shedded at Ardrossan but the engine complement remained low, many of the turns into the town involving engines working in from their home districts with empties and returning loaded, as soon as maybe.

No more than a dozen locos were accommodated at the shed (renamed Ardrossan North following Grouping), details of which have been recorded in notes by W. L. Callan in the *Journal* of the Stephenson Locomotive Society, 1959, and by W. L. Callan and G. Robin in the *Railway World* of 1961. In the 1920s three or four 4–4–0s were in use, 'Dunalastair I' Nos. 14312, 14315 and 14317 and a 'Dunalastair II' No. 14326. There were also 0–6–0Ts for dock work, 0–6–0s on goods and an 0–4–4T for the Kilwinning East-Irvine Bank Street Branch.

Amalgamation with the rather larger GSWR establishment was inevitable but the old CR shed survived the decade to be closed at the last in July 1931, locos and men transferring to the ex-GSW premises. The Caledonian shed remained intact (a store for idle locos) for several years at least, before demolition; indeed, the turntable was usable, and listed as such by the Scottish Region, as late as 1953.

BAILLIESTON

Baillieston was a two-road engine shed 'ordered to be erected' on 10th December 1872, to coincide with pits being sunk nearby. Located at 'the Nackerty', it lay amidst colliery lines and waste bings, occupying almost the only level ground about. A 'pug' was outbased from Polmadie from the start and by the 1930s usually No. 16027 or 16035 was responsible for shunting Bredisholm and other pits to the east of Baillieston. The shed is little known and its 'status' is imperfectly understood – it is absent from LMS records and was linked directly to the activities of the adjacent pits. It could hold four 'pugs', and privately owned engines worked 'turn about' with the CR example; they were stabled and maintained at the shed, it would appear. The Polmadie 'pug' might very well have worked on a 'hire' basis, the shed effectively (even if it was not the original intention) maintained for the convenience of colliery locos. It closed in July 1935, together with the local collieries and was reported demolished in May of the following year.

'BALLOCH'

There were engine facilities at Balloch, on metals joint with the NBR comprising, by the mid-1890s at least, a 45 ft. turntable, on the west side of the line between Balloch station proper and Balloch Pier and, on the east side, by the River Leven, sidings and a coal stage. To the Caledonian 'Balloch' was no more than a locomotive yard, with water column, coal stage and turntable (enlarged with a 60 ft. Ransomes Rapier unit in 1938). In July 1915 the North British suggested a cover over the then-shared coal stage, the Caledonian's half amounting to £180.

At no time did the Caledonian use Balloch as a stabling point, all engines 'came or went' to Dumbarton. The line between Dumbarton and Balloch had become 'Joint' from 1896 with the existing NBR Balloch turntable thus transformed into 'joint property'. It had been put in (replacing one of 1850) by the Caledonian and Dunbartonshire Junction Railway in 1858 or thereabouts, and was renewed again under Caledonian pressure in 1895, for the forthcoming joint ownership and the larger CR 0–6–0s.

BALQUHIDDER

Balquhidder was built in fashion highly reminiscent of the replacement shed at Loch Tay (see page 95), though it was of a rather earlier period, the line opening from Crieff in April 1905. The shed was provided with a 60 ft. turntable and housed for many years a '2F' 0–6–0 outstationed from Perth, represented through July/August 1939, for example by No. 17453. At the start an 0–4–4T was also

The Balquhidder 0–6–0. A letter in *Trains Illustrated* of June 1956, from F. Turner recalls the Balquhidder crew roused from their beds to pilot an overloaded train Comrie-Oban only to be disciplined 'for bringing out an engine without permission!'   *B. Hilton Collection*

Balquhidder shed.   *B. Hilton Collection*

Bankfoot on 13th June 1936. From *The Locomotive* of 1931: 'For many years the Caledonian Railway operated one of the small Drummond tank engines, No. 173 of the 0–4–4 class but since 1920 one of the larger McIntosh engines No. 159 (LMS 15209) has been employed, this engine working local goods through to Perth.'   *W. A. Camwell*

there, working to Crieff and back with a single brake composite. The 0–6–0 stood as pilot for the Glen Ogle climb as far as Glenoglehead Box, when the train was over its load for the gradient. Banking was not permitted on this section.

Water was not available at the shed itself but would be taken from one of three columns at the station, one each to serve the up and down platforms and one the branch platform. The last cost £55 and dated from 1906. Despite such provision, by the summer of 1938 the LMS Scottish Committee could report that the supply at Balquhidder was 'inadequate' and approved £150 for a new 8 inch pipe 'to connect the existing reservoir feeding the storage tank direct to the water column at Balquhidder thereby increasing supply from 8000 to 21000 gallons. Formerly obtained from Lord Breadalbane's Estate at nominal rate of one shilling per annum. The new proprietors the Misses Watters, Edinample, Lochearnhead, want £20 p.a. ... Agreed.'

Many of these remote sub-sheds existed in Scotland and inevitably a large number did not survive the harsher economics of LMS rule. Balquhidder was accordingly abandoned in the early 'forties (dates available vary from June of 1940 to 28th February

1942) and the service worked by a Crieff locomotive. The building was demolished but the turntable (almost certainly out of use since the outbreak of war) siding, pit etc. remained in place increasingly lost amidst the vegetation.

BANKFOOT

The line at Bankfoot opened in March 1906, a light railway venture noted by the *Railway Gazette*. The account unfortunately does not mention the shed, a minute timber structure designed to house the single engine sent from Perth to work the branch service: 'The Bankfoot and Strathord Light Railway, which is worked by the Caledonian, was opened for goods, minerals and livestock traffic on Monday last. The line is three miles in length and connects with the CR main line at Strathord [where a separate platform beside the main line station was provided]. The station at Bankfoot has been designed to give accommodation to a considerable amount of traffic, and arrangements will be made at Strathord Junction to enable through excursions to be run from Perth and other large centres to Bankfoot. Although nominally a light railway, the construction and equipment of the line are equal to the CR ordinary branch line standard.'

The line was eventually purchased outright by the Caledonian, in 1913, but the responsibility for its construction and operation, in every detail, lay with the parent company – before the branch opened the Bankfoot Co had had to ask the Caledonian for a further supply of rails, to allow them to complete the line into the engine shed itself.

The first engine had been a Drummond 0–4–4T, replaced later by a standard example. This was certainly the case by 1915 and only at livestock sale times did an 0–6–0 appear for the 'cattle specials'. The passenger service was withdrawn in April of 1931 and although the shed, an attractive little building on a dwarf brick wall, still stood in 1936, it went out of use at an early date; obscure and ill-documented, it had effectively been abandoned by about 1920/21, a new bus service proving too much for the light railway. The only water to be had was from the trestle-supported tank outside and engines had recourse to this supply long after the shed itself went out of use.

BLAIRGOWRIE

In its proportions, appearance and layout the shed at Blairgowrie, with two roads, was thoroughly in keeping with CR practice. It was not built with the line, however, and in the mid-1860s a small, it is thought wooden, engine shed, some 50 ft. by 20 ft., sufficed. This building almost certainly dated from opening of the line in August 1855 but no turntable or coal stage was provided.

The whole terminus was subsequently rearranged and opportunity taken to completely rebuild the shed, with turntable and water tank provided at the same time. Stone-built, it was a through building with access direct from the 'table, a Cowans Sheldon balanced 42 ft. unit which bore the date 1887.

In Scottish Midland Junction days, the engine came from Coupar Angus and the Scottish North Eastern (formed upon the amalgamation of the SMJ and the Aberdeen company) also appear to have had an engine at Coupar for use on the branch. It is not known, however, if any shed accommodation was provided at the latter site; certainly none existed in 1850. From around 1868–1869 the Blairgowrie trains were worked through from Dundee via Newtyle; this was in Caledonian days and 2–4–0s were used on passenger runs with 0–4–2s on goods, in accordance with period practice. The arrangement appears to have been that passengers for the Perth or Aberdeen directions were put off at Coupar Angus while the train went on to Dundee. There are also suggestions that displaced 4–4–0 'Oban bogies' worked through to Blairgowrie prior to the arrival of 0–4–4Ts. In the period before Grouping, a single standard 0–4–4T was stationed at Blairgowrie for the branch service and by 1935 two of the ex-

Blairgowrie on 21st September 1935.   *W. A. Camwell*

CR passenger tanks were normally in use. The shed, sub to Dundee, closed in January 1942 but survived in private use for very many years, at least until the 1960s.

BONNYBRIDGE

The Kilsyth and Bonnybridge line was not 'joint' in the usually understood sense – both

the Caledonian and the North British worked over it, with separate staff and stock and shared expenses. There was little passenger traffic but quite a bit of coal and odd (but not insubstantial) items like cast iron guttering and domestic stoves. The coal traffic declined, however, and the Caledonian had removed itself by 1921. The company had

Bonnybridge on 6th June 1949.   *W. A. Camwell*

Callander on 21st September 1935.

W. A. Camwell

shunted the small yard at Bonnybridge from the start (1888) and a small shed had been put up – it was in effect an outstation of Denny, in its turn an outstation of Stirling.

The first engine is said to have been an 0–4–0ST, followed by 0–6–0STs of Conner vintage, replaced in time by a standard 0–6–0T.

BRAYTON

This was a little known shed, in the northern part of the English Lake District, reached in circuitous fashion from Kirtlebridge via the Solway Junction Railway and a stretch of North British metals, to meet the Maryport and Carlisle Railway some yards east of Brayton station, a single track connection known as 'Brayton Junction'. The two-road shed, barely able to accommodate a pair of 0–6–0s, lay with some sidings in the fork formed by the CR and M & C lines. Both roads continued through the shed, one of them onto a 42 ft. turntable and a well sunk nearby supplied a tank and column on the turntable approach.

The shed, remote from the rest of the Caledonian system, was contemporaneous with the line from Annan of September 1869, taken across the Solway Firth in July of the following year. The shed itself reportedly came into use on 13th September 1869 but was abandoned in 1895/1896. It was demolished around 1904, leaving only the turntable in place (it was still in position indeed in 1923) but engines continued to stable over-

night until at least 1909 and probably to 1921, when the Solway Firth viaduct closed. Four men, it turns out, a driver, a passed fireman and two passed cleaners, continued to be based at Brayton, long years after closure.

BROCKETSBRAE

The line through the valley of the Nethan, 'the Lesmahagow Branch', opened in stages from 1853 to 1856, carrying only minerals until the mid–1860s when a sparse passenger service began. The shed opened in 1877, following a Board instruction of 7th November the previous year for 'an Engine Shed and Turntable'. The first known engine based at 'Brocketsbrae' was one of the 2–4–0Ts, later replaced by a former Oban line 2–4–2T, replaced in its turn by an 0–4–4T and occasionally an 0–6–0. There may have been almost enough space for two engines, with an 0–6–0 or some kind of engine for mineral purposes, shedded along with the tank. The 1888 working Timetable suggests that an 0–6–0 was needed for mineral work.

The station was known as 'Lesmahagow' until 1st May 1905 when a station of that name opened on the 'New Lanark Lines' to the west. The older station was then renamed 'Brocketsbrae'.

The shed, which lay on the east side of the station, was part of the Hamilton district and closed early in the LMS period. In November 1929 the 'removal of the engine shed' was discussed and in August 1932 the final

removal of 'engine shed pit and the siding' was authorised.

BROUGHTON

See Peebles. A temporary shed serving the then terminus of the Peebles branch. Opened in November 1860 and put out of use early in 1864.

BROUGHTY FERRY

The original shed and works of the Dundee and Arbroath Railway, largely dispersed to Arbroath by the 1860s.

CALLANDER

Callander was the terminus of the Dunblane Doune and Callander Railway, promoted by the Scottish Central with more than half an eye on the through route to Oban. A shed of suitably generous proportions, matching this erstwhile gateway to the west, was accordingly provided at opening, in the summer of 1858. It was massively built in stone, with two roads and stood on the north side of the Dunblane Doune & Callander station, more or less in open fields and overlooked by only a few primitive terraces – 'soldiers settlements'. A well nearby served the shed, but the turntable, 40 ft in diameter, lay in the station itself, at the extreme end of the line.

The extension to Oban (the first section came into use in 1870) took its leave of the main line some yards to the east, where a much better alignment could be obtained,

Dalmally station and engine shed.   *B. Mathews Collection*

leaving the old terminus a goods station, isolated on a short spur. The old 40 ft 'table, based on the dimensions of Scottish Central engines, proved an early problem and on takeover by the Caledonian in 1865 a fresh survey generated much discussion as to a suitable replacement. A spare 45 ft example was suggested at one point but it was said to be too small for the passengers and goods classes then in use. The company eventually settled on a new 50 ft unit, installed upon the shed approach; it afterwards controlled access to the building which now found itself on the south side of the running lines. In common with the Oban 'table, the Callander example was enlarged in 1902 (to 60 ft), for new McIntosh '55' class 4–6–0s, a Cowans Sheldon balanced unit costing, with extra siding, £1,967.

An outstation of Stirling throughout its days, Callander, prior to the opening of the first section westwards in 1870, housed only two engines, a passenger and a goods. There was presumably some increase between 1870 and 1880, for work to Tyndrum and then to Dalmally prior to completion through to Oban in 1880. 2–4–0s were in use in this period and, of course, in 1880 the ill-fated 2–4–2Ts arrived. In June 1880 four 2–4–2Ts

Dalmally shed on 28th September 1935.   *W. A. Camwell*

Dumfries ex-Caledonian, 20th June 1936.

W. A. Camwell

were at Callander for Oban trains, Nos 156, 159, 160 and 161, but by January of the following year only one remained, No. 158, which had been placed on the Stirling service. Three '670' class 0–4–2s worked the Oban services but with the arrival of Brittain's 4–4–0 'Oban bogies', the workings shifted to Stirling, Callander returning to the practice of earlier years with only a pair of locos for the former Dunblane Doune & Callander section.

The passenger engine around the late 1880s and early 1890s was one of Conner's 2–4–0s with 7 ft wheels but, with the advent of the 'Dunalastair II' 4–4–0s, one was sent to Callander – No. 779 (LMS 14335) of 1898, named *Breadalbane* after Lord Breadalbane, a CR shareholder, a former director and member of the LNWR board. *Breadalbane* remained the Callander engine until 1924 when, on receiving crimson lake livery, it was removed to Stirling. Its departure in that year probably marks the closure of the shed – goods working by a Drummond 0–6–0 also ceased at this time, given over to an Oban pick-up engine – though the shed still stood, in fine condition, well over fifty years later.

DALMALLY

The shed here, a substantial and lengthy stone building with 48 ft turntable outside, presumably dates from May 1877 when the relevant section of the Callander and Oban opened to Dalmally. The extension on to Oban was begun about a year later, opening finally on 30th June 1880. Once traffic was underway, the shed seems no longer to have been necessary for regular work – it was not put out of use altogether but rather kept available for the regular sheep sales. An extra engine was then required, having to act as shunter and fetch trucks stored at stations in the area. This is believed to have been the only use to which the shed was put but it must be mentioned that timetables of the late 1880s show early morning departures from Dalmally, suggesting that an engine could have stabled overnight.

The shed was finally abandoned around 1930/1931, when road lorries took over most of the sheep transport, but it remained intact, with turntable, for a number of years, the building itself until at least 1938.

DENNY

There was a small shed here, measuring some 50 ft. by 30 ft., apparently of two roads, one of which terminated inside the building. The line was built as part of the Scottish Central Railway tapping an ironstone pit and serving mills and other works by the River Carron. The shed, to the east of the station near the 'Denny Branch Extension' (the SCR Ingliston Branch, opened 1st January 1860), did not open immediately. It was built at a time subsequent to September 1862 and had long been in use by 1913. Since it was of 'CR pattern', 1869 is seen as a likely opening date. By the time of the First World War the branch had prospered indeed, and sidings, goods yard and two goods sheds had appeared. No turntable was provided, engines off mineral trains turning on a series of colliery connections which made a rough triangle. A water column stood at the shed, an outstation of Stirling over many years. Denny was closed 'on 28th July 1930' and the building subsequently demolished.

DOLPHINTON

The Caledonian line from Carstairs made an end-on junction here with the North British and at one time both companies maintained small one-road engine sheds. The CR building lay on a lengthy siding to the west of the station; plans of 1896 show only a turntable, its single spur occupied some ten years later by an engine shed, approximately 40 ft. by 20 ft. A water column fed from a small tank was provided on the turntable road.

There are further possibilities here, in that the OS plan of 1896 is in error, omitting the building, for on 10th November 1868 the old Dunblane loco shed was ordered 'to Dolphinton'. Certainly an engine was based there at an early date, reputedly a 2–4–0 at first. Its duties were not onerous, the line passing through farming land with only three trains daily, probably mixed. The former Solway Junction 0–4–2s were later sent to Carstairs for the branch, shedded weekly (or fortnightly) about at Dolphinton. 0–4–4Ts, 0–6–0s and occasionally 4–4–0s were subsequently employed and after 1915 Carstairs used almost any available engine – Dunalastair I, II and III 4–4–0s were common and latterly Compounds were seen at work.

Dolphinton closed on 31st December 1915, the final removal of the building and turntable recorded in LMS minutes of May 1933.

DUMFRIES ('ST. MARY'S')

The Caledonian maintained a single-road engine shed here, a solid building in stone for the use of the company's engines working down from Lockerbie. Opened in August 1863, it was a through building and lay off

Greenhill on 20th September 1935. The allocation on closure is given as: '17233, 17283, to Stirling, 17301 to Motherwell, 17274 to Grangemouth, 17366 to Dawsholm.'   *W. A. Camwell*

the CR goods station spur north of St. Mary's Street. A 42 ft. turntable was installed a few yards to the north of the shed with (originally) an open coal stage at the very extremity of the yard. A water column fed from a tank stood alongside the shed road where a small hand crane was later provided, presumably to assist coaling. The turntable was enlarged in 1902, a new 60 ft. Cowans Sheldon unit being approved in May at a cost of £900. On Grouping, the shed was immediately redundant, engines making use of the nearby (and more conveniently sited) ex-GSWR shed. The LMS Scottish Local Committee (Traffic and Works) considered what to do with the building at the end of December 1923, ordering it 'to be made suitable for use by the Carriage & Wagon Department in connection with the repair of wagons'. This ensured its survival and it remained, in excellent condition, until at least the mid-sixties, when the entire site was offered for sale.

DUNBLANE

The Scottish Central Railway maintained a small shed here, housing engines required for banking up to Kinbuck. On 10th November 1868 the shed was ordered removed from further use (see Dolphinton); since 1865 it is believed the banker (or pilot) operated direct from Stirling.

EAST KILBRIDE

A shed was authorised here and a tender accepted, on 27th November 1877. It reportedly opened in May 1878 but by 1896 no trace existed.

EDZELL

A tiny single-road shed was erected here, terminus of the 'Brechin and Edzell Railway', opening with the line in June 1896. It stood on the west of the yard, south of the station itself; the building could barely accom-

modate a single tank engine and no turntable was provided. It appears to have been dispensed with around 1910 and was demolished by 1922. Brechin engines afterwards worked the service.

EGLINTON STREET

A shed was maintained here, on the southern approaches to Central station, over some considerable period. It was opened in 1878 (the tender was approved on 22nd November the previous year) to relieve pressure on Polmadie when the new Central station opened. It was closer to the terminus and afforded engines a quicker turn-round than was available using the main shed and the bottleneck then existing between Bridge Street Junction and Gushetfaulds. Eglinton Street was thus an outstation of Polmadie, a convenient servicing/turning point related to the main depot as Buchanan Street to St. Rollox. The station lay between Lilybank Road and Crawford Street, the four-road brick shed occupying much of the ground on the west side. It was a constricted site, the shed and turntable (42 ft. at first, enlarged by 1915 to 51 ft.) fronting Crawford Street with every available piece of space put to use; spurs were led off the turntable and the coaling stage and ramp were positioned amidst the yard with very little room to spare.

Assuming Eglinton Street's principal role to be servicing point for the Polmadie depot is fraught with doubt; there is something odd about the place in that what usefulness it possessed in this regard vanished within a matter of five years or so. Perhaps it should never have been built, for on 18th November 1884 Drummond is found recommending its conversion for carriage storage and cleaning, to which the Board assents. Around 1902 the question of using the yard for locos once again arises: the shed was 'not to be opened' but the turntable etc brought into use for engines 'waiting over for a return working'. 'Local engines' would not be catered for.

In October 1914 two new pits had been ordered, 'to facilitate the Examination of engines' at a cost of £300 and in April 1920 'alterations' were authorised to the coaling bench 'In order to facilitate the Coaling of Engines'. 'At present prices' the cost was estimated at £840, compared to an estimated pre-war cost of £335. The difference was made up of a 'charge against the government', the changes having the added advantage of an estimated annual saving amounting to 'about £250'.

By now engines made frequent use of Eglinton Street yard but the shed itself was never reopened – even before the coaling bench alterations were considered, minutes of the CR Engineers' Western District indicate the disposal of the building: 'May 4th 1920: West of Scotland Aviation Co. have applied. . . . to be allowed to use the Engine Shed at Eglinton Street Station as a garage for motor cars and to form a doorway into the shed from Crawford Street. . . . . The Engine Shed at Eglinton Street has been disused for many years'. This application was approved, subject to a rent of £150 per annum. This was agreed by the lessee and the building latterly became a road motor depot, coming at last into the control of NCL.

The yard continued in use throughout LMS days – Carlisle local engines were often to be seen on Saturday afternoons and Compounds at times. The coaling bench was found convenient for 'special' loads of coal, for testing purposes, and a class '5' 4–6–0 was so occupied on 27th October 1948. Eglinton Street went out of use with the introduction of diesel sets from 1959–1960, Cook Street sufficing for day-to-day needs.

GARTSHERRIE

The Garnkirk and Glasgow Railway appears to have established an 'Engine House' here, about 1840, timetables indicating the presence of at least one locomotive, engaged on passenger and goods duties. A map of 1848

Irvine on 11th August 1937. *W. A. Camwell*

shows a two-road shed roughly 100 ft. long but no turntable (though there should have been one); the building was of the through type and lay just to the north of the station but south of the Summerlee Ironworks. Like the main line, it was doubtless built on arches, with a tank and pump house (water was drawn from the canal basin) alongside. It was closed in the mid-1860s on the opening of Motherwell.

'GOVAN'

There are references to a shed 'at Govan', on the GSWR/CR 'Paisley Joint Railway'. What details are to hand will appear in a subsequent volume covering sheds of Glasgow and South Western Railway origin.

GREENHILL

At Greenhill the Caledonian main line, leaving the Central Lowlands for Stirling, swept close to the Edinburgh and Glasgow main line of the North British. The two were connected by a loop owned by the Caledonian, from the CR 'Lower Junction' to 'Upper Junction' on the NB line, and a variety of sidings were in use by the early 1860s. The Caledonian established a major creosoting works between the loop and their main line and laid down a 40 ft. turntable close by, serving the yards west of the CR station.

There is little evidence to be gleaned from maps, such as they are, but the Scottish Central Railway had an engine shed in existence by 1852, when complaints were being made to Perth 'from the depot at Greenhill'. Something at least still seems to have been in

use in the early 1880s for there is a Board of Trade report regarding a derailment: contained within it are references to pilot engines customarily moving to the rear of the train for banking to Cumbernauld Glen, then returning to *Greenhill Sheds*.

A new two-road shed, in wood, was opened in 1900 nearer to the station, the contract having been placed on 13th June 1899. It again stood alongside the loop, opposite and facing the creosote works. The building measured some 160 ft. by 30 ft., and a 60 ft. turntable was installed at the head of the yard. One road led through the building, a siding was available for coal wagons in the absence of a proper coal stage, and water was taken from a substantial pre-existing reservoir alongside the new shed. Some half dozen 18" 0–6–0 goods were kept at Greenhill for local work together with 0–6–0STs for shunting, both in the important CR/NB exchange yard and at the creosote works. In 1928, much of the work was tranferred to Grangemouth though at first this seems to have been more in the nature of an official manoeuvre. Shunting engines, 'pugs' by now, remained for the creosote work and other engines were stored, it is believed, out of use. These may indeed be the 0–6–0s listed by the *Railway Observer* in 1933 as the Greenhill allocation:

18″ 0–6–0
17233, 17255, 17274, 17301, 17366, 17383.

0–4–0ST
16025, 16032.

The shed is considered to have closed in the early part of 1935, but the creosoting did not finally end until the 1939–1945 war

period and it would be reasonable to suppose that a 'pug' at least could have found some further employment until then.

IRVINE

Irvine, a single-road wooden shed with 50 ft. turntable, opened with the short branch from Kilwinning in 1890. It lay north of the station, separated from it by the Quarry Lane bridge. Traffic, even golfing excursions, proved ever a disappointment and a single Drummond 0–4–4T (No. 191 for many years) sufficed for the branch workings, stabled overnight in the little shed. A turntable was available for 0–6–0s and occasionally a smaller 4–4–0 on Territorial camp traffic; after the line reopened in 1919 an 0–4–2 tender engine was allocated, working the branch from Kilwinning with combined goods trips as required. This took it to Lugton but around 1925 the job was transferred to Ardrossan. Irvine shed was then closed, the engine travelling light to and from the branch.

KILBIRNIE

Caledonian ingress to this iron-producing district amidst the hills of Kilbirnie Loch came late, the 'Lanarkshire and Ayrshire Railway' branch a foray into GSWR country encouraged by local business interest. A two-road wooden shed, similar to the building at Kirtlebridge opened with the line in 1889; it was equipped with a 50 ft. turntable but coaling was at its simplest, from open wagons parked in the yard. Ostensibly the line ran as part of the Lanarkshire and Ayrshire

Site of Kilbirnie shed, 28th April 1936.

I. W. Hannan

company, but day-to-day operation was entirely in the hands of the Caledonian. On 10th January 1905 the Engineers Department of the Western Division discussed the provision of a new siding for the Kilbirnie loco coal wagons; costs were estimated at £155, eased in that 'the L & A have agreed to pay'.

Kilbirnie was an outstation of Polmadie from CR days into the LMS period and for many years housed only a pair of 0–4–4Ts. The earliest engines had been 2–4–0s on passenger services and Drummond 0–6–0s on goods and minerals. The latter continued on this work throughout the existence of the branch but 0–4–4Ts replaced the 2–4–0s from around 1906.

The line lost its passenger service toward the end of 1930 and the shed closed at the same time – it still stood, however, in the overgrown station area over six years later. The 50 ft. Cowans Sheldon turntable was listed 'available for use' as late as 1948 but its removal from the 'official list' of 1953 dates its final demise.

KILMARNOCK

There was a small two-road shed at Kilmarnock for the use of CR engines working the joint Glasgow Barrhead and Kilmarnock line. Stone-built with a slated roof, it measured about 160 ft. by 40 ft. and had a brick water tower outside. A 42 ft. turntable, listed in the CR Working Timetable Appendix as

Kilmarnock on 26th June 1937. Built in red sandstone, it was the only 'Joint' line shed to be used solely by the Caledonian. It is thus a matter of convenience to mention it here; the other 'Joint' line establishments will be described in the next volume, along with former Glasgow & South Western Railway sheds.

W. A. Camwell

'Kilmarnock (GB & K)', was provided in the yard, with a water column on the approach siding. With the much larger G & SW establishment close by, the shed on Grouping was rendered immediately redundant and as early as 27th December 1923 the LMS Scottish Local Committee (Traffic and Works) decided that 'the former Joint Line Engine Shed at Kilmarnock be made suitable for use by the Carriage and Wagon Department in connection with the repair of wagons'. The shed had opened in June 1873 but had been rarely used since 1910, when the G & SWR had, as an economy move, taken over the full maintenance of the GB & K.

KIRRIEMUIR

The shed at Kirriemuir opened with the short branch from Kirriemuir Junction in 1854. Labelled 'Carriage House' in the Town Plan of January 1866, it was at first a single-ended building, standing on a lengthy siding some yards to the east of the station, by the local curling pond. There was no turntable for many years and one was not authorised until October 1899 – a second-hand example shortly afterwards installed at the rear of the shed. A small lean-to was added to the building itself and a new tank provided closer to the shed. The turntable appears to have still been in use in 1915 but Kirriemuir, close to and an outstation of Forfar (it had a Drummond 0–4–4T available in 1894), went inexplicably out of use at an early date. It was roofless by 1901 and by 1922 'most everything – turntable, building – except the water tank, had been removed.'

KIRTLEBRIDGE

A shed to serve engines working into England over the Solway Firth, through Annan to Bowness and Brayton, was opened in September 1869, a two-road building for four engines demolished under a local order of 16th July 1895. It was replaced by a two-road affair, wooden cladding on a timber frame, its construction recommended following an estimate of costs, £230, produced on 10th July 1894. A 42 ft. turntable had been provided since 1869 but coaling was from open wagons stabled on an adjacent siding. This in turn required alteration, McIntosh on 10th May 1904 recommending 'that the locomotive coal siding be slewed nearer the siding in which the engines stand while being coaled'. This was to cost £20, whilst early on the locomotive water supply had been arranged, with 'John Irving of Burnfoot and others . . . . . . from a pond on the Estate of Braes', at £8 per annum. It was piped to a single column on the turntable road, the only engine water, indeed, available at Kirtlebridge.

The new shed could comfortably house two engines, though at times more may have been allocated. By 1914 there were two 'old Oban bogies' allocated to Carlisle, with one in use 'fortnight about' for the Solway Junction workings. They replaced 2–4–0s on the passenger work but goods had since 1869 been given over to the two Solway Junction Railway 0–6–0s of 1868. They survived into the late 'twenties as LMS Nos. 17101 and 17102, the only 0–6–0s permitted to cross the Solway viaduct (closed in 1921). Kirtle-

Kirtlebridge after closure.   *W. A. Camwell*

Leadhills, or Wanlockhead, on 19th June 1936. It was not unusual for the branch engine to be snowed up inside the shed in winter, forced to await the succour of the Beattock plough.

W. A. Camwell

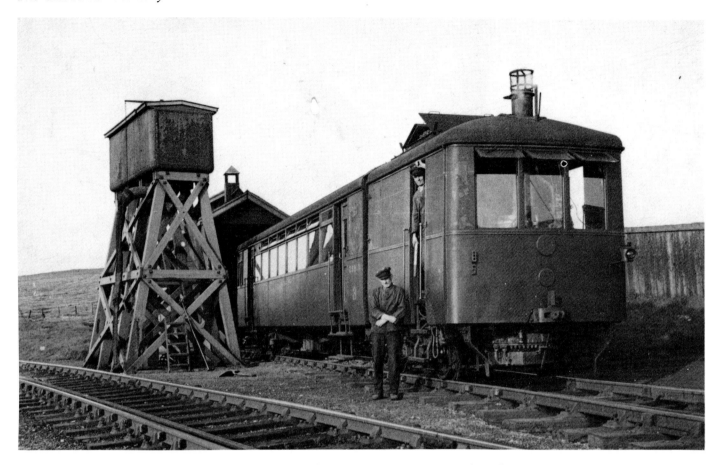

bridge had been an outstation of Carlisle since opening in 1869 but did not survive the LMS Depression stratagem, closing on 25th April 1931 when the truncated line to Annan was finally closed to passenger traffic.

The railcar (*above*) on 19th June 1936 and (*below*) an early branch train. *The Locomotive* of 14th January 1939 noted closure of the branch and its 'tramcar type' train, 'latterly a Knott End car'. Lead and silver had been mined about, it went on, 'with varying degrees of success for centuries . . . Tradition has it that during the reign of James V of Scotland, gold worth £100,000 was won and more recently has been found in sufficient quantities to make wedding rings for royal and ducal brides'.   *W. A. Camwell and J. Hooper Collection*

LEADHILLS

The Leadhills branch was a belated attempt to tap more closely the mineral wealth of Wanlockhead. The shed opened with the line from Elvanfoot in October 1901, the line being extended through to Wanlockhead a year later. There had long been a succession of lead mines (over several hundred years) to the south and west of Leadhills village, a high and remote miners' settlement, but only 'Wilsons Shaft' (according to contemporary maps) remained as a serious working when the railway arrived. The new Caledonian line crossed the tramway (the latter in a tunnel linking the mine with its washing mill) and in 1909 a second mine, Glengonnar Shaft, was in use, connected to the same tramway.

The little wooden shed, about 55 ft. by 18 ft., stood entirely isolated some distance to the east of the station, by the old 'Thief Slack Hass' quarry. Single 0–4–4Ts of various types formed the complement over many years, the engine outbased from Beattock. Various steam railcars were also tried on the line, in the 1930s, without conspicuous success. The shed had a rather charming trestle-built water tank, fed at first from a well and subsequently drawn from the local mine company supply. In 1916 the CR Super-

Lockerbie on 20th June 1936. From about 1920 until 1939/40 St. Rollox had a lodging turn to Lockerbie, leaving after midnight and, after many halts, reaching Lockerbie about 11 a.m. Local men took the engine over for shunting and got the train ready for departure around 1 a.m. the next day.
W. A. Camwell

intendent wrote regarding a proposal to pipe water from the Leadhills Mining Company, 'for use at the Leadhills Engine Shed'. The Engineer reported that 'the cost of laying a three-quarter inch connection between the Leadhills Mining Company pipe and the tank at the shed is about £27'. This was approved, along with the rental, 10/- per annum.

Leadhills, remaining a Beattock outpost to the end, was closed on 31st December 1938 with the abandonment of the line, the last engine being a McIntosh '2P' 0–4–4T No. 15217.

LOCKERBIE

Lockerbie shed, in period Caledonian style, is believed to have opened in 1863, in connection with the line to Dumfries. Stone-built in traditionally solid fashion, it had two roads, with a 42 ft. turntable, a balanced Cowans Sheldon product, provided alongside. Two short sidings led off this 'table to the rear of the shed and in latter days (after 1900) a low stone stage was built, served by the longest of the turntable spurs, and a new siding extended round the east side of the shed.

An outstation of Beattock, Lockerbie in its heyday operated some four or five locos,

0–4–4Ts and 0–6–0s in the main, though in its early days it saw CR 2–4–0 passenger and 0–4–2 goods engines as well as those taken over from the Portpatrick line. Through trains were run from Stranraer to Lockerbie, connecting with the main line services with corresponding workings in the return direction. Prior to 1914 unrebuilt Drummond 6 ft. 6 ins. 4–4–0s, along with an occasional 4–4–0, could be encountered, whilst during the Second World War several were stationed for the military traffic to and from Stranraer. All manner of work could be carried out on these engines, and lifting facilities (shear-legs) still existed as late as 1923. Of three rail-motors, Nos 2, 3 and 4 sent to Scotland for trial in 1928, one at least enjoyed a brief sojourn at Lockerbie, running to Dumfries on occasion and, 'according to rumour', was even tried out on the Kirtlebridge–Annan line. The Lockerbie motor was thought to have been used purely as an (unsuccessful) trial and is not believed to have engaged in any revenue-earning service. A variety of 'trial' engines could be found in the area over these years and, in addition to the railmotors, Lockerbie hosted an LMS 2–6–2T, used on regular trials, and two ex-LNWR engines, both 2–4–2T and 0–6–2T, tried out only with great temerity on 'dummy' trains.

The shed was effectively closed in April 1931, Dumfries taking over Lochmaben route duties; one road was cut short and buffered and the building closed up. The single 'Lockerbie Pilot', which shunted round about, subsequently travelled light from Beattock, worked for a shift by Lockerbie men. The turntable remained in working order and engines customarily stood on its approach road, where firebox clinker etc. could be conveniently dumped. The Lockerbie men transferred to Beattock in January 1951, though the 'pilot', usually an 0–4–4T, continued its daily visit. The shed building remains intact to this day.

METHVEN

The small brick shed at Methven opened with the terminus in January 1858, intended as overnight shelter for the branch engine. One of the early Conner/Brittain 0–4–4WTs was in regular use in the 1890s and 1900s, replaced in turn by a Drummond 0–4–4T. These became the typical inhabitants, out-stationed from Perth until replaced by Sentinel railcars in 1931. With this the shed closed, despite a later appearance 'under 29A Perth'. The 1938 *Railway Observer* described it as 'closed for some time now' and it still

The Caledonian Railway. Sheds Closed Prior to 1947

159

Methven shed and station.

B. Hilton Collection and W. A. Camwell

'Montrose LMS shed'.
H. C. Casserley Collection

stood, in fine condition, at least as late as the mid-1950s.

MONTROSE

This two-road shed, measuring about 52 ft. by 32 ft., opened along with the Aberdeen Railway branch from Dubton Junction in the latter part of 1849. A 15 ft. turntable at first lay immediately outside, on the southernmost road of the 'Engine House', a proper engine turntable, 45 ft. in diameter, not appearing until after November 1885 when a redundant unit at Perth was ordered to Montrose. When erected it had to be sited some distance away, on the north side of the line by the timber yard.

A sub-shed of Forfar, Montrose remained in use through to the eve of the Second World War, surviving Board instructions of 10th December 1872, to move the building 'to the west side of the line'. It remained firmly on its original site and continued to play host to the 0—4—2 types first sent there on opening. Scottish North Eastern Railway 0–4–2s of later vintage took over from the earlier Hawthorn (or similar) examples and by the 1880s and 1890s obsolete main line engines, 2–4–0s as well as 0–4–2s, could usually be found to work the line. As the numbers of these stalwarts dwindled, 0–4–4Ts came on to the work and a pair formed the normal complement in LMS days.

The Caledonian station at Montrose was closed to passengers on 30th May 1934 but the engines, working trains to the LNER station, continued to use the shed. The venerable building was, however, burnt down in May 1939, through the carelessness (it was said) of a nightcleaner; whatever the events, he redeemed himself by removing both engines before they could suffer serious damage. 'Regulars' Nos 15172 and 15200 were involved, the latter, as a result of blis-

tering, reappearing with tankside numbers. The 'shed' officially closed in September and the two engines, four sets of men and two cleaners, transferred to Brechin.

MORNINGSIDE

There was a shed at Morningside, for the Wishaw and Coltness Railway, from about 1842. Actually at Chapel, outside Morningside, its engine(s) were concerned with local ironworks traffic (the main goods incidentally, over the years); passenger work was sparse and the shed had been closed by around 1855.

By about the 1880s Caledonian engines (from Motherwell, no great distance away) stabled in the goods yard; in the early 1900s the North British began using the CR station (Morningside was an end-on junction between the two) and as a *quid pro quo* CR engines were able to stable overnight at the NB engine shed. There is a legend that before this arrangement was made, CR engines used the goods shed in the CR yard, vacated as traffic was cleared at the end of each day.

The NBR shed in turn suffered some disaster (it was sub to Bathgate) but following Nationalisation Morningside simply became a stabling point within the Motherwell 'catchment'.

MUIRKIRK

Prior to 1923 a Caledonian engine, off the CR Lanark–Muirkirk service, was stabled in the Glasgow and South Western shed here.

The story of this depot will be described in Volume VI.

NEILSTON

A turntable was provided at Barrhead in its period as a terminus from 1848, the Board of Trade inspector making it quite clear that

the 2–2–2 engines used on the line were not to work tender first. When the line was extended in October 1855, however, a small engine shed was put up at Neilston (Lower) at the far, or country, end of the goods shed, abutting or at least very close to the building itself. A small turntable lay outside the door. Space was very restricted, with steep hillsides and a road in the valley and the shed evidently occupied excavated ground. It held one engine and measured about 40 ft. by 20 ft., or less; it was removed in the making of the Barrhead and Kilmarnock Joint line, having in all probability gone out of use by 1870.

The line is indeed a little-known one, the paucity of minutes etc. a reflection of the dire financial situation of the company. There was no end of legal wrangling, one report describing it as 'a lawyer's Paradise'.

PAISLEY

There was a small shed close by Paisley St. James station; it did not have a turntable and engines took water from columns in the goods yard. Little is known of the site – it is absent from the CR's 'Fixed Plant and Machinery' list of 1917 but was certainly in use by that time. It would have arisen out of the Paisley and Barrhead, taken over from the promoters by the CR, opening, it is believed, around June 1905. It would thus allow the local handling of traffic on that line and that arising from the Clippens (Johnstone) branch and (later) traffic from the Ordnance Factory at Bishopton. The shed was small, holding only a single 0–6–0 with comfort and was in timber with one closed end. A second 0–6–0 was on occasion lodged partly inside, and the shed's exclusion from the fixed plant list is explicable only perhaps as an accounting device connected presumably with the erstwhile Paisley and Barrhead. It was still stand-

Peebles, 19th June 1936.   *W. A. Camwell*

ing in 1922, in use, and had indeed been
particularly busy during the Great War
period, dealing with Ordnance Factory
traffic.

The shed would appear to have been taken
down around the time of Grouping and,
although engines continued to stand there,
it was more after the fashion of a daytime
'layover' rather than overnight stabling,
which effectively ended around 1926. No less
than 'eight sets of men' were there in BR
days, an improbable number unless connected somehow with the shifts of Greenock
(Ladyburn) men. They were, in any case,
divided amongst Ladyburn and Polmadie
from January 1953.

G. H. Robin, writing in the *Railway Magazine* of 1958 refers to St. James as 'a sub-
depot', closing on 3rd January 1953, a principal turn, on 0–6–0 'Jumbo' working, being
the 8.50 daily freight. Polmadie afterwards
sent down a similar engine, but ex-NBR 'J35'
0–6–0s had been observed on the duty,
worked instead from Gallowhill, near Green-
law.

PEEBLES

A two-road stone-built shed, its construction
entirely in keeping with Caledonian practice
of the early years, was erected at Peebles more
or less from the first. The CR station was
effectively a terminus, served by a branch
opened throughout in January 1864,
extended on from Broughton where a temporary engine shed had stood since 1860.

A single track, the NBR-owned 'Caledonian
Branch' connected end on with the CR line,
via a girder bridge over the Tweed and served
for goods transfer with the North British
station, nearer the town centre on the north
bank of the river.

In LMS days services were worked by a
variety of locos, including ex-GSWR 2–6–0s
ending their days with a run to Peebles;
occasionally one of the 2–6–2Ts were to be
seen. In earlier times more substantial
engines were in use, a Ransomes Rapier 60 ft.
turntable being installed in 1906. This had
been ordered in October 1905 at a cost of
£430 and remained in place at least until the
early 1950s when 'flat bottom type rails' on
the 'table were considered worthy of note.

The original engines had been small
2–4–0s of 1847/1849 vintage and 0–4–2s for
goods, followed over the years by larger
engines of similar aspect. Around the 1890s
the smaller CR 4–4–0s of Drummond and
Lambie design were in common use on the
passenger turns and by the 1910s engines as
large as the 'Dunalastair IIIs' were employed
on through workings to Glasgow and vice
versa. Similarly goods engines got larger and
at sheep sale times the large McIntosh
0–6–0s were frequently to be found on the
Westinghouse-braked cattle trains. Peebles
shed appeared to have one 4–4–0 and two
0–6–0s as 'regulars', outstationed from
Carstairs.

Close by the south bank of the Tweed, the
shed site required some excavation, whilst the

turntable lay at the extreme end of the yard,
the two separated by a covered coal stage.
Water was pumped to a tank from the river
a few yards away. The new 'table of 1906 was
installed immediately beyond its predecessor
and, when ready for use, the old girders were
removed, the pit filled in and a replacement
length of track laid across.

Peebles survived the costing assaults of the
'thirties but, as with many small sheds in
Scotland, closure was finally precipitated
when the Second World War began to press
even harder. Peebles shed closed in 1940 and
engines subsequently ran light as necessary
to and from Carstairs.

'SOUTH SIDE'

A little known establishment, a predecessor to
Central station and Polmadie (see Polmadie,
p.115).

There were two separate sheds, the two
South Side stations not being connected (by
a loop) until 1853. The Glasgow Barrhead
and Neilston had a small wooden building
in the fork formed by the Pollokshaws and
Cathcart roads. Three 2–2–2s had been
stabled there, the shed measuring about 50 ft.
by 20 ft., two roads with a 15 ft. turntable
outside. The building was removed in 1853.

STRATHAVEN

There had been a shed at Strathaven since
the railway's early days, a terminus near to
the site of what later became 'Strathaven
North'. Close by the village of Flemington

Site of Strathaven, 8th June 1949.   *W. A. Camwell*

(one of many so named in Lanarkshire) and a $\frac{1}{4}$ mile or so east of Strathaven itself, the shed opened under Board orders of 27th October 1871, 'also a pit'. Yet another obscure, single-road affair, it stood to the north of the station with access from a 40 ft. turntable positioned outside.

The line was extended southwards to Strathaven Central, etc, in 1904, effectively bypassing the old terminus; the new line took its leave of the old route some $\frac{1}{2}$ mile north of the terminus but ran more or less parallel as far as Flemington. Thus a new, through station, 'Strathaven North', could be built only yards from the original, now isolated on a lengthy goods spur. The shed remained in use throughout all this but was evidently no longer in the best of condition – this led to some curious proposals in the summer of 1907:

> 'Strathaven. Proposed . . . to convert the old Goods Shed into an Engine Shed . . . and repair the old Engine Shed.
> Conversion of old Goods Shed into Engine Shed   about £205
> Repairing old Engine Shed   £10
>   £215
>
> Approved'.

Various alterations were carried out at Strathaven, sidings reduced and cranes removed, but the goods shed, which stood on the west side of the yard, nearer to the station, appears not to have suffered the proposed conversion. Instead, the engine shed was

simply rebuilt – the single road was extended through the old shed and a new building erected at the rear, what remained of the old shed being subsequently removed. Three 0–4–4Ts and an 0–6–0 were afterwards stabled at Strathaven.

An outstation of Hamilton in Caledonian days after Grouping, Strathaven became the responsibility of Motherwell. Work had declined enormously however and by 1930 the 'branch' was really little more than a generously appointed coal siding. The shed was finally closed around 1931 and on 13th February 1934 its final end was discussed: 'Engine Shed Turntable and Sidings at Strathaven North no longer required. Should be removed, cost £275. Materials = £226, net outlay £49.'

TYNDRUM

Tyndrum was the terminus of the Callander and Oban Railway from August 1873 until May 1877 when a further section (on which work had started in the spring of 1875) was opened to Dalmally. Tyndrum shed was built to serve this temporary terminus, being erected around July of 1873. It was solidly built in stone with a 42 ft. turntable immediately outside, listed as serviceable and 'of 45 ft. diameter' in Scottish Region records of 1948; by 1953 it had disappeared.

The shed was more or less put out of use on completion of the new section (in May 1877), afterwards used only at periods of

sheep sales and, for an intermittent period in the early years of this century, for engines working engineers' trains in the district. It was finally closed, as a war economy measure, on 31st December 1915.

WEMYSS BAY

The line to Wemyss Bay opened in May 1865, a dash to the Firth of Clyde designed to secure steamship traffic from an encroaching Glasgow and South Western Railway. The company, the Greenock and Wemyss Bay Railway, was worked from the first by the Caledonian, and the single-road stone-built shed dates from opening, designed to harmonise with 'Inverclyde House' and similarly built mansions nearby. The Caledonian did not officially absorb the Wemyss Bay company until 1893, widening most of the line at the end of the decade, and the turntable, immediately outside the shed and controlling access to it, remained inconveniently small over many years. It had proved awkward operationally for some time and in the 1890s indeed had been linked via rodding to a signal box lever, for the protection of the running lines when engines were turned. In 1924 serious efforts were made to discover a suitable alternative site: 'The present turntable is of insufficient capacity for the turning of larger classes of modern engines and the site which is on the west side of the railway is too restricted in extent to permit of a larger turntable being installed'. The site in mind was, it turned out, being 'rapidly fenced in' by a land agent and 'urgent acquisition' was forcefully suggested. This turntable never materialised but was finally enlarged in 1938 after closure of the shed, with a Cowans Sheldon 55 ft. unit ordered the previous year. Articulated and vacuum-fitted, the long-standing space restrictions required the retaining wall to be cut back and the running lines slewed slightly. Throughout Caledonian days at least the only engine water supply was from the shed tank, and locos certainly made use of the siding and pit well into the 1930s.

A sub-shed of Greenock Ladyburn, the building was officially out of use for locomotive purposes by 1927, though, as already intimated, locomotives requiring turning, water or fire cleaning, of necessity visited the site. A single wagon, for coal or ash disposal could subsequently be found, lavishly accommodated inside the shed itself.

Wemyss Bay shed, 16th June 1936.   *W. A. Camwell*

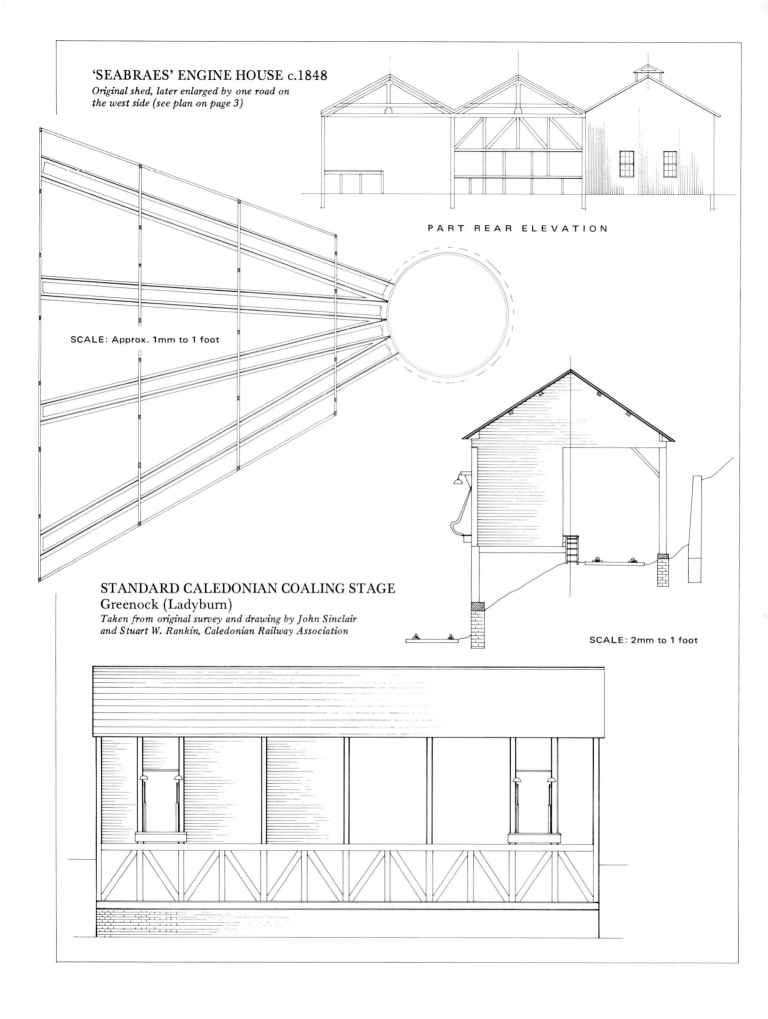

'SEABRAES' ENGINE HOUSE c.1848
*Original shed, later enlarged by one road on
the west side (see plan on page 3)*

PART REAR ELEVATION

SCALE: Approx. 1mm to 1 foot

STANDARD CALEDONIAN COALING STAGE
Greenock (Ladyburn)
*Taken from original survey and drawing by John Sinclair
and Stuart W. Rankin, Caledonian Railway Association*

SCALE: 2mm to 1 foot

STIRLING
Scottish Central Railway 1850

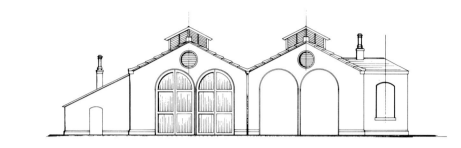

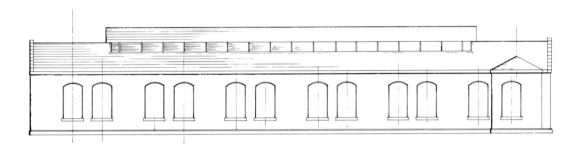

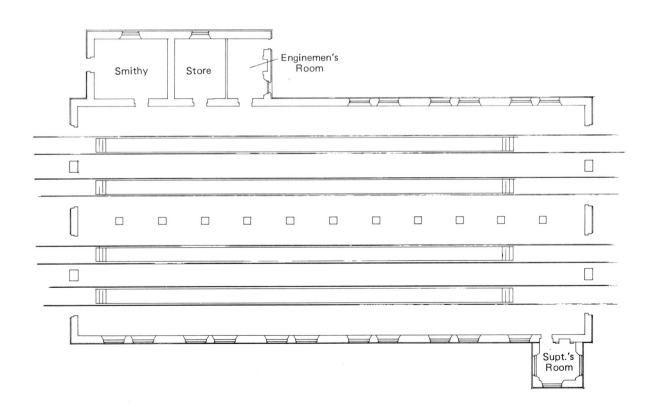

Smithy

Store

Enginemen's Room

Supt.'s Room

SCALE: 1mm to 1 foot

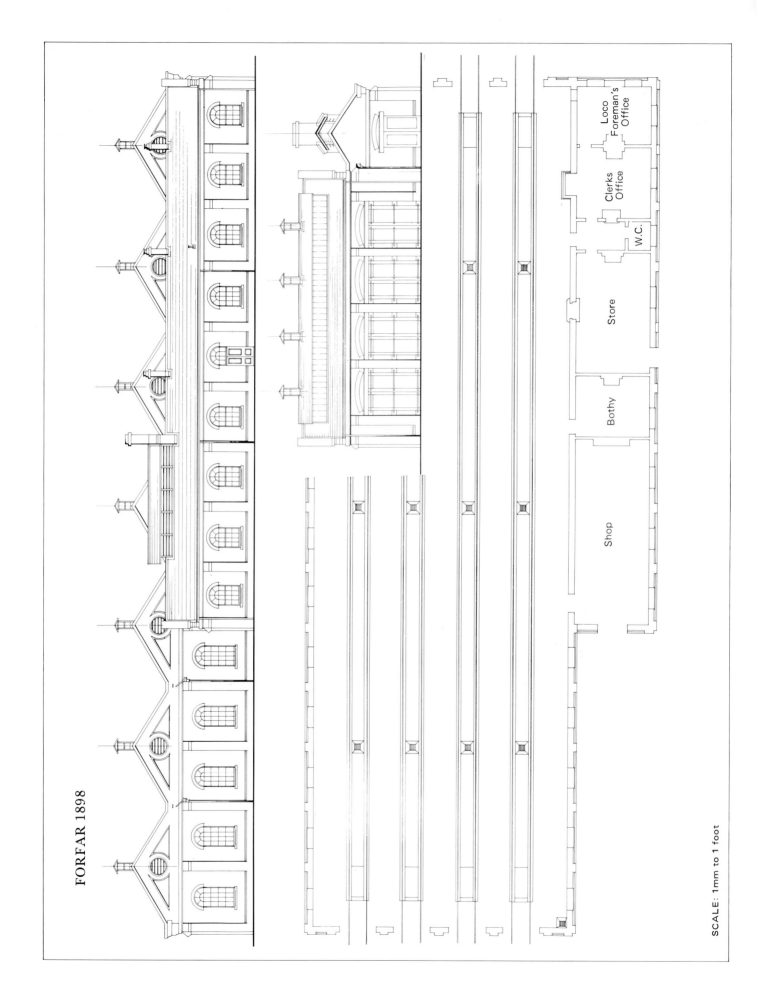

FORFAR 1898

Loco Foreman's Office

Clerks Office

W.C.

Store

Bothy

Shop

SCALE: 1mm to 1 foot

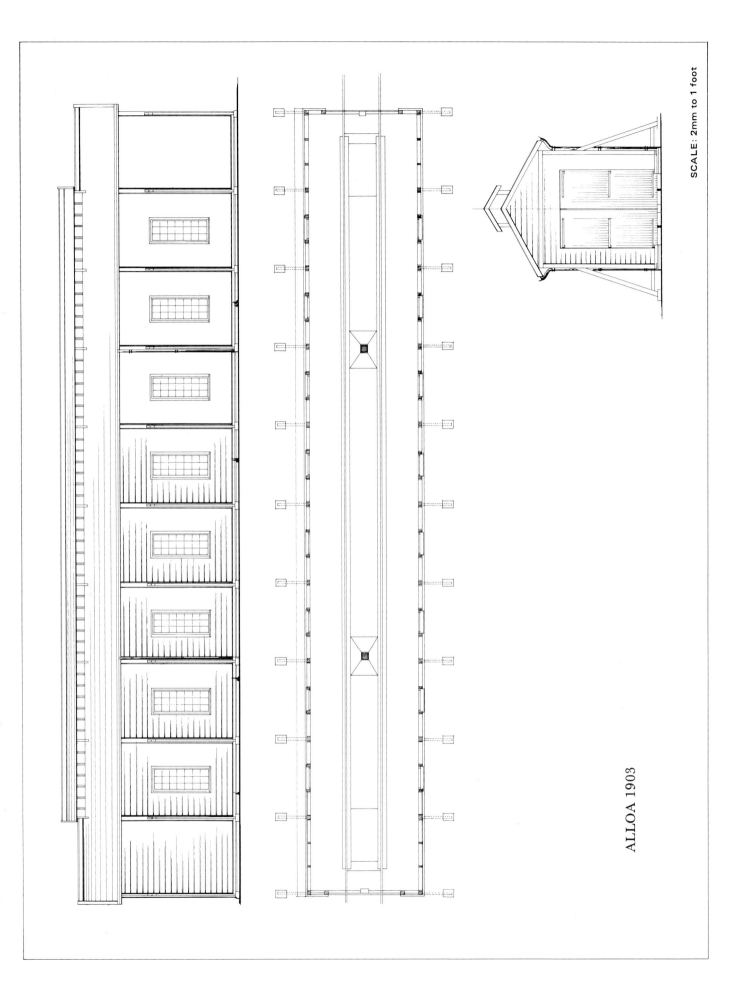

SCALE: 2mm to 1 foot

ALLOA 1903

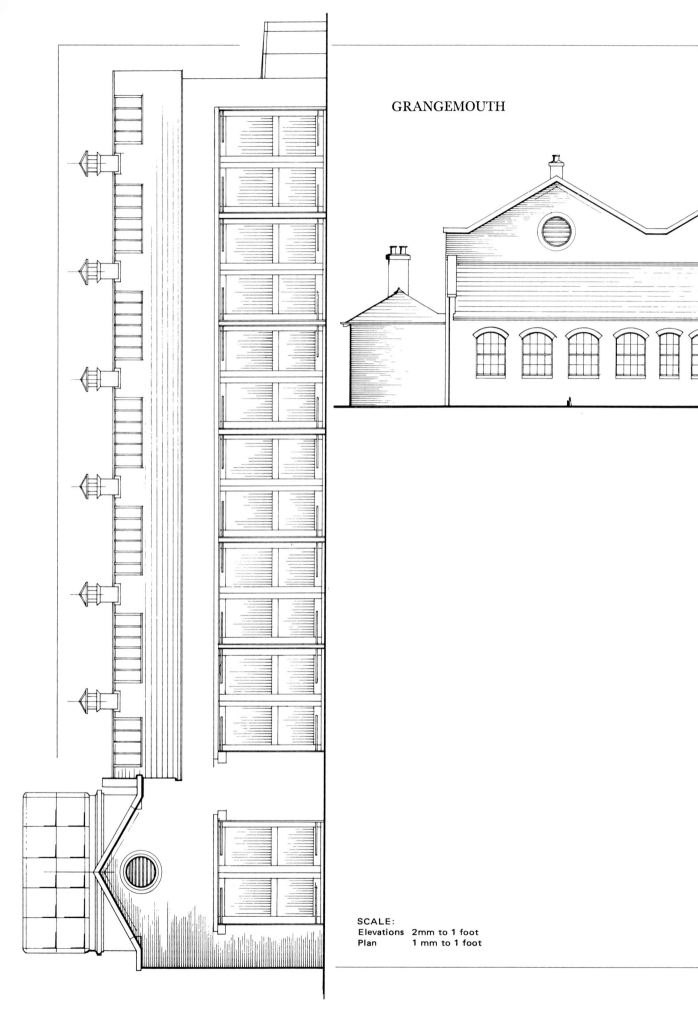

GRANGEMOUTH

SCALE:
Elevations 2mm to 1 foot
Plan   1 mm to 1 foot

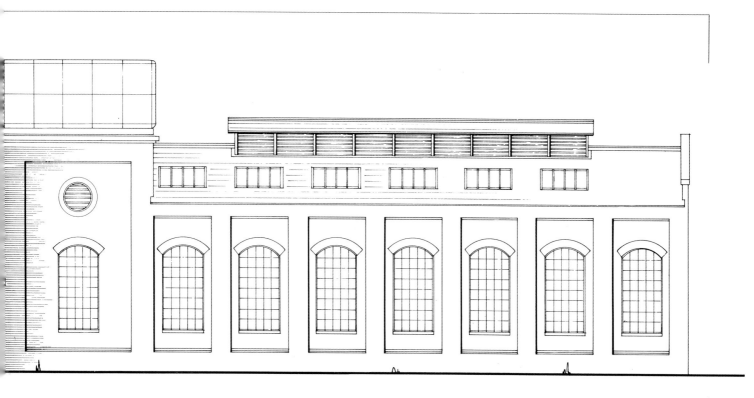

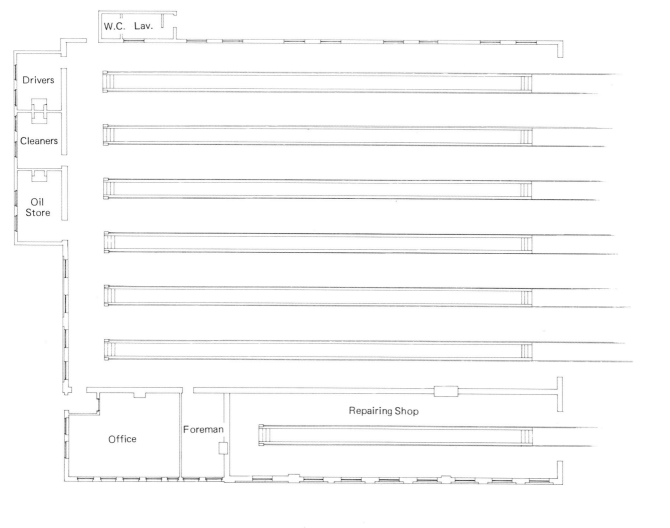

W.C. Lav.

Drivers

Cleaners

Oil
Store

Office

Foreman

Repairing Shop

ACKNOWLEDGEMENTS

The Caledonian is for Stephen Summerson, who gave much of his time to an appraisal of this and most other volumes of *LMS Engine Sheds* with courtesy and hospitality. J. F. McEwan spent a great deal of his time on some less than comprehensive accounts of Scottish sheds; much of the earlier material, in particular, derives from his own specialist knowledge and notes gathered over many years. It is with particular gratitude that we acknowledge his help and guidance. J. L. Stevenson proved an invaluable guide through much that was otherwise only dimly perceived, and Alan Wilson once again was able to comment to great effect upon various technical mysteries. All provided much encouragement, with a laconic good humour and great forbearance. John Hooper made available a number of documents, references and photographs, gleaned from his own Scottish delvings, and John Sinclair of the Caledonian Railway Association made freely available material gathered over a number of years, particularly illuminating with regard to Greenock. Much of the Ladyburn detail, including 'John Street', 'The Blitz' and the 'Puggie Line', are through his good offices. Albert Greig and his colleagues examined a draft of the book to considerable effect, averting at least one particularly embarrassing *faux pas*.

The travels of W. A. Camwell once again made possible a photographic record of places wholly obscure and remote, more inaccessible in the 1930s than many parts of the continent of Europe. His early pioneering work has left a unique record.

Special thanks go to H. C. Casserley, Bernard Mathews, W. Potter, Roger Carpenter, H. N. James, H. F. Wheeller, Bob and Peta Skelton, and *The Gallery* for readings on 'Boysnacht', Scottish Record Office, R. M. Casserley, N. E. Preedy, B. Hilton, A. G. Ellis, T. Middlemass, Tony Wright, Ken Fairey, Brian Morrison, T. J. Edgington, H. I. Cameron, W. H. Whitworth, W. T. Stubbs, Pendon Museum, Photomatic, Dave Banks, G. S. Lloyd, G. Coltas, W. A. Hannan, P. J. Kelley, William Sinclair, James Venn, R. J. Essery, D. F. Tee, J. F. Henderson, W. A. Brown, E. Wilmshurst, M. Mensing, J. Scott, D. J. Montgomery, Monty Smith and J. Robertson.

Paul and June worked wonders in their usual behind the scenes role, combining merciless taskmaster with counsellor/advisor, whilst Beverly and Wendy manned the field kitchens.